Royal Blood

ROYAL BLOOD

GORY PATH TO THE THRONE

E. L. Withers

1964

DOUBLEDAY & COMPANY, INC.

GARDEN CITY, NEW YORK

For their valued help in the writing of this book,
most grateful thanks are offered to:

T. O. CRAMER

MARGOT JOHNSON

EMILY W. POTTER

JAMES SCOTT

Preface

In the 1898 edition of his massive work *Murder in All Ages*, Matthew Worth Pinkerton (of detective fame) has this to say about the dangers attendant on kingship: "Many kings and potentates [have fallen] at the hands of assassins; poison being the means most commonly employed. A large number of the Emperors of Rome were thus removed from the scenes of their crimes, while not a few truly good rulers have been assassinated. Julius Caesar fell beneath the daggers of his one-time friends and supporters, at the foot of Pompey's statue. After that time the Emperors felt all the anxiety that disturbs our modern czars, and guarded by every means in their power, against the knife and poisoned cup of the assassin, but too often in vain; the ambition of rivals, who were able to excite the venality of the rabble, and, more especially, the army, generally proving superior to all their precautions." It is one of the prophetic coincidences of recent history that twenty years after Pinkerton's writing, presumably without second sight, his "modern czars" too were dragged down and executed, for in one sense the destruction of the house of Romanov marked the end of autocratic royalty which as a historical strain ran back from that point to an age in pre-history of which time has no recollection; the royal houses surviving into more recent years exist as shells of their former importance, emasculated now, shaped by the law instead of themselves shaping it. Matters were not thus regulated in the great days of kings.

But those great days were not all power and splendor. Pinkerton's summary of royal deaths makes clear the gloomy expectations of the men and women who wore crowns and sat upon thrones (and among the women gentleness of sex was in itself neither a protection against violence nor the guarantee of a gentle heart); yet such prospects of danger, treachery, and a terrible death have nevertheless proved throughout history to be no deterrent to the ambitious. The crown has always existed as a goal above any other in the physical world, above wealth or influence, combining force and grandeur, forever the hub of intrigue, rapacity, and sudden attack. After every other concern has been disposed of, when individual eccentricities have been gratified or exhausted, when loves of the heart have been won or lost, there yet remains in the young and the aging, the rich and the poor, the clever and the infirm this one last feature of personality: ambition. Thrones exist to be taken; kings reign to be deposed; and like a rattle of drums, the fall of kings punctuates the drama of history.

If the sanctity of royal blood gives its possessors no safety, no immunity from harm, it is mildly astonishing that those attempting to seize crowns should not observe in their own acts the pattern for their future destruction, too, at the hands of just such other aspirants as they themselves now are. But the lesson seems never to have been learned. In every time the pretender and the usurper have schemed for thrones, murdered their kings, and lost their own lives. To consider a single, compact instance, in Rome after the overthrow and death of the emperor Nero, his destroyer and successor, Galba, survived him for only a few months; he was assassinated by Otho, who then committed suicide when he grew convinced that Vitellius was about to win the empire for himself; and soon after Vitellius's succession he was seized in his palace by the soldiers of Vespasian's party who dragged him off through the streets, tortured him publicly, killed him, and pitched his body into the Tiber. By the time of Vespasian's rise to the throne less than two years had passed since Nero's death, so brief and disastrous were the reigns which followed it.

In the face of such businesses as this, however, there was still never a shortage of persons aspiring to imperial rank, persons of every kind, from every station in life, scholars and peasants, generals and administrators and madmen (no aberration was so frightful as to put a crown absolutely beyond reach); and brutal as the fate might be of those Romans who wore the imperial mantle and carried in their veins the royal blood of the moment, classical Rome was no more vicious in this regard than were other countries where the throne stood similarly high in the public veneration. In the eastern Roman empire, which had its seat at Constantinople and endured for eleven centuries after Rome itself had been abandoned to the sack and annexation of barbarians, the throne was occupied by twelve full, different dynasties, as well as by innumerable unrelated emperors; murder and violence were necessarily recognized as the dangers lurking under the crown, and the wearers of that crown were obliged to adopt an almost Oriental fatalism, an indifference to safety, and a willingness to gamble their lives for the title of emperor.

Alexius II was strangled with a bowstring by his father-in-law who usurped his realm. Alexius III captured his brother, the legitimate emperor, while he was off hunting, and put out his eyes; he seized the throne, but eight years later he was deposed by the brother's son; he lived, however, until another claimant to the throne had overturned and murdered this son; but then the luckless new emperor, failing to keep his crown, fell into Alexius's hands, so he too was blinded and then died after being hurled from the top of a pillar. And still another victim of blinding was Constantine IV, who was rendered thus by his mother's command, since she desired to rule in his place. Constantine III was poisoned by his stepmother. Romanus III was poisoned by his wife because she was in love with one of her servants, whom she married and who thus became Michael IV. Indeed, the staggering fact is that of all the 107 emperors and empresses who reigned at Constantinople, no more than thirty-four died of natural causes.

In other latitudes, also, conditions of an equally violent nature prevailed. In the Russia of the fifteenth and sixteenth centuries, following the long, eventful reign of Ivan the Terrible, there came a period of such turbulence that it was known as "the time of the troubles," a period of no more than twenty-four years in which one child of the imperial family, one regent of the empire, two pretenders to the throne, and two (or perhaps three) czars were murdered, two other czars were deposed and imprisoned, and one more died supposedly of guilt and terror. In all this tangle the country was swept with warring armies and embattled factions. Foreign troops fought one another as well as the domestic armies, and it had grown so unmistakably clear that Russia was dying from this unruly course that peace had to be enforced at any cost, and a new czar was at last chosen by general consent (this choice lighted upon the youthful Michael Romanov, who was to found the three-hundred-year Romanov dynasty which, after it had completed its own course of deposings and assassinations, was at last to be brought to the final and total destruction of all czardom).

But these confused and bloody events were no more of an exclusively Russian type than the dreadful ends met by the emperors at Constantinople were exclusively Byzantine: the events in the history of any land may appear to possess a certain nationalistic coloring, but such events in general can be seen to have repeated themselves over and over again in country after country. England was torn in two by the Wars of the Roses, and at last the whole mighty house of Plantagenet was tumbled by the grandson of a Welsh gentleman-farmer. In France during the sixth, seventh, and eighth centuries the kings themselves were relegated to positions of so little importance or dignity that they were kept half-imprisoned on outlying farms while their governments were run and their splendors methodically usurped by the so-called "Mayors of the Palace," who made it their concern to see that the kings remained besotted, debilitated, and inert. In Renaissance Italy such a grand superabundance of royal crime was brought into being (Cosimo I de' Medici, for instance, is said to have murdered two of his own children and driven their mother to a death of shock and grief, while two of his sons and two of his sons-in-law also murdered members of his immediate family) that it is possible for the student of such matters to become at last almost surfeited with blood—indeed, that risk exists not only in Renaissance Italy, but in almost every area of that field, so that a certain selectivity, a restricted consumption amounting to a diet, becomes necessary if one violent deed is to be distinguished from the next one. Death, after all, is still death; and even among emperors and empresses, kings, queens, princes, and all the rulers of the earth, this final ending is the same. Inescapably it has the monotony of the ultimate grandeur, and persons interested in pursuing the subject are wise to sip rather than to gulp it.

As the threat of death hangs over a throne, however, a balance of compensation necessarily also exists. And in fact it is evident that some particular magic has to dwell in a crown and invest those who wear it—a magic of such properties that it makes all dangers worthwhile—and that magic is not any of the desirable aspects of royalty customarily included in the definition of that term: it is not a facet of the king's strength or his wealth, or of the majesty of his circumstances. Instead it is an intangible possession, not subject to purchase, not available to persons within the structure of law. Yet it is the seat of desire in the hearts of men, women, and children alike, of every race and nation; it surpasses every human ambition including ambition itself, for even ambition serves only to bring one near this single goal—and that is to be able, as royal personages were, without counting the cost or checking the risks, to perform any act of whatever kind or nature one might choose.

If the child wish he may founder on sweets; if the man wish he may decimate his kingdom; if the woman wish she may enjoy lovers till they stupefy her, and no one can intervene to call a halt. In the days of vital sovereignty the king was neither bound by legality nor subject to reprisal by his people (other than the single major reprisal of overthrowing him which, by the cumbersomeness of its nature, was not designed to operate with the restrictive adaptability of constitutional processes) so that he was actually beyond the law and at perfect liberty to follow any course he desired, however vicious or savage or destructive, as Henry VIII of England disposed of his wives by divorce or beheading apparently at the dictates of his fancy's whim—or as the emperor Commodus murdered his brother in his mother's arms —or as Philip II of Spain, after marrying two cousins and outliving them both, married a princess of France and then, imagining that she was conducting an affair with his son, poisoned the two of them and went on to marry his niece—or as the empress Theodora, who was so chagrined at having borne an illegitimate son that when he visited her in her sacred palace, she caused him to be strangled in the basement there—or as Attila used his father-in-law's skull for a drinking cup.

But this unimaginable freedom did not exist in a vacuum. In its twinings were caught animate beings whose unfettered license had the side effect of allowing their personalities to develop an exuberant individuality so baroque, so extravagant and vivid that it has no counterpart among the great figures of modern times. A Hitler lacks the prodigality of a Caligula, or a Stalin the grandeur of a Louis XIV; and so the great kings and queens— reigning with contemptuous pride, flourishing their vices as conspicuously as they lavished away their treasures, murdering and being murdered with brilliance or irritability or sometimes with the mere indifference of the jaded—are recognizably a part of the past. Their oddities may share some common denominator with the rest of humanity and time, but the expression of those oddities, the unhampered violence, the unabashed cruelty, the privileges and excesses and immunity and unconcern all date them remotely in the past, fixing them there for the scrutiny of the ages.

And because of this fixed removal it is difficult to come to any sort of personal grips with these legendary figures as flesh and blood, to see them eating and drinking and resting as simply as modern men do. They seem a little larger than life, rather like works of art than of nature, their tremendous appetites and limitless energies whirling them through life like a throng of giants—more story-book material than creatures of fact. Even the physical objects with which they associated themselves, the instruments of torture and death by which thrones were filled or emptied—rack and hot iron, poison ring and dagger and sword— are bizarre in their mere distance from today's mundane realities, for there are fads and fashions in death as there are in architecture or dress or any other sphere of human affairs, and fashions come and go. Crowns themselves are no longer objects of moment; they have taken their place among the curiosities of the historian's notebook. The castles and palaces have become drawing cards for tourists. The dark rivers into which bodies were furtively thrown are now well patrolled, and the famous streets and squares ring with the peaceful sound of fountains and the steps of sightseers rather than with the clash of arms.

The figures which once peopled these scenes have retreated from them now; in their removal from life thay have gone to a distant, uninhabited place of their own where, a breed apart as the Titans were, vastly proportioned, human-like and yet non-human, each figure presides forever from the recesses of a well-sunk, sculptured niche in a row with others of his kind over a company of echoes—the niches themselves stretching with geometrical evenness down the sides of the long, cold, gray gallery of the centuries where the human visitor seldom goes to wander or to gaze. Here with stone eyes and motionless limbs sit the plump, petulant ones such as Nero; here with their carved robes spreading at their feet sit the wicked queens such as Catherine de' Medici and Catherine the Great; here sit brooding the unredeemed monsters such as Ivan the Terrible; here are represented such great houses as the slothful Borgias and the lively Plantagenets, all these beings now silent, unmoving, unforgetting, swallowed in a gray light which comes from no visible source.

Along that gallery of time they are all turned to marble, restricted at last, with their own times drawn irresistibly away from them so that in this withdrawal crowns are scattered among the ages like withered petals, and the figures themselves are left naked before the distant stare of the critic, the doctor, and the connoisseur. The divine right of kings, like a discovered thief, flits down the long stone floor, retreating from shadow to shadow, at last vanishing discreetly in the distance; and with the exit of this thief, the light in the gallery is seen to be already fading. The moist chill of the marble enters the air, and with it comes the slatey odor of a room unvented. Absolute silence becomes strangely audible in its emptiness, and with this silence, darkness slowly falls upon the place. The great kings and queens in their niches do not move or blink, but imperceptibly dissolve into the gathering shadows; individualities merge in the dimness, personalities fade, and the strong lines of character and action become a blur. The dimness dwindles to the end of twilight. Finally the scene is darkened altogether, and in that black, eternal silence the occasional straying visitor can hear only the soft, prolonged, sad murmur of the ebb of time.

CONTENTS

~~~~~~

PART 1

~~~~~~

Nero and Agrippina

Nero and Agrippina

Near the spot where the great shell of the Colosseum now stands, the emperor Nero built a palace called the Golden House which was one of the marvels of the world. Yet when its construction was finished, and the masons and goldsmiths and artists and sculptors had taken themselves off from their completed labors, and the time arrived for the dedication to the household gods, Nero at his most churlish merely remarked offhandedly of his sumptuous new dwelling: "I finally have a house fit for a human being to live in."

But this was not honestly to suggest that heretofore he had been living in a style less than suitable to the grandeur of his position. He had inherited a variety of palaces within the city of Rome, as well as more scattered villas, country houses, mansions, and manors; and as it happened the Golden House was not originally even intended to be another palace. It was to have been a passageway between the Palatine and Esquiline hills, known as the House of Passage; but this first building was consumed in the fire to which Nero is supposed to have fiddled, and the resurrected House of Passage became so gigantic that it spread up onto the hills on either side, and even encroached on the Forum. Pliny says that it threatened to swallow up the whole of Rome, and jokes were made about the chance of it engulfing the town of Veii twelve miles distant.

The portico, for example, was sufficiently large to contain a statue of Nero 120 feet tall, so the ceiling must have been somewhat over the height of a twelve-story building. There was, besides, a triple colonnade of such vast proportions that it extended for a full mile in length, while the building itself, in addition to enclosing more than the customary number of courtyards with the appropriate (and, it may be supposed, the most ostentatious) gardens, fountains, pools, terraces, and plantings, was also extensive enough to embrace a lake which was intended to look like an inland sea; there were groups of buildings along its shores constructed to resemble foreign cities, and upon its waters mock naval battles were enacted for the emperor's amusement—this whole immense pastiche giving him the gratifying sense of holding all the lands of the earth immediately under his hand.

Nor was that the end of the resources which the palace grounds had to offer. On one side of the inland sea there were open lawns with cultivated vistas extending into the far distance fully ornamented by the choicest specimens of the gardener's craft. And by way of contrast to these formal conceits, there lay upon the farther side of the huge lake, all closed within the circling arms of the palace itself, an elaborate and artificially natural-appearing countryside of grain fields, forests, vineyards, and pastures, with the appropriate animals running loose in each and constituting a sort of uncontained menagerie. In the forests there were wild and semi-wild beasts rooting and snorting and scampering among the tree trunks; and in the pastures and open scenery there were horses and cows and domestic livestock of every kind.

The blatancy of these landscapes and exteriors, however, faded in comparison with the interior of the palace. The ostentations of the Caesars had long since vulgarized the use of gold and jewels, but no production on this scale had ever been carried out before. There were rooms in which nothing was to be seen anywhere except gold and more gold. The walls were cased in gold. The ceiling and furniture were plastered solidly with it. The floors, when they were not gold, were mother-of-pearl, beautifully tesselated and inlaid; and precious gems were used in the most spendthrift way imaginable to supplement the building's decoration.

The supper rooms and banqueting halls had the most elaborate and precious ceilings—gold, needless to state, often set with ivory, pierced and carved. They were coffered, like the ceilings which can still be seen in the ruins of some of the baths around

Rome, and in the Pantheon. Some of these were so designed that their panels rotated slowly while scattering the petals of flowers, which wafted down upon the heads and shoulders of the revelers as they feasted. Other ceilings had complicated plumbing inside them which sprayed out perfumes and unguents and such luxuries. And to complete this chaotic picture, with the ceilings discharging all manner of bounty, the chief banqueting room was circular, and revolved continually day and night without stopping so as to provide the emperor with the delicious sensation of flying around the universe like one of the heavenly bodies.

A fair amount of conjecture has been spent on this amazing room. By what mechanical device did it rotate? And at what pace? It has even been suggested that the chamber might have been difficult to enter because of the speed of its spinning—as if one were trying to leap onto a merry-go-round whirling at full tilt—but it may be guessed that it did not rush round at quite that heady rate. The ancients envisioned the planets and stars as progressing upon their heavenly courses with immutable leisure and tranquillity; and if Nero enjoyed picturing himself as a celestial figure, without doubt he appreciated the full stateliness of that position, for the contemplation of his own importance ranked as a significant item among the activities of his mind.

In the most obvious sense the construction of the Golden House was one of the ultimately grandiose expressions of human vanity ever to be made; but in another sense the Golden House existed in relation to the ordinary domestic residence precisely as Nero existed in relation to the ordinary human being: all his life he had been a special person, a boy and then a man apart, descendant and relative of emperors, heroes, and gods, who could no more be measured by normal human criteria than his palace could be judged by the utilitarian standard of providing shelter from the elements. Fanciers of architectural oddities will find few examples odder or more noteworthy than the Golden House; and in the same way (for the palace, preposterous and tasteless as it was, reflected precisely the strangeness of Nero's character) this emperor achieved a unique position not only when compared with ordinary men, but even in comparison with other personalities of bizarre or fantastic nature.

He was born in December of the year A.D. 37, the son of Gnaeus Domitius Aenobarbus, a Roman nobleman, and his wife, Agrippina, and lived to become the fifth emperor and sixth Caesar to reign over Rome. It was a matter of chance that he was not born in a hovel, or even in an everyday house, but that at the time of his birth the emperor himself was none other than his own uncle, Caligula, his mother's brother; but upon such accidents of blood-relationship as this Nero's entire career was based. Caligula, being the current representative on the imperial throne of the family of the Caesars, also represented the family's descent from Aeneas, the legendary founder of Rome, through him from his mother, the goddess Venus, and finally through Venus from her father, Jupiter, king of the gods. Many of the Caesars themselves were also gods; Nero was not, but Caligula was. He was accustomed to converse privately with Jupiter in that god's temple, first placing his ear to the sacred statue's lips, then whispering into the statue's ear; and finally he announced that the statue had suggested that the two of them should live together, so he built a bridge between his palace and the temple for direct access. On this same metaphysical plane he decided to wage war against his cousin, the sea-god Neptune, so his army waded out into the ocean, gathered up shells and driftwood as if they were trophies of war, and withdrew to celebrate a military triumph.

Being thus demonstrably a god, and because the gods of the Pantheon were allowed innumerable (indeed, limitless) eccentricities, Caligula chose to avail himself of this latitude to the utmost. He had gained the imperial throne by murdering his granduncle and benefactor, the previous emperor, Tiberius, and it was said that he had also disposed of a grandmother, a sister, a father-in-law, and cousins without number as well as more distant relatives. To this list it may also be added that as well as laying low his own family, toward folk of lesser degree he showed no pity, no mercy, and no compunction, torturing and killing without restraint for his personal delectation.

Caligula's extravagance was so prodigious that he not only

soon squandered the billions of his inheritance from Tiberius, but also the annual revenue of the empire, so that he was then obliged to discover new sources of income. One of these was his corps of professional informers, who gave evidence which might bring rich men to trial, and prison or death, such men's wealth reverting to the emperor. Another was a scheme whereby he auctioned off furniture and effects which were no longer required at the palaces, making a handsome profit by selling these things to the provincials, the socially aspiring, and the unwary (including those who dozed during auctions) for their snob value. And the third was a yet more novel method of raising money: he opened his palace as a house of prostitution, where the vessels of pleasure were none other than his sisters Lesbia, Drusilla, and Agrippina (mother of the baby Nero).

These ladies were all living incestuously with him, in any event, so it was really not such a great step beyond that to outright prostitution. In fact, he had been discovered in bed with Drusilla by his grandmother when he was in his early teens (subsequently he forced the old lady to kill herself) and matters had progressively worsened. So now, making the most of his unusual attitude, he obliged all those persons who sought the imperial favor not only to utilize the facilities of the palace, and to pay heavily for using them, but then to lend their own wives, daughters, and even sons to swell the voluptuous assets of the establishment. But finally this venture began to pall on him. Drusilla, his favorite sister, was dead by this time (there was a rumor that he killed her, and as if in remorse he did cause her to become a goddess after her death), and Agrippina and Lesbia did not fare much better. He grew tired of them and banished them to the island of Pontia where they were subjected to the rigorous and potentially fatal life of political exiles. Undoubtedly it was at this time that Agrippina became an expert swimmer—and this accomplishment was to have an effect on her future.

The banishment of Agrippina was followed in a short time by the death of her husband, Domitius, leaving Nero a virtual orphan at the age of three. (For his part, Nero's father was known to be one of the wickedest men in Rome, the scion of a family even more wicked than the Caesars; he was utterly dishonest in every matter, large or small; he was incestuous with his sister; he was charged with treason by Tiberius; he was insanely cruel and subject to fits of murderous rage in which he liked to gouge out eyes with his own thumbs, or slay deliberately any bystander upon whom his wrath might fall—on one occasion he was known to have whipped up the horses drawing his chariot purposely to run over a little child in the road. At Nero's birth he pridefully announced that nothing could have sprung from his union with Agrippina which was not an abomination and a public curse.) Nero, being thus thrown upon the world by his father's death, went to live with an aunt, in whose house he received only the most cursory and offhand scraps of attention, being educated (if that word serves to describe the slight training he received) by a professional dancer and a barber.

As to Caligula, in the fullness of time the excess of his vices drove his subjects to revolt. The Praetorian Guard turned against him, and he was brutally slaughtered in a palace revolution—first he was hacked across the neck, then run through the chest, then a part of his jaw was slashed away; and finally the attackers, furious at all his sexual outrages, attacked his genitals with their sword points as he writhed on the pavement, whimpering for mercy.

While this butchery was taking place, Caligula's uncle, Claudius, who had heretofore been considered the fool of the family, was hiding terror-stricken behind a drape in a room of the imperial palace, and there he was discovered cowering by a soldier of the palace guard, dragged forth, and hailed as emperor. In fact, the guards always shone conspicuously in the murk of the imperial succession: it was a captain of the guard who was thought to have helped Caligula smother Tiberius under a pile of dirty clothing and steal the imperial ring from his finger; and the guard was to turn against other rulers in time, as it did against Caligula, and help new men to seize power.

While Claudius was being made emperor, Agrippina and her sister Lesbia continued, of course, to suffer their exile on the island to which Caligula had banished them; but although

Claudius, in the period following his elevation, was fully occupied by the caprices of his current wife, the terrible Messalina, still he had sufficient consideration for his female relatives to rescind the banishment. His nieces returned to Rome, and Agrippina entered upon that long season of her life through which she waited and intrigued and coaxed from fate a prosperous future not only for herself, but also for Nero who, all this while, was growing up.

Claudius was a tolerant husband, but after some years of condoning or blinding himself to the sins and perfidies of Messalina's life, she overstepped even the broad bounds of his good nature, his carelessness, and his inertia (publicly she went through a mock wedding between herself and her favorite lover, and lest anyone should remain in doubt as to her sexual agility, the marriage was consummated before hundreds of drunken, but nevertheless astonished, guests on a stage hung with vine leaves and leopard skins), and Claudius was forced to have her killed. Thus he was in the market for a new wife as he approached old age, even though he had already been three times married.

Messalina, who had had no intention of sharing either the power or the consequence of her position as empress, had taken good care to see that no increase of influence should come Agrippina's way after her return from exile. Upon Messalina's death, however, Agrippina's stars seemed to come into propitious alignment. There were three candidates for Claudius's hand, and one of these was his ambitious niece, Agrippina. Each of the three contenders possessed a strong political backing, and for a time the issue of his choice seemed in doubt; but at last, after a struggle of some dimension, Agrippina carried the day, not neglecting to prevail upon her aging uncle with the kisses and caresses to which the closeness of their relationship entitled her. They were married, and not long afterward (significantly) one of her previous competitors died without warning—supposedly by poison. The other was persecuted at great length by the new empress; she was stripped of her possessions, sent into exile, and finally Agrippina in a passion of vengeance sent a tribune to force her to commit suicide, and had her beautiful head cut off and

brought back to the palace so that she should be positively able
to identify it and be sure that the deed had been carried out—an
act which she accomplished by wrenching open the dead mouth
and examining the teeth.

Now that Agrippina was actually married to Claudius, the
range of her power was much more extensive than it had ever
been before, for a great difference existed between merely being a
member of the imperial family, and actually reigning as empress.
Her personal ambition could carry her no higher than this; but
her son's future was still to be assured, and so she set further
intrigues afoot. Through the years which had passed before
Agrippina became empress, the young Nero was developing to the
edge of manhood, so now he had arrived at an age where his
mother might practically begin to think how she could go about
placing him on the throne, with or without legality. In order to
accomplish this, she connived for his marriage to Claudius's
daughter, Octavia—a move cleverly designed not only to
strengthen his claim to the throne (Claudius had a son of his
own blood, Britannicus, who should have been his successor),
but also to strengthen the power of her control over her son
through his wife, for poor Octavia was soon entirely in her wicked
stepmother's thrall. The foolish Claudius raised no objection to
such a marriage, and so this extraordinary event took place, and
Octavia became simultaneously Nero's wife, his sister, and his
aunt since Claudius was both his stepfather and his granduncle.

It only remained now to persuade Claudius to name Nero as
his chosen heir, and then the old fool would no longer be of any
use; he could be murdered, and Nero could be placed upon the
throne; and this was actually brought about when Nero was
seventeen years old. Claudius was induced to make such public
statements as would suggest that he chose Nero as his successor
over Britannicus, and in so doing he sealed his own fate.

A famous poisoner named Locusta, already under sentence
for a previous crime, was called in. A dish of poisoned mushrooms
was prepared, and served by the emperor's taster. Claudius ate
them unsuspectingly. For some time it had been his habit to lie
down after dinner and have his throat tickled with a feather to

induce vomiting. This was done now; but to counteract the loss of the mushrooms, the feather was dipped in poison, and the poison thus swabbed on his throat. To speed matters along, he was next fed a dish of poisoned gruel with the suggestion that it might settle his stomach. And then a poisoned enema was administered as the *coup de grâce*.

His death was kept fiercely secret until everything had been made ready for Nero's succession. No one was allowed to leave the palace. Bulletins were issued regarding the state of the dead emperor's health, and entertainers were hired to amuse his fictitious last hours. Finally, restraining Britannicus inside the palace, Nero sortied forth in the midst of the Praetorian Guard and gave the news to the Senate and people. Since there was no contesting heir present to raise opposition, he became the sixth and last of the true Caesars. (The emperors who followed him, and who called themselves Caesars, were merely assuming what had been a family title of the Julian and Claudian houses, and which was in time to be permuted into such titles as Kaiser and Czar.)

Nero had, of course, been privy to the poisoning of Claudius, although Agrippina had been the main force behind that plot. But his first solo murder was that of his stepbrother, Britannicus, whom he not only feared as a source of political danger, but of whom, on account of his own musical aspirations, he was wildly jealous because Britannicus had a vastly superior singing voice. Even though he was only fourteen years old, Britannicus showed every sign of becoming one of the few noble members of his family, and from the moment of his father's murder he had been sequestered in complete retirement so as to keep him from performing any good actions which might swell his popularity. His attendants and slaves were all creatures of the new emperor or the dowager empress, and he had no friends anywhere to stand by him. This made the murder simpler to commit than it might otherwise have been.

That same Locusta who had prepared the poisoned mushrooms for Claudius was called in again. After Claudius's death she had been sent back to her imprisonment; but it was handy to keep her alive. She stewed up her poison, gave it to Nero, he gave it to Britannicus's tutor, and the tutor fed it to the young prince. But either because Locusta had made a mistake, or because Britannicus had taken the precaution of fortifying his system with antidotes (there appear to have been almost as many antidotes as there were poisons) the stuff had no effect upon him except to act as a laxative. Nero flew into a violent rage and flogged Locusta with his own hand, while she whined that she had only been trying to protect his good name. Finally he commanded that her equipment be brought to his bedroom, and he forced her to manufacture a new and better poison while he watched. When the poison was ready, he had a young goat, a kid, brought in and fed this poison to it. The kid became very ill indeed, but did not die for five hours, which was not quickly enough; so Locusta was put to work again on a third brew. This time it was given to a pig, which gobbled it down and dropped dead instantly. Nero was satisfied.

The poison was administered at a banquet. Britannicus's taster was involved in the plot, just as Claudius's had been. A cup of extremely hot broth was set before the boy, already tasted and proved to be harmless. It had been anticipated that he would ask to have it cooled, so the poison was added to a pitcher of cold water, and the water was poured into the broth. Britannicus drank, and immediately fell back, dying. Naturally this caused a great commotion among the other persons present at the banquet; but Nero, reclining on his couch, merely smiled his quiet, humorless smile and blandly assured everyone that Britannicus was subject to the falling sickness, and that it would presently pass away. The boy, himself, passed away instead. Everything which was to follow had been designed beforehand, including the funeral arrangements: the body was carried out from the banquet and buried that same night in a driving rain before anything could be done about it. The emperor was so pleased with Locusta that he granted her a full pardon for her services to him, and gave her large estates in the country where she set up a kind of school and instructed pupils in her art under the emperor's benign protection.

With the murder of Britannicus, Nero's position on the imperial throne was once and for all established; there were no other male heirs with a claim comparable to his own, and the heiresses such as Claudius's daughters could not, by law, put forward their claims (that was why Agrippina had wanted her son to become emperor, and had worked with such ardor toward that end—not that she was altruistic or had any family feeling, but that knowing she could never be empress in her own right, she was determined to be at least the force behind the throne). And with absolute power in his grasp, Nero—who had been, up to this time, something of a shadowy figure—began to emerge instead as a concrete personality.

In his flesh Nero was not appealing to look at. Although his legs were skinny, his belly was protuberant, and his ponderous head sat on a very thick neck. Under a dome of yellow hair arranged in tier upon tier of artificial curls, his round moon face was blotchy with pimples and boils; and his blue eyes were nearsighted so that he was obliged either to squint or to wear a vacuous look of incomprehension as bleary figures crossed his vision.

Nor was the mind which animated him any more attractive. Nero was the sort of person who suffers from a chronic discontent. While Claudius was alive, the young man's whole ambition had been bent toward dispossessing Britannicus and becoming emperor himself. Once this had been achieved, and Britannicus killed, however, it no longer seemed so alluring; and while he had certainly no desire to return to private life or relinquish any of the benefits of his lofty position, still he was unable to keep his eyes from turning toward greener pastures. His merry, wandering fancy lit upon the profession of singing, and he decided that his next triumph should be in this field. He sent for the greatest masters to teach him, and began to affect an air of poetic melancholy. Although his voice was not good, he never became aware of that fact.

When he concluded that he was ready to make his public debut, he went to Naples for this purpose, where a large crowd gathered to hear him. The occasion was unpropitious. His concert was no more than started when an earthquake occurred; the theater commenced to tremble and totter, and everyone except Nero was much alarmed. Not he, however. He went on singing until he had gone through the entire concert as planned. The moment he was finished, though, there was a frantic scramble for the exits. Providence was plainly taking care of the innocent spectators, for the building was no sooner emptied than, with a terrible noise, it collapsed upon itself in an avalanche of stones and mortar and clouds of dust. Nero was in no way dismayed by this, but continued breezily in his new career.

Having completed his series of Neapolitan concerts, he next returned to Rome where everyone dutifully applauded his "divine voice" and then, since he had Rome already well under his thumb, he proceeded to Greece. Here the theater did not collapse, but other strange events took place. As a matter of policy he refused to allow anyone to leave the theater while he was singing, and this led to a number of dire situations since he was sometimes in the habit of singing for several days or a week at a time. Not even advanced pregnancy was a satisfactory excuse for leaving, and several children were born in the audiences. To some persons this musical imprisonment was so hateful that escape by any means was preferable, and they climbed secretly up and threw themselves off the roof or out windows, happily risking the effects of the fall in order to get away. But the most enterprising were those who went through complex acts of illness and collapse, and were carried out as if really dead.

Then in addition to singing in concerts, Nero also entered into the singing competitions along with the true professionals, where naturally he won every prize which was being given. Now that he was acknowledged as the greatest singer in the world, however, this business also seemed no longer quite so engrossing to him. Distant fields once more beckoned. He decided that he wanted next to be the world's greatest chariot driver, and to achieve this end he began entering the races. Lamentably he had no more talent for this pursuit than he had for singing; during one important race he so far undid himself as actually to fall out of his chariot; he was propped back in again, and was still unable to hold out till the end of the course; but the judges wisely awarded him the victor's crown just the same.

By the time he returned to Rome again after all this protracted junketing he had garnered enough prizes that, as if he were a conquering general, he ordered a triumphal procession for himself with the purpose of showing them off. For a long time now it had been his custom to hire trained claques to applaud him in the various stylized ways (that is to say with hands cupped, with palms flat, and so forth) and he had now organized the crowds which attended his procession in much the same way, so that the garlanded throngs lining his road to the palace all, as Dio describes them, chanted in unison: "Hail, Olympian Victor! Hail, Pythian Victor! Augustus! Augustus! Hail to Nero, our Hercules! Hail to Nero, our Apollo! The only Victor of the Great Tour! The only one from the beginning of time! Augustus! Augustus! Oh, divine voice! Blessed are they that hear it!"

Now while all these public events were taking place, Nero also found time to enjoy a remarkable private life. He was fond of sneaking out of his palaces at night, disguised, to frequent taverns, break into shops, steal their contents, and beat men and women he met in the deserted streets—sometimes beating or stabbing them to death and throwing their bodies into the sewers. At first he did this only with a small company of intimates; but after one of the men whom he started to beat turned on him and beat him instead, he took to carrying off his pranks under the protection of an escort of the guard. This was symptomatic of the growing carelessness with which he exposed his vices as his reign wore on.

As well as abusing in the spirit of the moment young boys, married women, and even a Vestal Virgin, he conceived an attachment for a comely youth named Sporus. He next developed the notion that the two of them should get married; with this in mind he had Sporus castrated and—in Suetonius's somewhat mysterious wording—"attempted to make a woman of him." Finally he did marry the fellow, with the full wedding ceremony. Sporus wore a bridal veil and brought a dowry; and afterwards Nero took him home and treated him exactly as he treated his wives, decking him out in the finery of the empresses, riding with him in the same litter, and publicly kissing and fondling him. Subsequently he married at least two other men—Pythagoras and Doryphorus—but in each of these cases he, rather than the object of his passion, wore the veil, brought the dowry, and enacted the part of the bride.

While these unnatural marriages were taking place he also married three women. The first was Claudius's daughter, Octavia. This move was entirely political. He never cared much for her, and he dispensed with her—although after a good deal of difficulty—as soon as he dared. He then married Poppaea Sabina, who was so magically beautiful that it was hard to believe she was human; but he killed her in a moment of irritation. And last of all, he married Statilia, murdering her husband in order to make her available for marriage.

Statilia outlived him, but the other two were not so lucky. Poppaea was dispatched in a quick and carefree fashion, although he loved her as devotedly as his volatile nature allowed: he kicked her in the stomach while she was pregnant because she scolded him for coming home late from the races, and she died as a result. Previously, Octavia's end had not been so easy. First of all he banished her from Rome, although not very severely; he did not divorce her at once, and the only important stipulation of her exile was that she should stay outside the city. He remarked that she ought to be content with the title of empress, even if she was one in name only. But she was not content; and the populace was not content either. Octavia was widely liked, and the general feeling was that she had been treated shabbily. There was so much ominous muttering around the city that Nero was forced to recall her.

He did not like being forced to do things. It was a situation which so seldom confronted him that he had no chance to get accustomed to it; and now, as soon as Octavia—only twenty years old, and not very dangerous—was re-established in the palace, mobs of people came to congratulate her on her return and her safety, and the emperor was so frightened at the sight of her popularity that he banished her in real earnest, having first tried several times unsuccessfully to strangle her. She was shipped off to a singularly desolate island in the Mediterranean; he divorced her officially; and twelve days later he married Poppaea, on whom his sights had been set for some time. This did not go over very well with the people. The mutterings became more ominous, so cowardly Nero annulled the marriage to Poppaea and canceled Octavia's divorce. But this, too, did not have the desired effect. The people were so jubilant that they forced their way into the capitol, knocked over the new statues of Poppaea, and set up the old statues of Octavia again. Nero was trapped between the will of the people and the will of his beloved Poppaea, who was something of a shrew. Poppaea prevailed: Octavia had to be killed so as to settle the controversy once and for all.

But there had to be a legitimate excuse for doing it; people were growing weary of indiscriminate murders. The only practical course now was to accuse her of adultery and execute her, but this was not easy to do, for her life had been altogether virtuous. After a number of slaves had been tortured in an effort to extract some damaging information and none was forthcoming, one of Nero's minions—Anicetus, by name—was persuaded with bribes and threats to say that he had seduced the empress. A hollow punishment was meted out: he was banished to Sardinia where he lived the remainder of his life amid the greatest luxury, like a minor king, his reward for his services. But on Octavia's island her punishment was of a very different order: when the messengers of death arrived from Nero, they commanded her to be tightly bound with cords, and then the veins in every part of her body were cut open that she should bleed to death. She bled slowly, however, too slowly for her impatient tormentors; so without more ado she was killed outright by being scalded to death in boiling water.

By the time of Octavia's death, Nero had long since become a virtuoso in the field of murder, demonstrating there all the talent which he so conspicuously lacked at singing and chariot racing. The initial success of Britannicus's murder had encouraged him to the point that for the rest of his life he showed neither discrimination nor moderation in putting to death anyone he chose. He ordered that Poppaea's son by a previous marriage should be drowned by his own slaves while fishing simply because the child had played at being an emperor. To one man to whom he had promised a soothing cough syrup, he sent a flask of poison instead. He killed Claudius's other daughter, Octavia's sister, Antonia, because she declined to marry him after he had murdered Octavia and Poppaea. His tutor and guardian, Seneca, the famous stoic and philosophical writer, earned his hatred by amassing too much money and because it was said that he made fun of Nero's singing behind his back. He was ordered to commit suicide. The situation would have been farcical had it been less sinister.

The old man opened the veins in his arms; but he bled such a trickle that he had plenty of time to dictate to his secretaries, visit with his friends, console his wife, and one thing and another. Finally, when it seemed that he was never going to die, he took a dose of hemlock, but by now he had lost so much blood that the poison, also, was unable to kill him. Then he took a hot bath, but this too had no effect; and at last, bleeding monotonously all the while, he was carried to an even hotter bath where the steam suffocated him. He used up the better part of a day in dying. His wife had intended to commit suicide at the same time he did; but she must have bled even more slowly, and after he was gone she decided to have her wounds bound up and live for a bit longer. Nero did not object to her living, so long as Seneca was out of the way, and she enjoyed a safe if colorless old age.

Perhaps the most playful murder committed by Nero was that of an elderly aunt, a semi-invalid who was obliged to spend her days in bed because she suffered from a chronic complaint of the bowels. She seems to have been a gentle person, fluttery and affectionate; and one day when her imperial nephew had come to visit her and seated himself demurely on the edge of her bed for a chat, she stretched out a loving hand, stroked his chin upon which a fuzz, not yet a real beard, was growing, and said quaveringly in the sort of fond voice in which old ladies do speak to adored nephews, even though they may be scamps as well: "I only hope I live to see the day when you shave for the first time. Then I shall die contented."

"Very well," said Nero, smiling his sinister half-smile, "in that event, I'll have myself shaved at once."

Thereupon he issued orders to the courtiers surrounding him, a barber was fetched, and the fuzz was scraped off without more ado. Doctors were also summoned, and in a perfectly genial way the monster commanded that the sick old lady be given violent purgatives and overdoses of physic. Her surprise and dismay were short-lived, as was she herself; her natural indispositions were so aggravated that they carried her off in a very brief time, and her body was not even cold before Nero had seized all her property and suppressed her will in order that nothing she owned might find its way into other hands than his.

The full roster of Nero's murders runs on at almost endless length, and after a time it becomes unavoidably repetitive. But there is one crime, one particular murder, which stands out above all the others as the most spectacular crime of his career, even the focal point of his entire life. For this one rises above all the others—and, indeed, over most of the great crimes of history—not only for elaboration and bravado and color and inventiveness, but for a grand confusion of deeds and motives as well: this colossal act was the murder of the emperor's mother.

Personally and politically Agrippina was a fearsome woman. Not only was she what the French designate as *Madame Mère* (a term of status for which there is no precise English equivalent), but she was also the dowager empress in her own right; not only was she the mother of an emperor, but she was as well the wife of an emperor, the sister of an emperor, the niece of an emperor, the grandniece of an emperor, and the great-granddaughter through different branches of the family of both an emperor and an empress. Few persons in history have enjoyed loftier connections than these. Because of all this, and because of the strength of her personality, she was a great force to be dealt with.

She was not the sort of woman who would choose to remain

tactfully behind the scenes. She bound herself to dominate Nero, and through him the empire, at whatever cost; and since he was only seventeen years old when he succeeded, for a while this was not difficult. But as time wore on and he became annoyed with the restraint which her influence placed upon him, she had recourse to more devious methods. Incest was run-of-the-mill after her relationship with her brother Caligula, and her marriage to her uncle Claudius; so now, repeatedly, she took advantage of her son's fondness for drink to array herself in diaphanous finery and seduce him. Matters arrived at the state where the two of them, casting all discretion aside, rode together in a closed litter and were seen, upon dismounting, to have the most telltale stains upon their rumpled clothing. All this increased her ascendancy over him, but it also increased his resentment of her domination.

She was supposed to be very beautiful, although after the life she had led—debauchery interrupted by her spartan exile—there can have been but little bloom left on her by now. Being hard to start with, she had become coarsened to the texture of steel; and this steeliness, in the form of her ambition, separated her still farther from her son when she championed his marriage with Octavia. Originally Nero had been all in favor of this marriage, but after he became emperor he started resenting Octavia, too. He had fallen in love with, and wanted to marry, Poppaea, but his mother would have none of this. She laid herself out to him more lavishly than ever; she and Seneca between them found him a mistress who was almost exactly Agrippina's double, although younger. But Nero was suffering from his chronic discontent: he never had what he wanted, nor wanted what he had. There was now no substitute for Poppaea. Octavia had to be done away with. Agrippina would not allow this. Therefore, logically, Agrippina had first to be put out of the way. It was a touchy situation, but appealing at the same time. Thomas De Quincey describes the events which led up to the murder:

"It would really be pleasant, were it not for the revolting consideration of the persons concerned, and their relation to each other, to watch the tortuous pursuit of the hunter, the doubles of the game, in this obstinate chase. For certain reasons of state, as Nero attempted to persuade himself, but in reality because no other crime had the same attraction of unnatural horror about it, he resolved to murder his mother Agrippina. This being settled, the next thing was to arrange the mode and the tools. Naturally enough, according to the custom then prevalent in Rome, he first attempted the thing by poison. The poison failed: for Agrippina, anticipating tricks of this kind, had armed her constitution against them, like Mithridates; and daily took potent antidotes and prophylactics. Or else (which is more probable) the emperor's agent in such purposes, fearing his sudden repentance and remorse on first hearing of his mother's death, or possibly even witnessing her agonies, had composed a poison of inferior strength. This certainly had occurred in the case of Britannicus."

There was, in fact, a strange mingling of affections among Nero's hatreds; and after the murder had been accomplished and all of Rome was congratulating him upon this daring deed— Agrippina's friends trying to change sides, the Senate never more obsequious, nor the populace more servile—he suffered horrible tortures of remorse, wallowing in a swamp of self-pity and paying the murdered woman, who was certainly no martyr, every conceivable honor. He fancied that her ghost haunted him, and he performed many magic rites in an effort to entreat its forgiveness.

Meantime: "On Agrippina, however, no changes in the poison, whether of kind or strength, had any effect; so that, after various trials, this mode of murder was abandoned, and the emperor addressed himself to other plans. The first of these was some curious mechanical device, by which a false ceiling was to have been suspended above her bed; and in the middle of the night, the bolt being suddenly drawn, a vast weight would have descended with a ruinous destruction to all below. This scheme, however, taking air from the indiscretions of some amongst the accomplices, reached the ears of Agrippina; upon which the old lady looked about her too sharply to leave much hope in that scheme: so *that* also was abandoned."

So as to prepare the ground for the murder a little more thoroughly, Nero now decided that she should be harried in other ways for a bit while he was hatching further plots. Accordingly he banished her from the palace, snatched away all her titles and dignities (he could have done nothing more calculated to enrage her), and finally forced her to retire in ignominy to one of her country houses, almost unattended. At this point his sense of humor came to the fore; the game was to become even more diverting. He bribed various men of the city to bring false lawsuits against her in the courts, and he hired bands of vagrants to go out to her country house and make alarming noises under the walls at night, at other times jeering and mocking and screaming abuse which she—the proudest of the proud—was powerless to stop. All this time, though, his fertile brain was still contemplating the murder.

"Next he conceived the idea of an artificial ship, which, at the touch of a few springs, might fall to pieces in deep water. Such a ship was prepared and stationed at a suitable point. But the main difficulty remained, which was to persuade the old lady to go on board. Not that she knew in this case *who* had been the ship builder, for that would have ruined all; but it seems that she took it ill to be hunted in this murderous spirit; and was out of humor with her son; besides, that any proposal coming from him, though previously indifferent to her, would have instantly become suspected. To meet this difficulty, a sort of reconciliation was proposed, and a very affectionate message sent, which had the effect of throwing Agrippina off her guard, and seduced her to Baiae for the purpose of joining the emperor's party at a great banquet held in commemoration of a solemn festival."

For once her acumen seems to have deserted her. She was completely taken in by his repeated hypocritical assurances that he was contrite, that children ought to bear with the irritability of their parents and smooth over little disturbances. She bragged about her son's repentance and the recovery of her influence over him; and she set out to join him for the magnificent feast of Minerva.

She came to Baiae by water in a sort of light frigate, intending to return in the same way. Nero went to meet her, embraced her with seeming joy, and conducted her to the site of the ceremonies, having first slyly prevailed upon the captain of her galley to wreck it as if by accident, but right away, so that she should have no choice as to the vessel in which she was conveyed home when the time came. Everything went according to plan, and the festivities started to take place. The dowager empress was graciously received by all her son's cohorts, and seated at table above the emperor. The near success of his scheme made Nero frolicsome. He prolonged the feasting with playful conversation and youthful exuberance until he knew that the galley had been destroyed. All this time the collapsible ship was floating in plain sight near the shore.

"What was to be done? The great lady was anxious to return to Rome, and no proper conveyance was at hand. Suddenly it was suggested, as if by chance, that a ship of the emperor's, new and properly equipped, was moored at a neighboring station. This was readily accepted by Agrippina: the emperor accompanied her to the place of embarkation, took a most tender leave of her, and saw her set sail."

As a matter of fact, he had delayed the proceedings until nightfall so that the evil deed might take place in the dark; it had a greater chance of success this way, and of appearing to be an accident. In high spirits, then, he broke up the banquet, and trailed by the entire glittering court he escorted his mother down to the water-gate where, the night being brilliantly lit by slaves bearing torches, he made protracted farewells, clinging to her with every sign of the most fervent adoration, kissing her eyes repeatedly and at last even opening the front of her robe to place lingering kisses on her breasts, crying deceitfully: "Strength and health to you, mother! For you I live, and because of you I rule!"

"It was necessary that the vessel should get into deep water before the experiment could be made; and with the utmost agitation this pious son awaited news of the result. Suddenly a messenger rushed breathless into his presence, and horrified him by the joyful information that his august mother had met with an alarming accident; but, by the blessing of Heaven, had escaped safe and sound. . . . The ship, it seems, had done its office; the mechanism had played admirably; but who can provide for everything? The old lady, it turned out, could swim like a duck; and the whole result had been to refresh her with a little sea-bathing. Here was worshipful intelligence. Could any man's temper be expected to stand such continued sieges? Money, and trouble, and infinite contrivance wasted upon one old woman, who absolutely would not, upon any terms, be murdered! Provoking it certainly was; and of a man like Nero it could not be expected that he should any longer dissemble his disgust, or put up with such repeated affronts. . . . And, unquestionably, if people will not be murdered quietly, and in a civil way, they must expect that such forbearance is not to continue forever; and obviously have themselves only to blame for any harshness or violence which they may have rendered necessary."

De Quincey is mistaken in giving the impression that Agrippina was a sweet, frail, elderly lady: she was only entering middle age: she was tough, statuesque, mean, and arrogant. It can scarcely have surprised anyone that she could swim after her island exile, although that phase of her career had been somewhat glossed over lately. And she was, in addition, still very much alive, so the real murder had yet to be committed.

She had, meanwhile, swum furiously to the land, with her wet draperies clinging about her. News of the business was out the instant the ship sank, and the shore was thronged with people along the beach, some even walking out into the water, some climbing piers, and some setting forth in boats while public prayers for her safety wailed through the darkness. One of the boats picked her up just as she was reaching the shallows and conveyed her along to the Lucrine Lake where she had a villa. There was no moon, but the stars were out in silvery brilliance, and the black sea was as smooth as obsidian. The whole affair had not been very arduous except that during the ship's sinking she had been wounded in the shoulder by a falling timber. So now, safe for the moment, she entered her house, rigid with fury, and tried to think what she should do next.

When she had been relieved of her honors, she had also lost her bodyguard; the villa was full of slaves and women upon whom she could place no dependence. To be sure, the army owed her its loyalty, but even more it owed its loyalty to Nero as emperor. Her position was frustratingly impotent; and upon consideration it seemed to her that the wisest course was to pretend that nothing had happened, that the ship had collapsed by accident, that there had been no construction in her ceiling to make it fall on her, that she had not been insufficiently poisoned three times, that in brief everything was fine. Her only safety lay in seeming to ignore all. The advantage of this was that it might disarm Nero for the moment, and in the ensuing delay she could rally her forces for the inevitable battle. In line with these plans, then, she sent for her most trusted freedman, Agerinus, and dispatched him to tell the emperor that she had escaped death by the favor of the gods, and that she begged him to put off a visit to her for a few days, however distressed he might be at her narrow scrape, because she needed rest. Then she applied remedies to her wound and went to bed, pretending to feel perfectly secure.

What she had not counted on, however, was that the infuriating news was bound to have reached Nero already, considering the number of people who knew she was safe. Thus he had had plenty of opportunity to make new plans by the time Agerinus arrived with the message. Nero was, in fact, as frightened of what she might do as she was of him; and Agerinus was shown into the imperial presence to find the emperor toying with a pretty dagger and casting frenzied glances this way and that. While Agerinus was standing at attention repeating the empress's message to her son, the son was ranging and loping about the room, the dagger still in his hand. Finally he crept up behind Agerinus and stealthily dropped the dagger on the floor just beside the messenger's feet.

The stage was now set for the final treachery. Nero let out an awful bellow which brought a multitude of soldiers and courtiers flooding into the room. He pointed an accusing finger at the innocent Agerinus and screamed that he had

brought a dagger into the imperial presence at Agrippina's insti-
gation, and that she had sent this man to assassinate him. This
made everything more or less legal: Agerinus was taken off under
guard to be killed; and Agrippina's execution was formally and
publicly ordered.

The throng which had gathered along the shore had, by now,
begun to stream inland toward Agrippina's villa with the intention of wishing her joy and congratulating her on her good fortune in surviving. These people, advancing, had almost reached
the house when the approaching sight of Nero's armed and
threatening force halted them. There were countless witnesses
to what followed.

The leader of the murderous horde was one of Nero's bloodiest henchmen, Anicetus, the inventor of the collapsible boat,
a fierce hater of Agrippina, and the man who was later to bear
witness against Octavia. He had brought with him a considerable number of the guard, and he deployed them to surround the
house; then, being sure that no inmate escaped, the gates were
forced open, and the soldiers tramped clanking into the building.
It was dark and silent except for the ring of the boots on the
pavement; the women and slaves were clustered, trembling
with fear, in whatever hiding places they had been able to con-
trive. Such slaves as tried to defend the empress were slaughtered.
At last, with Anicetus leading, the soldiers marched down the
long gallery to the closed doors of Agrippina's bedroom. The
few persons who had gathered around the doors were hurled
aside, and bursting through, Anicetus strode in with the soldiers
at his heels.

Agrippina was in bed, but not asleep. She was attended by
a single slave-girl, and the bedroom was in semi-darkness, lit only
by a small oil lamp. As the soldiers entered, the girl sprang up,
cringing away from them; and the empress said icily: "Are you
leaving me, too?"

Then raising herself on an elbow and turning toward
Anicetus, who was flanked by a captain on one side and a centurion on the other, she said with gracious firmness, determined
to brazen it through as long as possible: "If you have come from

my son to find out how I feel after my accident, tell him that I am quite recovered."

They came slowly on toward her, their faces gray and blurred in the dim light, without answering her.

She went on a little more loudly: "But if you are here to do me harm, I will not believe that my son has sent you! He would not order his mother's murder!"

They were almost on top of her now, one at the foot of the bed, and one at either side. The captain had a club; he raised it, swung, and struck her violently across the head. She fell back against her cushions; but then, marshaling the last of her nearly exhausted energy as they leaned over her with drawn swords, she tore open the front of her gown to expose her still-beautiful body, and through bared teeth screamed savagely: "Stab me in the womb that housed such a monster!" The centurion plunged his sword into her belly; the others followed his example; and with many wounds she died.

Years earlier she had been forewarned of her doom, and had spurned the idea. While consulting the soothsayers about Nero's future she had been told that he would one day be emperor, and would kill his mother. Upon hearing this she had exclaimed scornfully: "Let him kill her, so long as he *does* become emperor!"

Nero's reign continued for yet another nine years after the murder of Agrippina; but when the end began to approach there was no stopping it. By an agreeable coincidence, it was on the very anniversary of his mother's death that word reached him of the revolt of the armies and the peoples in France, and it was on the anniversary of Octavia's murder that he, himself, died.

He was at Naples when the news came from France, and for eight days he loitered there, declining to answer the messages which arrived hourly, evidently finding the matter to be of no interest whatever. Finally the dispatches from France became so threatening that he dropped a note to the Senate, asking sulkily why that body did nothing to avenge these insults to its emperor. At last he was obliged grudgingly to return to Rome. He appeared to be seized with genuine panic at the state of affairs which he found there; but once back at the Golden House he did not bother to visit the Senate or in any way try to rally his forces, but spent his time playing with a new musical instrument which had just been invented, a water organ.

The second blow came with the news that the Spanish provinces under Galba (who was, in fact, destined to become the next emperor) had also revolted. At this point Nero flew into a fit of dramatics, fainted dead away, came to, tore his robe, beat his brow, and moaned that no one had ever suffered as he was now suffering. His nature was too volatile for these vapors to last for long, however, and presently he was back at his customary activities of feasting, giving concerts, and driving in the races; and since he was acclaimed supreme in these last two categories, he was now, he decided, ready to become the world's greatest gladiator, and he commenced to make plans toward that end, chief among which was the training of a tame lion which the emperor, advancing naked and empty-handed into the amphitheater, was to pretend to kill with superhuman strength using only his bare fists. The lion would dutifully roll over and play dead.

But while he was trifling with such fancies as this, his brain was also producing various plans for subduing the revolution: all the governors and heads of the army were to be massacred; all exiles everywhere and all Roman residents of foreign birth were to be slaughtered as a precautionary measure; the provinces were to be turned over to the army for pillage; the entire Senate was to be poisoned at a great banquet; and finally the city was to be set on fire, after a vast number of wild beasts had first been released on the people. All this came to nothing, however, and next he resolved to take the field himself, and upon meeting the rebels to throw his person upon their mercy: the sight of his piteous weeping would bring them all over to his cause once again. So he began to assemble his customary thousand baggage carts, and to think upon which of his musical instruments would be most suitable for the journey. All his current mistresses were to be dressed as soldiers and to form his escort. But he had no money for this undertaking, and as he was neither able to raise any nor to enlist any soldiers on his side, this plan also fell through.

His third plan was to assemble a fleet and sail away to some remote spot where he could establish a new kingdom of his own; but he had no ships, so he was necessarily obliged to stay at home. His fourth plan was similar to his second: he would appear in the Forum, dressed in black, weeping tragically enough to soften the most hardened heart, and loyalty would rise triumphant in the disloyal breasts of his subjects. But he was finally afraid to attempt this because his subjects might tear him to pieces before he could really engage their attention. Then, as a last possibility, he considered sneaking away to Egypt (a most musical country) where he could earn his living as a singer. But before this scheme could be developed to any degree, matters had come to a head.

In the face of his blithe certainty that he would somehow outwit his enemies, he cannot have realized the nearness to which his own doom had approached, for in spite of all his extravagant plans he still took no concrete action which could have resulted in his defense, but continued without interruption his life of frivolity. In line with his usual practices, one night shortly before his end he summoned to his palace suddenly and with extreme urgency, in greatest haste, a group of prominent senators and knights. These worthies naturally supposed that he had at last settled upon a definite course of action, and that he had called them to be present in order either to consult with them or to announce his decision. This was expecting too much of him, however, as they were soon to see; when they had assembled before him, he made his momentous pronouncement: "I have discovered a means by which the water organ will produce louder and more musical tones!" Dio adds incredulously: "In such jests did he indulge even at this crisis."

Matters, of course, were rapidly worsening all around him. Such men under arms as he had been able to send against the rebels deserted his cause and joined the uprising. At last even the Senate was moved to action against him; it withdrew its support of him, and various of its members approached the palace guard and persuaded them, also, to desert the emperor. The prefect of the guards' camp was loyal to Nero, so he was straightway killed, and the soldiers declared themselves for Galba.

This seduction of the guard had, unavoidably, been done in secret and very hurriedly, so that Nero was unaware of what was taking place around him; and on his last night as emperor he retired to bed no more alarmed than he had been, and went to sleep, hopefully anticipating that the morrow would bring him good fortune. At midnight he waked to discover that all his guards had left him. He sprang from his bed and rushed out through the empty, echoing halls and corridors of his great palace. He was able to raise a handful of followers—Sporus, whom he had married, and two or three others—but all those among his friends who owned any influence had fled. Mournfully he returned to his bedroom, only to find that now even his personal servants had run away, taking with them all the loot they could carry including his bedsheets and a little gold box in which he kept some of Locusta's poison against just such an emergency. So next he sent for a gladiator to come and kill him, but when the gladiator did not appear, Nero, in a frenzy, quitting the palace altogether, dashed off toward the Tiber intending to hurl himself into its depths; but he was deflected from this, too. Rather than die, he now decided that he needed to find some retired spot where he could collect his thoughts. His handful of followers was still with him, and such an asylum was offered by his freedman, Phaon, a villa a few miles outside the city; and so the emperor with his last remaining attendants set forth on horseback in the small hours of the night, snaking their way along the dark, ominous streets, through one of the unguarded gates in the city walls, and out into the open countryside.

Once they were beyond the walls their winding route took them perilously close to the mutinous guards' camp; fires flickered dimly through the intervening trees, and the riders could hear the drunken shouts of the soldiers themselves as they cursed Nero and made bets on Galba's success. The camp was safely skirted. Nero had paused in his flight only to wrap a dark cloak around him, and shroud his head and shoulders in a long scarf, and these garments concealed him in the blackness. It was a wild and fearful night, as if even the heavens were concerned with the deposing of an emperor: the tremors of an earthquake caused the ground beneath the horses' hoofs to quiver and dance, and at one point a bolt of lightning spurted down almost in Nero's face.

Here, outside the city, fighting had been engaged the day before, and dead bodies lay sprawled at the edge of the path. At one of these the emperor's horse shied violently, almost unseating him, and causing the scarf to fall away from his head. By an unlucky chance a retired soldier of the guard, an old half-pay officer, was at that moment picking his way along through the brush at the path's border; he glanced up, recognized the emperor, and saluted him. The little party hurried on without returning the salute, all the more frightened now because the course they had taken would certainly become known when this soldier reached the camp. The scarf was hastily secured in place once more; and when, presently, they passed a small band of marauders heading toward the city, the fugitives were unrecognized in the darkness, and the strangers only stopped them long enough to shout a question to them above the rising howl of the wind through the trees as to whether there might be any news of Nero's actions from Rome.

At length, as a gray dawn was beginning to break, they drew near to the villa. A barely visible trail led around to the back of the property. The riders dismounted, turned their horses adrift to graze among the scrub, and set out to follow the trail. Before they had gone any distance, however, forcing a passage through thorns and bramble bushes which whipped uncontrollably in the wind, they came to a reedy stretch of marshland which it was only possible to navigate after they pulled off their clothing and threw it in front of them to cover, successively, each space they crossed. Finally they came onto firm ground again, and in a short time reached the rear wall of the villa.

But there was no opening here, no way to get through; they were stranded on the outside. The only hope was to break a hole

in the wall, and while his attendants set to work at this task, the
emperor squatted on the damp, sandy ground and picked the
thorns out of the shreds of his cloak. By the time the sun was
fully risen, concealed behind banks of dull and heavy clouds, an
entrance had been forced. But it was only a small gap in the
masonry, and Nero, descendant of the gods, had to crawl through
on hands and knees, only to reach the bleak, deserted courtyard
where the slaves had formerly been kept.

He could go no farther. He had barely the strength left to
creep into one of the miserable cells where the slaves had slept,
and there he collapsed on a verminous pallet. His attendants
left him and went in search of food; but they could find only
water and the coarse black bread which had been fed to the
slaves. He took some water, but rejected the bread, turning his
face to the wall until, emotion overcoming his weariness, he decided that he must prepare to meet his end. He struggled out
into the courtyard once more and, with the help of his attendants, began to dig a grave for himself there. The tears which had
been intended to move nations streamed unnoticed down his
face; he had already begun to take on a deathly pallor in that
gray light. Weeping continually, he gathered together such shards
and bits of broken marble as he could find for the lining of the
grave, and begged anxiously that wood and water be brought so
that, upon his death, his body might be cleansed and ritually
burned.

Just as these preparations were being completed, there came
from the distance the rattle of horses' hoofs: a courier bringing
news from the city. The emperor's hiding place was known; he
had been proscribed as a public enemy by the Senate, and sentenced to execution by being stripped naked, impaled on a forked
stake, and beaten to death with rods. It was too much . . . *almost* too much. Two daggers were produced, and the sharpness
of their points tested. But he could not bring himself to commit
the final act.

In sheer imbecility of purpose he flew moaning around the
courtyard and back into his cell, then out once more, wailing
that the time had not yet come, and finally pleading that one

of his poor, faithful attendants should set him a good example by committing suicide first. The attendants unanimously and firmly declined to do any such thing. There was nothing for the great playactor to do now except act, so on the spot he composed and delivered a mournful soliloquy: "To live on thus, despoiled, disgraced, does not become a Nero! The times need resolution! Up, Nero! Rouse yourself!" and so on. Everybody stood around and listened politely, but the effectiveness of the scene was somewhat spoiled because at best Nero never smelled very good, and after all his exertions he positively stank.

Finally, as the monologue was drawing to an end and the exhausted body was flopping and posturing more weakly, an interruption occurred. The thunder of many horses was approaching the villa's gates; the echoes rang round the courtyard; the declaiming voice dwindled away. It was the troop of soldiers sent out to take him captive. He whirled about, snatched up one of the daggers, and held it to his throat. But still he lacked the courage, and after a moment one of the attendants stepped forward, placed his hand on top of the emperor's, and shoved the blade into that fat neck.

But Nero was not dead yet. He lost neither his voice nor his dramatic propensities, but sank back, gushing blood, while he contrived a beautiful, willowy decline, sobbing in his most soulful voice: "O, Jupiter, what an artist perishes in me!" and gesturing with graceful pathos. The imperturbable attendants laid him carefully on the ground beside the open grave. Meanwhile the party of horsemen had dismounted and forced open the gates, and now they came striding through the halls and apartments of the villa and out into the rear courtyard. All this time Nero was frenziedly talking on and on, weeping and lamenting at intervals, so that the centurion who was in command of the corps of soldiers rushed up to where the bleeding figure lay, whipped off his cloak, and held it to the wound. The emperor, choosing to take this as an act of renewed loyalty, said with lofty condescension: "You are too late!" When the centurion seemed somewhat taken aback, he added more graciously: "But you are faithful."

Then his eyes, always protuberant, bugged out still farther, and he expired.

The news of his death spread, of course, very rapidly. A messenger was dispatched to inform Galba, and while the body continued to lie on the ground of the courtyard, an immense crowd gathered from every side to see it and rejoice. In Rome the people ran wild with relief and thanksgiving; statues of the hated emperor were torn down and destroyed utterly; and many of the populace, in rapture, went so far as to wear the caps customarily worn only by newly freed slaves, to show that they had now emerged from the bondage of Nero's reign. It was only curious that the body of the dead ruler was not mutilated by the throngs which so detested him, but was instead allowed a decent burial.

He was not laid to rest in his homemade grave at Phaon's villa, however. Two of his old nurses deposited his ashes in a porphyry and marble tomb on the Pincian Hill, where the gardens of the Villa Borghese lie today. From this tomb (the family tomb not of the Caesars, but of his father's house, the Domitii) there was to be seen a magnificent panorama of the Tiber Valley and the lovely marble city of Rome spread out below; and in the serenity of this setting it appeared that at last a peaceful end had been reached to the violence and iniquity of the past fourteen years. Yet the terror generated by Nero had been so enormous that for a long time after his death was known to have occurred, and other emperors ruled in his stead, there were those who cautiously continued to place flowers at his tomb, venerate his statues, and make public his edicts, finding themselves unable to believe that a being so monumental in wickedness could be merely mortal, but confident that he would, like an avenging god, someday return to confound his enemies. And this aura of wickedness remained so persistently attached to his name that as much as a thousand years later, in the eleventh century at the depth of the Middle Ages, his murderous spirit was still reported to haunt the summit of the Pincian Hill.

PART 2

Catherine the Great of Russia

Catherine the Great of Russia

Peter the Great, more than any other Russian czar, directly influenced the path of his nation's history when, in the late seventeenth and early eighteenth centuries, he forced European customs, manners, and thought upon the backward and semi-Oriental peoples over whom he ruled. But as his political activities were triumphant, his personal life was disastrous. Only one of his sons survived childhood; and that son, Alexis, he detested with all his heart.

Alexis, in turn, equally detested his father; but since Peter was czar, it was inevitable that in a struggle between the two of them he should win, and so the event transpired. Peter announced that Alexis was the ringleader in a plot against his life, and accordingly he and five hundred other persons, ranging from the Bishop of Great Rostov to Alexis's stableboy (all of them archconservatives in violent disagreement with Peter's determination to westernize the country) were arrested, tortured, and killed. The weedy Alexis was not executed outright, but was rather tortured beyond his capacity to endure, so that at the last his father could with ostensible virtue withdraw his own destroying hand still technically clean of filicide, while at the same time he could await with perfect confidence the end which he was rendering inescapable. Within a period of less than a week Alexis first received twenty-five strokes of the knout (as this was administered in those days, the leather thongs of the whip interlaced with wires, it was physically impossible to survive thirty strokes), and then shortly he received fifteen more. The czar's reputation was salvaged, for his son died in bed rather than at the hands of the executioner.

Prior to these evil events Peter had ridded himself of his first wife, Alexis's mother, by shutting her up in a convent, and had chosen as his second wife a peasant woman who had begun the long, ascending line of her career under the protection of a Swedish dragoon, had graduated to the position of mistress of, respectively, Generals Shermentev and Menshikov, and finally engaged the affections of the czar himself who, in his rough, forthright way, married her and crowned her empress with the name Catherine I (not to be confused with Catherine II, the Great). They had altogether twelve children; and here the struggle for the succession of the Russian crown becomes immensely complicated.

The murdered Alexis had had one son, so that upon the death of Peter the Great there were left behind him two important claimants to the throne: the widowed Empress Catherine, and the late czar's grandson, another Peter. As seems often to be the case when the destiny of a throne is being decided, in Russia the imperial guard played a major part as a balance of power between rival claimants; and on this occasion, for the sake of old times and old loves, the empress had the guards on her side. While the Senate was deliberating over the succession, the guards lined up outside the palace, pounded on their drums in an ominous manner, and the Senate hastily arrived at the obedient decision that Catherine was the proper heir.

But her life of pleasure had ruined her health, and she lived to enjoy her accomplishment for two years only. Thereupon Peter, the grandson, who was now twelve years old, succeeded with the name Peter II. He was a disagreeable boy, just as his father had, in fact, been a disagreeable man; instead of staying in the new Europeanized capital called St. Petersburg which Peter the Great had built, he dragged the court back to the medieval gloom of Moscow and the Kremlin, with the result that he contracted smallpox in that unhealthy setting, and died on the very day set for his marriage, having reigned less than three years.

The succession now becomes even more tangled, and out of all the welter of would-be czars and czarinas a niece of Peter the Great's, Anne of Courland, ascended the throne, reigned ruinously for ten years, and died unmourned; she was succeeded by her grandnephew, Ivan VI, who was only two months old and who did not last for long on the throne.

Of all the twelve children born to Peter the Great and his Catherine, only two had survived, both daughters. The elder of these was comfortably settled as Duchess of Holstein; the younger, Elizabeth, had been living in a retirement which was not altogether voluntary through the last several reigns. Now, however, she saw that her opportunity had come. She was already the center of a large and optimistic, if not very wieldy political faction, and she decided to risk all on a gamble for the throne. Either she would become empress, or she would at best be shut up in a convent, or at worst be put to torture and death.

She descended upon the most important of the guards regiments to secure its aid, and one of those characteristic, awesome Russian scenes of utter emotional abandon took place: the aspiring daughter of Peter the Great appeared out of the night in full military regalia, escorted to the guards barracks by her coterie of plotters, her face flushed with the anticipation of triumph. The soldiers, fervid with enthusiasm, brandished their arms, cheering her, and swore oaths of everlasting loyalty. Tears flowed copiously, and everyone set out for the palace through the silvery light of dawn in a high state of stimulation after the emotional orgy in the barracks. There was no one to stop them, and upon reaching the palace they marched directly in, waked up the baby czar and his parents, sent the child off to imprisonment, banished the parents north of the Arctic Circle, and the newly made empress ordered the rest of her household to join her at her imperial home in time for lunch.

Elizabeth reigned for twenty years, and was a popular ruler. She was a beautiful woman, very vain and somewhat eccentric: she cut out the tongues of persons whom she suspected of lying to her, and enjoyed dressing as a man, although when she died it was found that she possessed more than fifteen thousand dresses. Long before the end of her reign she had, being unmarried and childless, decided on her heir: her nephew, the son of her sister, the Duchess of Holstein; and she brought him to Russia and found a wife for him. In due time he became Czar Peter III, and it was by this path that his inexperienced little German bride became Catherine the Great, enlightened empress, friend of Voltaire and Diderot, thinker, writer, politician, conversationalist, voluptuary, and committer of one of the most notorious crimes of the eighteenth century.

It was common gossip that the Empress Elizabeth had three hundred lovers, and in this instance the gossip was surprisingly accurate. Through her career she had five principal lovers, but she by no means limited her favors to these five; and to vary the possible monotony of her life, a constant stream of men poured up and down the back stairs of her palaces; her only regret can have been that, unlike the Empress Faustina in Rome, she could not run her practiced eye over great numbers of sailors and physical laborers, all stripped perfectly naked for inspection, and pick the one whose assets struck her most favorably just as she might have picked the best vegetables for her table. Still, with three hundred lovers she maintained a certain standard of her own.

It was also common gossip that Catherine the Great had three hundred lovers. But here the gossip and the truth parted company. Elizabeth was promiscuous in the general sense, Catherine in the particular. Whereas Elizabeth had five major lovers and a host of lesser ones, Catherine had twelve major lovers and no lesser ones to speak of. She was as faithful to each of her lovers in turn as if he had been her husband. The husband himself was the only one to whom she was unfaithful.

In her slickly plausible memoirs she says blithely: "I was very affectionate, and gifted with an appearance which was very attractive. I pleased at the first glance without employing any arts or pains to that end." She must have found it agreeable to think so kindly of her own appearance; but either she believed what she wrote because she had hypnotized herself into it, or she was flatly lying, for she was by no means so lovely as her description suggests. Elizabeth had been a beauty, but Catherine was a frump. She had a big, square head with straight, heavy, black eyebrows like a coal miner, and as she grew older she became positively dumpling-faced, very pudgy and jowly, with double chins.

Catherine's beginnings were somewhat lowly when viewed by royal standards. She began life as a Princess of Anhalt-Zerbst, a petty and indigent German state; her father was a big, wooden, slow-thinking soldier, and her mother was an ambitious, dissatisfied, sharp-tongued woman. It was her mother who immediately saw the possibilities when the Empress Elizabeth selected the Holstein Peter as her heir, and began unctuously and obsequiously making up to the empress on her daughter's behalf. The empress had a certain fondness for Germans. She had once been in love with a German. Peter was going to need a wife, of course, and Elizabeth was warily casting about in search of one. Catherine seemed to suit the requirements, so she and her mother set out for Russia where the girl, being pronounced acceptable, painfully underwent the necessary conversion from Lutheran to Russian Orthodox and married the young grand duke, who was even more of a nitwit than anyone had supposed. As soon as Elizabeth had the girl in her hands she sent the odious Princess of Zerbst packing, and that was the end of her so far as history is concerned. The incompatible newlyweds settled down to a life of total and mutual misery.

But much as Catherine disliked her husband, her strict Lutheran background had by no means been completely overcome. Peter was retarded in every way: he had both the physique and the mentality of a ten-year-old destined never to mature, and it was scarcely surprising that he was sexually impotent. All the same, Catherine put up with him, and they went their own separate ways as much as possible. It seems likely that she would never, of her own accord, have come up with the notion of taking a lover to fill the conspicuous gap in her life; but whether or not she would have, the occasion did not arise, for after several years, when the young couple had no children, Elizabeth put forward the idea herself.

It was Catherine's plain duty to produce an heir to the throne, and if her husband were incapable of helping out, somebody else would have to be called in to do the job instead. Elizabeth, after all, had lovers by the hundreds; why shouldn't Catherine have one? The Lutheran background put up a token struggle, but it was quickly defeated by the power of sheer, innate voluptuousness, and Catherine dulcetly surrendered herself to her first lover.

The moral jolt which this hurdle involved was really much smaller than it would have been a hundred years later. The Victorians with their standards of behavior would have seemed both silly and impractical. The eighteenth century in all its frivolous objectivity looked upon such matters with beaming tolerance. There was, for example, the celebrated case of Voltaire's mistress, Madame du Chatelet. For a long while this lady lived harmoniously in her château with both her husband and Voltaire at the same time; and the good-natured husband once said to Voltaire, upon discovering that she had yet another lover: "We have been betrayed!" Finally Monsieur du Chatelet drifted off by himself with his own mistress, but he never completely lost interest in his extraordinary wife. She was a notably ugly woman, and she wore so many diamonds that she glittered like the heavenly firmament. But she possessed a brilliant intellect. She was a writer, a translator, a scientist. And she was also of an excessively amorous disposition. At last she found herself pregnant by still another gentleman, with whom she was wildly infatuated.

So she and Voltaire retired to the château once more, and put their heads together. The Chatelets occupied a lofty social position, and moved freely among the court at Versailles; this latest affair had, in fact, taken place while madame was visiting the queen's jovial father who maintained a separate court at Luneville. Plainly the child was going to have to be provided with a legitimate parentage, and there was only one person who could accomplish this. Monsieur du Chatelet was formally invited to come home for a visit. Everything possible was done to insure an agreeable setting; and when his coach came trundling up the drive his favorite foods were cooking in the kitchen, a great supply of wines and spirits lay ready to hand, and his wife had decked herself out in even more diamonds than usual. Voltaire flitted discreetly about in the background acting as master of ceremonies and seeing that everything ran along smoothly.

The inevitable took place. Madame was glad to see her husband again. She was affectionate. She was fetching in her hideous way. They were still married, even though they had not been living together for a long time. They went in to dinner. Monsieur du Chatelet ate a large amount of his favorite foods, grew rather drunk and nostalgic and maudlin, and was then gently led off to bed by his scheming wife. The embryo was made legitimate, and Monsieur du Chatelet went away again without having the least notion of what was going on.

Everyone was very well pleased with this arrangement; and when the story got out, as of course it did, it was regarded as the tidiest and most polite possible way of dealing with such an awkward circumstance. This bit of rococo flummery had taken place some five years before Catherine, in Russia, became pregnant by her first lover; and however strictly her background might have inclined her, she could scarcely help being influenced by the knowledge that such occurrences were taking place not only in the Chatelets' domestic life, but in so many other situations all over the continent. The crowned heads were doing nothing to set a good example: there was Elizabeth with her three hundred lovers; there was Louis XV with a string of dazzling mistresses— the Mailly sisters, Pompadour, du Barry; there was Frederick the Great pursuing his strange if niggardly vices at Potsdam; England was run by the mistresses of the bovine Hanover kings; and Maria Teresa, herself a paragon of unbending virtue, produced two scandalous daughters—Marie Caroline, Queen of Naples, and Marie Antoinette, Queen of France.

What was to be expected of the innocent and unhappy Catherine? Her first lover had everything that his position could have demanded. He was a handsome and charming and exceedingly romantic young nobleman; in addition, and this was a considerable asset, he was in favor with the Empress Elizabeth; and finally, he gave Catherine a son, the future Emperor Paul, so that the Romanov dynasty, which is courteously supposed to have lasted until the Russian Revolution of 1917, was not the Romanov dynasty at all, but, after Peter III, the Saltikov dynasty, for that was the young gallant's name.

Unfortunately, however, he lacked the firmness of purpose to keep up with Catherine, who was now beginning to exert her political influence. He was sent to Sweden on a diplomatic mission, and there his predilection for philandering immediately caused him to form a new attachment. She did not tolerate this infidelity. She threw him over without delay, although it cost her great pain to do so. He had been her first real love. She was not so pained, however, that she didn't presently find a second lover, who lasted until a short time before the Empress Elizabeth's death, when Catherine fell in with the five Orlov brothers—great, virile, cursing, singing, drunken soldiers who were in sympathy with her political ambitions. The handsomest of these brothers was Gregory, and he became her third lover, and up to this time her most important one.

The two of them lived together from her last drab days as a grand duchess until long after she was firmly established and permanently accepted as empress in her own right, a period of some ten years. Orlov was masterful and passionate as a lover, but his character had many drawbacks; he was thoughtless, vain, arrogant, and unfaithful. After the first bliss, dissatisfaction grew slowly upon Catherine, until at long last he went *too* far. He seduced his thirteen-year-old cousin. Catherine determined to be rid of him at any cost—and the price of his dismissal was enormous: the title of prince, a yearly income of fifteen thousand rubles, six thousand serfs from any of the crown domains, and many smaller items. But her offers in this matter were also her commands, and he never returned to the position he had held for so long.

On the rebound from this rift she fell immediately into the arms of the first handsome man she saw, and this was one of her mistakes. They found each other mutually unsatisfactory. To avoid the repetition of such a thing, it was at this time that it became customary for her lovers to take what amounted to an entrance examination before commencing on their duties. They were first subjected to a thorough physical inspection by her Scottish physician, and then they went through a trial run of several days' duration with two of her maids of honor to see if their sexual capabilities were up to her expectations.

The first man who passed this examination became her fifth

and most important lover. His name was Potiomkin, and he was the one man of all whom she loved most completely and honestly. He was a giant in stature, and strong, as all her lovers had to be; but there the pattern ceased to be followed. He had only one eye, and at his best had been far from handsome. He was a wild, restless, moody creature, violently jealous of his imperial mistress, and as thoroughly in love with her as she was with him. His character was composed exclusively of paradoxes. He was a thundering general, but frightened by the sound of cannon; he was so lazy that for days on end he would never dress or comb his hair, but loll about his apartments fingering his jewels and muttering in the depths of Slavic melancholy, and then suddenly be seized with such energy that he would dash off to the farthest corner of the empire at a moment's notice; he was harsh but sensitive; alternately he wallowed in debauchery and purified himself through religion; he was, in brief, everything a non-Russian like Catherine thought a Russian lover ought to be: brutal and tender and half mad. He chewed his nails incessantly.

Gregory Orlov had been a passionate bully, too, but he lacked Potiomkin's intuitive understanding of Catherine's needs. When Orlov chose to give the empress a present he selected the Orlov diamond. To this day it is the fourth-largest cut diamond in the world. It cost him four hundred thousand rubles, and even with his resources it took him seven years to pay for it. Catherine, for her part, was passionately fond of jewelry; she bought so many emeralds that she upset the international market; but still, considering the hoards of jewels already in her possession, this magnificent diamond (which she mounted in the imperial scepter) was not an imaginative gift. Such thoughtless tactics were not for Potiomkin. He wrote poems and composed songs to her. He sent her roses from Italy in midwinter, and a basket of cherries on New Year's Day. A dancer from Paris was imported to amuse her, and a violinist from Rome; a vine of rare grapes from the Crimea was brought for her delectation. An officer was employed by Potiomkin who did nothing but scour the earth for the most wonderful and imaginative of gifts for the empress (this dizzy gentleman suggested that his epitaph should read: "Onward, coachman! Whip your horses faster!").

Orlov had always been somewhat under foot, but Potiomkin was never that. He possessed palaces so magnificent that the imperial grandeur shrank in comparison. His chef was reputed to be the finest in the world. The first oranges in Russia were served at his table. And aside from his trappings, he was a wit; he could always make Catherine laugh. Theirs was, altogether, a great love in the grandest sense of the term. He was incestuous with his niece, but this did not appear to bother Catherine in the slightest. She, herself, was always faithful to him while he was in the neighborhood. She only took her last seven lovers while Potiomkin was tearing off to the ends of the world to wage a war or negotiate a peace; and most of those seven were picked with Potiomkin's knowledge, sometimes even with his assistance.

But the twelfth and last of the lovers, named Zubov, proved to be Potiomkin's undoing. He was twenty-two, small, lithe, and egotistical; Catherine was in her sixties, fat, sagging, and magnificent. Potiomkin rushed home for the last time, demanding his dismissal as he had demanded the dismissal of the others when he felt that they had been in office long enough, but for once the empress failed to honor his request. It was war between Potiomkin and Zubov, and only one of them could survive. Zubov had the imperial ear and the aging body, but Potiomkin had the hitherto unfailing magic of his personality to support him. He set furiously to work, wooing his mistress all over again. His ranging imagination slipped the leash. His palaces were thrown open to the most splendid entertainments of his career; there were balls, banquets, masquerades, comedies, fireworks displays so brilliant that they were only outshone by Potiomkin's coat studded with diamonds from collar to hem, and his diamonds only outshone by the brilliance of his wit. Potiomkin did not need money. He did not need the imperial patronage. He was almost as powerful as the empress herself. He did it all for love of a toothless, swollen old woman.

And he failed.

The last of the banquets was one of the most resplendent in

history. It had taken hundreds of workers months to prepare. A thousand guests were invited to Potiomkin's Taurian Palace; the empress's arrival was heralded by a three-hundred-piece orchestra. Meat, drink, and clothes were distributed to the mobs outside. The festivities began with a masked ball which Catherine viewed from her throne. Then followed a ballet led by her grandsons, in which the dancers were adorned in ten million rubles worth of jewels. At length the company moved into a tapestried hall where a life-size artificial elephant covered with rubies and emeralds introduced yet a grander pageant involving two more ballets, an original comedy, the singing of choruses, and culminating in a vast costumed procession depicting all the groups and races subject to the empress's sway. The guests, attended by hundreds of footmen, strolled through the dozens of reception rooms and state apartments. At dinner the table service was all of gold. Potiomkin was defiantly dressed in bright red; but despite the grandeur of the entertainments he could not prevent his nervousness from overcoming him: at the end of the evening he escorted the empress to her carriage, and after she had driven away into the night he stood alone on the brilliantly lighted steps of the palace for a long time, trembling with apprehension.

His efforts had been of no avail. Early the next morning he received a terse note which ended everything. She thanked him for the entertainments, and was pleased to consider this last as a farewell feast. His presence was more urgently needed with the army than in the capital.

She should have realized that it was the beginning of the end for both of them. Potiomkin was ill, and now he seemed to court death; it came to him during a quixotic carriage dash across country; the greatest man in Russia died on coats hastily flung down for him at the roadside, without doctor or priest in attendance, and his single eye was closed by that same devoted niece with whom he had been intermittently living for so long. Catherine's end, when it came, was more peaceful. She died without pain after spending her last night of lovemaking with the silky Zubov. Neither Catherine's nor Potiomkin's personality was quite complete without the other. He had been one of her earliest supporters; even before she came to the throne he had loved her from a distance; and along with the Orlovs he had stood over the freshly murdered body of her husband so many years before. He had even helped to instigate that murder.

For Peter III had long since been put out of the way. That deed had been the necessary, the inevitable gateway through which Catherine's reign had been reached. So long as Peter lived and ruled she was no more than his wife, a czarina but not, to draw the distinction here, an empress. Nor would even her life have been certainly safe. If she had not killed him, he would have killed her. His nitwit malice had expanded to fantastic proportions, not only because of his impotence and her lovers, but because he resented the weakness of his own character and the strength of hers, her ability as a ruler and his inability, her popularity and the odium in which he was held by his subjects.

But he had earned that odium. He reigned for six months between the death of the Empress Elizabeth and Catherine's accession, and in that period he committed almost every conceivable folly, public and private. He had not the least interest in Russia; his total interest was in his German duchy of Holstein; he did not want to be czar, he wanted to be duke; he insulted fatally the all-powerful guards regiments by importing Holstein soldiers; he assembled his armies in preparation for war against Denmark for a tiny strip of Holstein soil, when Russia herself had infinitely greater need of those armies; and finally, in sheer insanity, he presented the whole Russian empire to his hero, Frederick the Great, King of Prussia, who had been Elizabeth's mortal enemy and was to become at best Catherine's uneasy ally. Frederick had the good sense to decline the gift.

Peter's private life was more pitiable than shocking. Without being a thoroughgoing, happy drunkard as the Orlovs and Potiomkin and so many other lusty Russians were, he managed to stay intoxicated, or at least muzzy, a great part of the time. Having just lately graduated from playing with lead soldiers, he treated his beloved Holstein guards as toys, and spent hour upon foolish hour deploying them about the grounds of his palaces, as if the Czar of all the Russias had no more serious matter with which to deal. He wore the Holstein uniform in preference to the Russian. He dismissed all his capable advisers, ostentatiously ignoring the most capable of all, his wife, and allowed himself to be guided by those courtiers who flattered him, however incompetent they might be. And, although he lacked the capacity to take a mistress in the customary sense, he surrounded himself with doubtful ladies, and his titular mistress was one of the homeliest women in the land: she was pockmarked, and had a bust as large as an alp.

He treated Catherine disgracefully. It had been plain for some while that trouble was brewing, but now it came out into the open. The psychological point beyond which there was no turning back was the famous banquet in honor of the Russo-German alliance. Five hundred guests were invited. The flower garlands were works of art; there were fireworks and salutes of cannon; the court poet had written a drama for the occasion, and the court composer had set it to music; everything was as festive as could be. Catherine sat at the center of the vast banquet table, and Peter at the head. When the toast to the imperial family was made, Catherine did not rise to drink. Peter, already fuddled, sent an equerry to demand why. Catherine replied with strained politeness that as she was, herself, a member of the imperial family, she had not considered it courteous. The equerry took her answer back to the head of the table; and Peter sent him down immediately once more to tell the empress that she was a silly fool. And then, fearful that this message might not be delivered in all its crudity, he leaned forward and shouted down the length of the table between the rows of glimmering guests: "Fool! Fool!"

In the shocked silence that followed this outrage Peter was irrevocably doomed. But Catherine did not want to move prematurely; she had to be sure of her resources. Yet delay brought danger. The next insult, during another banquet, was Peter's bestowal of the Order of St. Catherine upon his ugly mistress; only members of the imperial family were permitted to wear the Order of St. Catherine; the empress had not even received hers until she was officially betrothed to Peter, so this gift could only mean that the mistress was to become, in fact, a member of the family, and that Catherine was either to be divorced and banished, as Peter the Great's first wife had been, or killed.

Catherine preserved a stony silence throughout the festivities, and blankly watched her slavering husband pin the order to that huge breast. The one thing Peter now wanted from his wife was a reaction. It made no difference to him what sort of reaction it was—no form of admiration or affection, certainly; the time for that was past—it was not too late, however, for a display of fear or anger or jealousy or hatred. But Catherine sat on, bleak-faced, unreacting.

As the evening passed and the czar grew drunker, his irrational rage mounted until, at last, mad with useless fury, he ordered the arrest of the empress. The adjutant to whom the command had been given dared neither to obey nor to disobey, and went to the czar's uncle, Prince George of Holstein, for advice. It was only with the greatest difficulty and the most intense persuasions that this old man prevailed upon the czar to rescind the command. Catherine was allowed to depart unmolested, but the sign had already been made, and the whole court knew that it could now be only days before outright war was declared. Catherine overthrew her husband's government six nights later.

She could wait no longer. For all Peter's incompetence, he had inherited from Elizabeth a first-rate spy system, and even without his attention it continued to function as it had done during the previous reign. The fact that there was a plot afoot, although not the details, had become known; and a certain Lieutenant Passek, one of the plotters, was arrested for making "treasonable speeches against His Majesty." Within twenty-four hours everything Passek knew would be tortured out of him, and the plotters, including the empress, would be either dead or on their way to exile.

Neither Peter nor Catherine was in St. Petersburg that night. The following day was the czar's name-day; exquisite celebrations were scheduled, and he had withdrawn with his Holstein guards and his covey of ladies, all giggling and flirting with him, to the palace of Oranienbaum some miles outside the city. Catherine, not imagining that the hour of the revolution had arrived, was alone at the Peterhof palace to which the czar would proceed with his retinue the next day. (Oranienbaum was the palace which the Empress Elizabeth had given to Peter and Catherine when they were newly married, and in which they had spent their miserable years until her death. Peterhof was a huge, Italianate palace at the coast built by Peter the Great.)

As usual, drink had overtaken the czar that night. Catherine had gone to bed and to sleep. In St. Petersburg the news of Passek's arrest spread rapidly among the conspirators, and Gregory Orlov went at once to the barracks of the Ismailovsky regiment (one of the most powerful ones) to bring the guards round to Catherine's side. He sent his youngest brother, Alexis, to Peterhof in a hired carriage to awaken the empress and return with her to the capital in all possible haste. It was after midnight when he set forth, driving slowly to protect the horses for the return trip, through the crisp, silvery brilliance of a June night.

But when he arrived at the great pillared palace he found it deserted. The avenues and gardens were empty; the fountains were still. The empress was sleeping not in the palace itself, but in a little red pavilion called *Mon Plaisir* whose terrace was soothingly lapped by the starlit waves of the Gulf of Finland, and there Alexis found her. The tiny pavilion was unguarded, and her waiting woman, recognizing the familiar figure, admitted him without a word. In the dressing room the elaborate gown for the celebration of the czar's name-day lay ready to be put on; without ceremony he strode into the bedroom and, bending over the sleeping empress, said loudly: "Get up, Little Mother. Everything is prepared in the city."

She was awake instantly: "What has happened?"

"Passek has been arrested."

She dressed hurriedly, not in the elegant costume laid out for her, but in her simplest black dress, and slipped, silent and unobserved, through a french window onto the terrace and across the damp grass to where the carriage waited. The sky was graying in the east as they galloped back toward the city, growing slowly, steadily into the freshness of a golden summer dawn. The czar would have had perfect weather for his festivities.

They passed a few isolated vehicles, but no one recognized the plainly dressed woman in the hired carriage. At last, on the outskirts of St. Petersburg, in the full, slanting light of early morning, they were met by Gregory Orlov, who escorted them to the barracks of the Ismailovsky regiment. While Catherine stayed in the carriage, he went into the guardroom, and in a few minutes he returned with a handful of officers, followed by several dozen soldiers, half dressed, rubbing the sleep out of their eyes. Catherine stepped down from the carriage and addressed her drowsy audience briefly. She had come there for protection; would they renounce their allegiance to the czar? The drowsiness evaporated like dew. A surge of wild devotion swept over the scene. The soldiers pressed forward upon her, kissing her hands and the hem of her dress, hoarsely swearing their loyalty when a priest with raised crucifix appeared at the side of the regimental colonel; and the oath of fealty was administered there on the bare ground of the barracks yard under that bright sky.

Catherine returned to her shabby carriage; Orlov and the colonel rode beside it; the priest with his crucifix walked ahead; and the excited soldiers followed on foot. This little crowd proceeded next to the headquarters of the Semenovsky regiment, but the news had gone ahead of them, and before they reached the second barracks they were met by the wave of a jubilant throng, heavily armed, which in turn placed itself at the empress's disposal. At the head of her two faithful regiments Catherine rode on to the Preobrazhensky regimental barracks.

Here there was a slight check, for the brother of Peter's buxom mistress was one of the principal officers, but before a true struggle could be engaged the enthusiasm had overflowed, and the third regiment was in the empress's hands. The Guards' Artillery came next, and the keys of the arsenal were surrendered. The whole of the city was aroused by now. Houses emptied their occupants out into the streets and squares, and the procession grew longer and more exultant with every minute until the hired carriage was the center of a vast, cheering horde.

At length the procession made its heavy way to the Kazan Cathedral, where Catherine was annointed empress and autocrat of all the Russias, and from there took its course to the Winter Palace where the Senate was gathered, waiting. The palace doors were thrown open, and the crowd with Catherine at its head took possession. At noon the patriarchs of the Church arrived with the crown, scepter, and holy books. Ten thousand soldiers had congregated in the great square outside the palace. The day had grown hot and sultry, but not one member of the huge crowd stirred from the spot. The entire series of events had taken no more than five hours.

At Oranienbaum, meanwhile, Peter slept on into the morning while his throne was being stolen from him, arose somewhat the worse for the amount he had drunk the night before, attended a parade of his Holstein soldiers at eleven, ate a leisurely lunch, and at two set out with twenty of his ladies for Peterhof in a large open carriage, precious complexions guarded from the sun by bright parasols, gay laughter ringing across the parklands. But Peterhof was deserted. No preparations had been made for the czar and his company. The name-day festivities had been forgotten. Servants reported that the empress had been missing since early morning.

Peter could not believe it. He ran round the palace, looking for his wife in cupboards and under beds, while the ladies strolled on the terraces among the fountains and statues. At last a messenger arrived, dust-covered and limp with exhaustion, bringing the news that Peter had been deposed. The tranquillity of the scene went all to pieces. Peter would hasten to the city, show himself to the guards, and restore their loyalty to him. No, that might miscarry. One of his aides went to "talk seriously" to Catherine; a second went to bring the guards to their senses; a third went to try to assassinate the empress. Peter, pacing along the upper terrace, began issuing useless manifestoes right and left, sending letters to his wife telling her to stop whatever she was doing. In this fashion the afternoon passed. The more astute courtiers had thought of plausible reasons for leaving. To those who remained, a light supper was served on the lawn. Again, Peter got a little drunk.

Finally another idea was advanced. The navy and a large section of the army were at the island port of Kronstadt. The czar should retire there and request the protection of the garrison. A yacht was procured, and at eleven o'clock—after considerable delay in getting the ladies, the palace kitchens, and the wine cellar aboard—they set sail. They arrived at Kronstadt at one in the morning. Chains were stretched across the harbor; Catherine's emissaries had reached the garrison first.

Peter demanded entrance: "It is I, the emperor!"

"There is no emperor. Move off, or we fire!"

The alarm was sounded in the fortress, and as the yacht pulled away into the darkness of the night, hundreds of voices could be heard shouting in the town: "Long live Catherine II!" In the lowest cabin on the yacht, Peter buried his head in his mistress's lap, and was comforted to sleep. There was nothing to do, nowhere to go. To return to Peterhof would be futile. The boat made its hopeless way across the cold, black, silent water to the pretty, indefensible pleasure palace of Oranienbaum, once more.

Meantime, in the Winter Palace, Catherine had spent the afternoon in a council of state with the Senate. What was to be done with Peter now that he had been deposed? He must be taken prisoner; the formality of an abdication must be observed; and he must then be interred. He could not be allowed to wander about on the loose, but at the same time it was too much to hope that he would voluntarily place himself in the hands of his enemies. A military campaign to Peterhof was necessary, and at ten o'clock in the evening, just when the yacht was being fitted out to sail for Kronstadt, the expedition started forth from the capital.

Catherine had assumed the title of Colonel of the Guards. Mounted astride a white, dappled horse, she made a quick circle of inspection around her troops, some fourteen thousand in number, and then led the march out of the city in search of the czar. She wore oak leaves twined in her dark hair, and silhouetted bravely against the night, she seemed to be everything the soldiers wanted in an empress. That march to Peterhof was a brilliant political move. The revolution had been accomplished, and now there existed the danger of a backswing; but there was no time for a backswing with fourteen thousand troops on the march.

They spent the night along the road. The advance guard, riding ahead, reached Peterhof at five in the morning, and finding it deserted went on without dismounting to Oranienbaum. There the ornamental, useless Holstein soldiers had no ammunition, and had only been trained with wooden rifles in any case, so no resistance was offered. Peter sent a cringing letter to Catherine at Peterhof, and his envoy prudently deserted to the empress's cause. Then he sent a second letter renouncing the throne. In return Catherine coldly sent back to him a formal abdication, already written out, ready to be signed, and a stern message that he was to come to her immediately. He signed the abdication without a murmur of protest, meekly delivered himself into Gregory Orlov's power, and was driven away to imprisonment in a heavily curtained carriage with armed grenadiers on the running boards, on the step behind, and at the driver's side. Frederick the Great, to whom he had tried to give Russia, remarked tartly: "He allowed himself to be deposed like a child being sent to bed."

Catherine's position was now absolutely secure except for one glaring point: She had not the most remote legitimate claim to the throne of Russia. By deposing her husband she had committed an overt act of treason; but to gloss over this, the heir should then have been the young czarevitch, Paul. There was no question of her remaining in the background as regent, however. All the power was hers. But to make matters yet more difficult, Ivan VI—the baby czar who had been deposed by Elizabeth—was still alive, a prisoner in the Schlusselburg fortress. So at this moment there were three genuine claimants to the throne alive in the country.

Paul was sufficiently under her thumb that he was never to become a source of trouble. And in time Ivan VI, who had grown into a tall, stuttering, redheaded man, was to be killed during a fanatical effort to rescue him (but regardless of that then-unknown prospect, he had been so long imprisoned that he was almost forgotten). But Peter was a very different matter, and a very obvious focal point for any discontent which might subsequently materialize. Catherine was heard by a number of persons to refer to the unlikely event of his demise as "the best of all possible solutions"; and the empress's wish was his sentence of death.

Ostensibly he, like Ivan VI, was to be imprisoned in the Schlusselburg fortress; but in the meantime, until suitable quarters could be arranged there for him, he was taken to the little estate of Ropsha a few miles from St. Petersburg, under the guardianship of the same Alexis Orlov who had ridden to Peterhof with the news of Passek's arrest. This Alexis was a devil. On one side of his face he was as handsome as his brothers, but on the other side his face was warped and twisted, as the result of a dueling scar, into a perpetual snarling leer. And he gave as good as he got: it was he who put out Potiomkin's missing eye. This ruffian was the deposed czar's head jailer.

Precisely what took place at Ropsha has never become known. Peter was held there under close guard; it had been agreed before the signing of the abdication that he was to have his mistress with him, but they were instantly separated; he was shut up in one small room, the windows closely draped so that the guards on duty outside would have no chance of seeing him and, perhaps, feeling sympathy for him. His captors sat in an outer room, monotonously drinking and playing cards. Catherine had, of course, returned to the capital as soon as the prisoner was secured; and toward evening a week after the abdication she received a hastily scrawled note from Alexis Orlov at Ropsha: " . . . I tremble before Your Majesty's anger that you do not believe something awful of us, and that we are not the cause of the death of your rascal. But now the lackey Maslov sent to serve him has fallen ill, and he himself is so sick I do not believe he will live until evening . . ."

So Peter's murder had already begun.

And shortly later a second letter came: ". . . Little Mother, he lives no longer in this world . . . it came to a quarrel at table . . . we, ourselves, can not remember what we did . . ." It seems a convenient piece of forgetfulness concerning a murder so freshly committed.

Catherine was preparing herself for the evening when Alexis's terrible letters arrived; she locked them away in a secret drawer of her writing table, never again to be mentioned, and there they were found after her death by the Emperor Paul. An hour later she attended a magnificent reception. She was animated, brilliant, gracious, calm, regal. Gregory Orlov was at her side throughout the evening; and on the following morning, Sunday, a statement was released to the public: "On the seventh day of Our reign we received the information to Our great sorrow and affliction that it was God's will to end the life of the former czar Peter III by a severe attack of haemorrhoidal colic."

The body was brought to St. Petersburg and publicly laid out in the Nevsky cloister where the dead czar's rebellious subjects paraded past the bier for a final half-awed look. Keen observers noted, through the candlelit gloom of the place, that Peter's face was darkly mottled, like the face of an apoplectic, and that above the collar of the Prussian uniform in which he was to be buried, his long, skinny neck was hidden behind a broad, black bandage.

What was it that actually happened in that sinister seclusion at Ropsha, in that house so tightly sealed off by its guards and soldiers, in that room with the heavy, dark green curtains which were never opened?

In the first of Alexis's letters there is the subtlest imaginable suggestion that the czar and his servant had both been poisoned —why else should the two of them sicken simultaneously?—but if this were true, the czar must somehow have thrown off the effects of the poison. Perhaps the dosage was insufficient. Alexis was certainly not a poisoner by disposition, and finding himself in this unfamiliar element he might well have made a miscalculation. In any event, the czar was unexpectedly well enough by the hour of dinner to appear at the table.

It was not possible that he could save himself. It was merely a question of how and when the murder would be committed, although the actual method has never become known to this day. Perhaps he was stabbed, for there is a tradition of stabbing associated with the death, and Alexis's letter suggests a scuffle. But there was also the mottled face; and there was the black band about the corpse's throat as an established fact, so that strangulation cannot be ruled out. Regardless of the method employed, however, the result was unalterably the same: Peter III was dead, and Catherine sat securely on her throne.

While the tongues wagged, she went coolly about the business of organizing her reign as if nothing had happened. But her actions spoke her attitude: far from being degraded or punished, the Orlovs were heaped with riches, favors, and power. Only once, many years later, after the Orlovs had passed out of her life, was she known to refer to the matter.

Diderot, the French philosopher, writer, and encyclopedist, an intimate of her circle of intellectual friends, was visiting St. Petersburg; and in the middle of one of those endless conversations in which Catherine took such delight, she asked abruptly: "What did they say in Paris when my husband died?"

Diderot was so flustered by this unforeseen question that he could only gulp confusedly. The great empress, never more gracious nor more poised, instantly turned the subject to a joke, and there it rested, never to be renewed in her lifetime.

PART 3

~~~~~~

Edward II of England and
Isabella-the-beautiful

Edward II of England and Isabella-the-beautiful

In England before the time of the Norman conquest, King Edward the Martyr was murdered by his stepmother in the sturdiest tradition of royal greed. Four reigns earlier King Edmund had been murdered. A later king, Edmund Ironside, is believed to have been murdered, although the details of his dying are not known. King Harold was shot through the eye with an arrow and killed during the Norman invasion. The second Norman king, William Rufus, was shot (as if by accident) while hunting, but the fact of murder was deduced. Richard the Lion-Hearted was mortally wounded during an embattled siege. Richard II was deposed and imprisoned, and it is thought that he was then starved to death. Henry VI was done to death without, again, a record surviving as to the manner of his murder. Edward V, thirteen years old, was smothered under his own mattress by order of his wicked uncle. Then this uncle, Richard III, was slain in battle defending his crown. And finally Charles I was beheaded by his rebellious subjects. (It is only fair to add, however, that since the middle of the seventeenth century British kings and queens have uniformly and consistently died of nothing but natural causes.)

In the midst of this bloody contention for the crown of England, the kings themselves were not the only persons to perish; any who approached the steps of the throne too closely fell under the shadow of peril. Two of Henry VIII's wives were beheaded. Edward V's younger brother was smothered with him by order of Richard III. King John secured his crown by disposing of his rival claimant, Prince Arthur: having tried unsuccessfully to blind him, he stabbed him instead, tied a rock to his body, and dropped him into deep water. Mary Queen of Scots, attempting to rob Queen Elizabeth of her much-coveted crown, was imprisoned by Elizabeth for twenty years and then beheaded. (Mary had previously murdered her second husband by having him strangled and afterward blowing up with explosives the house where he was staying.) Queen Mary's rival, Lady Jane Grey, was beheaded. And there were many others who came to similar ends.

Yet even in situations of such tremendous drama as the plundering of crowns, differences and gradations of horror exist between the circumstances of one unthroning and the next. Not every toppled king is deposed with equal ease or difficulty; not every murdered king dies with equal suffering. Some, such as Edward V, smothered under his mattress, or William Rufus, shot in the hunt, have at least perished quickly; while others, less fortunate in the style of their misfortune, have, in addition to becoming victims of murder, first been obliged to endure the ordeals and mental anguish of their deposings and then sometimes made to live on, like Richard II in his presumed starvation, through protracted agonies before death wraps them at last in release.

But since kings have potentially the power to inflict willful pain upon a broader section of mankind than do ordinary persons, it is appropriate that this power should be counterbalanced by the hazard that when a throne tips and its occupant is dragged from it, his suffering may be greater than that of ordinary men, for as he was once above other men, now he may suffer not only all their pangs and torments—the physical torture, the emotional affliction, and the mental distress—but as well a sort of public anguish, which is the price he pays for the former enjoyment of greatness. Not individual enemies but whole nations rise to reject him and to proclaim his human insufficiency. And because of this magnification, what would be a virtue in another man becomes a weakness in the king; what would be a weakness in another man becomes in the king a monstrosity that must be plucked out and eradicated; and in this way are doomed kings brought to their most horrible ends.

Among such kings as these in English history, set apart as are great personages in a classic tragedy, none was more hopelessly doomed than King Edward II, none came to an end more horrible, nor suffered a tragedy more complete.

This luckless man was the son of one of the greatest of English kings, Edward I, lawgiver, conqueror, builder of a prodigious string of huge castles; and it was in one of these—Caernarvon Castle in northwestern Wales, where his parents had come to deal with the rebellious Welsh chieftains—that Edward II was born in 1284. The problem of the chieftains came to a speedy conclusion when they arrived at Caernarvon in a group, offering their submission to the king and requesting, in turn, only that they be given a prince who was in every way above reproach and who spoke neither English nor French. The resourceful king excused himself, and in a few minutes returned to the audience hall with his three-day-old son in his arms. Obviously this infant answered to the chieftains' description, and thus he became the first Prince of Wales.

Even with so auspicious a beginning, however, Edward II was soon to show himself as belonging to those ranks of men born to rule who have neither the talent nor the sense of responsibility for that post, nor yet any training which might cause them to overcome their defects. Edward's training was poorer than most. At the age of five he was given his own household, and his associates there appear to have been selected with the gravest lack of attention; they consumed in one year, for example, 239 casks (not bottles) of wine, as well as beer and ale in corresponding proportions—since the scale of the establishment was simple rather than majestic, this amount of drinking was being done by relatively few persons. It was scarcely to be wondered that the young prince grew fond of low companions, and was in no way sensible of the dignity of his heritage.

One of these companions, a youth of his own age, was Piers Gaveston, the son of a gentleman from Gascony (one of the provinces in France of which England was master at this time); coming to court with his father, he so impressed Edward I with the charm of his countenance and the distinction of his behavior that the king sent him to the prince's household that he might be a comrade for and beneficial influence on the heir to the crown. That charm and those good manners were deceptive.

Piers Gaveston was to become a thorn in England's side, for as it transpired Edward had strange appetites, and Gaveston was ambitious. The first real difficulty arose when Edward, at the age of twenty-two, after some years of association with his favorite, asked his aging but still hardy father if Gaveston might not, as a sign of regard, be given the province of Ponthieu in France, a grotesquely foolish and badly considered suggestion since Ponthieu was a strategic province in the then current wars.

Edward I, having heard some of the gossip about his son and Gaveston, screamed furiously: "You would give away land? You who have never conquered any?" He then dragged his son around the room by his hair.

Gaveston not only did not receive Ponthieu, but for the first of a series of times he was banished from England. This was the only desperate measure of the wise old king: the other banishments were to be by other hands. In those days it was customary for anyone under sentence of exile to hurry to the nearest port and embark on the first ship. In the event that no ship was leaving for several days, the sufferer must then strip to his underclothes and wade out into the water up to his chin every day as proof of his intended departure. The arrogant Gaveston was forced to accept this affront to his swollen pride, and eventually he did cross the channel; but he did not stay in his native Gascony for long once he reached it.

A year later the old king died, and Edward came into his own. His first act as king was to recall and reinstate Gaveston in opposition to his father's deathbed wish, and his subsequent acts were all to countermand or disregard the remainder of the dying requests. Gaveston, for his part, was created Earl of Cornwall, a title which was traditionally reserved for the royal family, and which carried with it an enormous income from tin mines; and close after this, the favorite was betrothed to the new king's niece as the ultimate proof of affection for him.

Edward was, like all his family, handsome of person; he was well set up, muscular, and pleasing of face, with what was to become known as typical English coloring and straw-blond hair. But as he was, himself, a follower rather than a leader by nature, so his appearance, too, had a certain lack of character; and as he grew older his muscles dwindled, his shoulders stooped, his gold hair lost its glint, and he became flatfooted. As a young man, though, he was attractive enough to foment a temporary throb in the heart of one who was, in her generation, thought to be the most beautiful woman in Europe. Her name was Isabella-la-belle; she was a princess of France, daughter of King Philip-le-bel, and sister of the future King Charles-le-bel.

Marrying into this dazzlingly beautiful family (whose men were as famous for their appearances as were its women), poor Edward was plainly cast into the shadow, and especially as all his new relatives had strong minds and imperious wills; but the marriage had been arranged by Edward I before his death, and the young king had merely to carry it through—crossing to France, there to be married in the midst of the French court in the presences of four other kings and three queens, and bringing his bride back to England with him. Not even he had the foolishness to take the insolent Gaveston along to the wedding, so instead he did something worse: he appointed the favorite regent of the kingdom with full and unlimited powers during his absence. Luckily Gaveston committed only minor mischief during this period; notwithstanding, the proud feudal barons, who wielded so much power in the kingdom, hated him with an awful hatred (not only did they resent his influence over the king, but he spiked their inflexible pride with his taunts and mockeries). For the moment, however, they were impotent against him, and when the king and his new queen returned to England, Gaveston was on hand at Dover, broken out in a perfect rash of jewels, to greet them. Edward flew from his wife's side into Gaveston's arms, kissing him and calling him brother in front of a great concourse of people; and the next day Gaveston appeared strutting in nothing less than the jewelry which Edward had been given by his French father-in-law as a wedding present.

The barons were in a very dangerous mood. Parliament met, and it was decided that Gaveston must be banished again, this time to be excommunicated if he should dare to return to England. The bishops had joined with the barons in this fierce endeavor, and Edward was forced to give in to them. Gaveston was sent off amid general rejoicing (he did not have to wade out into the sea this time), and it was only later that the truth came to light.

The sly but shortsighted king, far from degrading his favorite, had sent him to Ireland—which *was* a sort of exile, to be sure— but rather than going in disgrace, Gaveston went as the king's lieutenant, with all pomp and splendor. And once in Ireland he wrote immediately to the Pope, pleading in his most winsome way that the ban of excommunication be lifted. The Pope chose to be obliging in this matter, going contrary to the threats of the bishops; so a year after his second departure, Gaveston yet again returned to England with full ceremony, like a conquering hero, and was reinstated as Earl of Cornwall. The king was enraptured once more, and the barons were seething.

(This interminable see-sawing was carried out against the most flamboyant of fairy tale backgrounds: there were grim castles, and knights in armor, and tournaments with pennants fluttering in the dusty-sunny breeze, and a beautiful young queen in her floating robes, and a handsome villain swaggering about in particolored hose. But there was no hero; there was only Edward, stubborn and muddleheaded, causing matters to grow steadily worse and worse.)

Back from Ireland, Gaveston's position was no more secure than it had been before. By and by a new parliament convened; and because Edward had lavished away his entire treasury, he was obliged to apply to the barons for money. The barons, as might be expected, imposed conditions upon the granting of any funds. This time Gaveston was really to be banished in earnest, his life to be forfeit if ever he returned to England. So, with the king grieving bitterly, the favorite set forth on his third exile, this time to Flanders, that prosperous nation of weavers and merchants.

As might also have been expected, Flanders was too dull for the fiery Gaveston, and within a month there began to be rumors that he had sneaked back in disguise. The rumors grew more substantial and more pointed as he allowed himself to be seen here and there, openly flaunting his identity; and at last, with incredible folly, Edward announced that Gaveston had officially come back, and praised him for his return. *Again* Gaveston was made Earl of Cornwall. The country sprang to arms, and a state of war developed immediately.

The three principal figures in this drama—the king, the queen, and the jack—now all ran away together. They headed north, finally landing in Newcastle; but the barons' armies were pressing hot and close behind them. They had a few days' respite, but then, their situation being indefensible, Edward and Gaveston flatly deserted the queen, and the two of them put out to sea together, like the owl and the pussycat in the poem.

The fond couple sailed smoothly down the coast to Scarborough, where Gaveston, since the enemy was left somewhat behind for the moment, shut himself up in Scarborough Castle and prepared to withstand siege, while Edward scuttled off to the city of York to try to raise some sort of loyal following. But no following was to be raised, nor had Gaveston's preparations against siege been adequate. The barons arrived in Scarborough, attacked the castle, and took him prisoner. It was now agreed, after a certain amount of parleying, that he should be conveyed across country to be tried; but on the way his angry captors could no longer contain themselves; he was abducted from his nominal jailer, the Earl of Pembroke, and his head was cut off. On this violent note the first stage of Edward II's reign came to an end.

With the death of the favorite there was a sudden backswing in Edward's favor. Arms were laid down. The party of great nobles, having lost its focus for hatred on the night of Gaveston's furtive execution, now split into smaller, less powerful groups. And the good will of the people toward their king reached its crest when Isabella-the-beautiful gave birth to a son, the future Edward III, even though it had come to the public notice by this time that the king, besotted past belief, had actually given the crown jewels to Gaveston. The jewels were returned to the treasury, and for a time tranquillity was restored at home.

Its span was brief, though. There were terrible military defeats by Scotland; then came a year of floods and famine, starvation and misery. There were uprisings in Wales. And in the teeth of these cataclysms, Edward dreamily ensconced a new favorite in the niche left vacant by Gaveston's death, once more alienated the affections of his people, and began on the last drama which was to precede his downfall.

Hugh le Despenser, Earl of Winchester, a suave and sly old gentleman, was one of the very few great nobles who had remained loyal to the king through all his adversities and misdeeds. He had a son, also named Hugh, a brave and handsome young man, who had married a daughter of the Earl of Gloucester and upon the demise of his father-in-law assumed that title for himself. This young Hugh was appointed chamberlain of the royal household by the king's enemies as a result of the mistaken notion that the two of them disliked one another excessively.

They did nothing of the sort. Edward was primed and ready for a new favorite; and Hugh, like Gaveston before him, was ambitious and mercenary—so much so, indeed, that in a very short time he and his wily, smiling old father had between them shaken nearly all the plums off the tree of the royal favor. The ancient pattern repeated itself: the barons laid waste the land which the Despensers had taken, burned their houses, killed their livestock, and finally demanded the banishment of the favorites.

Edward allowed them to be sent into exile; but then, unexpectedly, he seized the initiative. He assembled a force of his own and went after his disloyal lords with such fury that the spine of the baronial party was broken, some of its leaders put to death, and others imprisoned. Among these last was a certain Roger de Mortimer, a scowlingly handsome rascal, dark as a gypsy, who came from the troublesome neighborhood of the Welsh border and had been the leader in the raids on the Despensers' property. He was imprisoned for life in the Tower of London; but even so, Edward was remiss in not paying closer attention to him.

The original Tower of London was an extraordinary structure, built as a fortress by William the Conqueror; and although it was a royal residence as well as castle and prison, it was notoriously one of the most dismal and uncomfortable buildings in England. For all its size, there was only one stairway, narrow and spiral, up and down which went not only the royal family and the court, but guards, servants, cooks, officials, errand boys, messengers, and every other functionary major or minor who might revolve around the presence of the king or the queen.

Thus when Isabella, unaccompanied by her husband who was tripping elsewhere with the newly recalled Despensers, came to the tower for the birth of a daughter, it was almost unavoidable that she should hear of the swarthy, moody, romantic prisoner, that she should become curious about him, that she should see him, then meet him, and finally fall in love with him—for that is precisely what happened. And not long thereafter the impossible, the unheard-of occurred. Mortimer escaped from the tower.

Some of his accomplices were presently discovered. One of them, a lieutenant of the guards, went with him in his flight. But before this flight from the heart of the royal stronghold could possibly be brought about, it was evidently necessary that a heart of something less than stone should be moved. Isabella-the-beautiful was even now only in her mid-twenties; and the train of events required some royal complicity. On the night of August 1, the feast of St. Peter, it was customary for the garrison to celebrate with particularly heavy drinking; and this special drinking appeared to be heavier than usual, for as the evening wore on the tower acquired a marked resemblance to the castle of the sleeping beauty in the legend: sentries fell asleep in their tracks, violent snores issued from the guardroom, cooks and scullery maids lay slumped among the pots and pans. The wine had been stiffly drugged. Mortimer and his friendly lieutenant escaped by a passage which led to the royal kitchens where, picking their way among the crumpled bodies and the debris, they climbed the chimney, emerged onto the roof, and dropped catlike to an inner court. From the battlements above them came the gusty breathing of the slumbering soldiers. The queen, cloaked and veiled, slipped out of the shadows, embraced her lover, and held steady with her own hands a rope ladder thrown over the wall while he climbed it. From the top, dimly silhouetted against the dark sky, he called down: "Now, fortune, be my guide!" and disappeared from her view.

The lieutenant followed him, and together they raced across the strip of ground to the river's edge where an open boat awaited them (the Bishop of Hereford, it transpired, had handled the outside arrangements), and they were carried swiftly and silently across the inky river. On the far bank a group of Mortimer's retainers had gathered, ready with horses. They rode without stopping, out of the city, across the countryside, through darkened villages and past darkened castles, black Mortimer blacker even than the night, until they reached the coast. Another boat lay here in readiness, and it conveyed them over the water to where a merchant ship, supplied by the bishop's good offices, lay at anchor off the shore. This ship, in turn, bore the fleeing lord to Normandy, and from there he made his way directly to the court of France. Shortly afterward, the queen also went to France for a visit.

Philip-the-beautiful, Isabella's father, had recently died, and had been succeeded by his son, Charles-the-beautiful. Now within the borders of France, England had great holdings, among them Gaveston's province of Gascony; and this was the ostensible reason for Isabella's journey. King Charles demanded that his brother-in-law, Edward, should come to Paris to do homage for these lands. The Despensers, on the other hand, had no intention of letting their pawn escape their grasp. So instead Isabella went as a compromise; and as soon as she arrived in Paris it became clear which way the wind was blowing. Mortimer was waiting for her, and casting discretion aside they proclaimed their love to the whole of Europe.

Meantime King Charles, who was glossily disregarding his sister's antics, announced that her homage was not enough. Edward would still have to come over. The compromise this time was precisely what Isabella had hoped for: her son, the heir to the English throne, who was now in his teens, was sent instead. With the young prince in their hands, Isabella and Mortimer lost no time. They went to the Netherlands, assembled an army, and invaded England.

Their intention was that the king be deposed, and the boy become Edward III. And such is exactly what took place. The army of invasion landed and was met with instant support. The English had had enough of their useless king. Barons and knights with their men-at-arms flocked to the queen's cause. Poor Edward scuttled here and there, looking for support and finding none. Only the Despensers adhered to him, and they had no choice. The queen's army surged forward across the land, while Edward retreated alone before it. The elder Despenser was captured and brought before the queen, still in his armor, sentenced to death, and hanged on the spot without even being allowed to remove the armor first. The shining metal form at the end of the rope presented a brilliant spectacle to the onlookers, and the royal princesses, Isabella's daughters, went into hysterics at the sight. The queen was enjoying her vengeance.

Finally the king and young Despenser, wandering about in something of a daze, were captured. The king was shut away; and Despenser was sent to the queen. His death was much worse than his father's had been: he was put into a black gown bearing his coat-of-arms upside down; a chaplet of brambles was forced onto his head; and he was dragged to the scaffold at the heels of galloping horses. There he was hanged by the neck, but not until dead, only until his handsome, lacerated face began to blotch from near strangulation. Then he was taken down. The black gown was discarded, his muscular abdomen was cut open, his bowels were meticulously removed, and ceremonially burned before his eyes. At last he was beheaded, and after that the emptied husk of his body was chopped into quarters and dispersed about the kingdom. He met his end patiently, but there was some question as to the point in this gruesome ritual at which he died. Anticipating his doom, he had almost succeeded in starving himself to death before his execution, and his grip on life was no firmer than the slipping away of a shadow. The queen, sphinx-like with contentment, watched every minute of his ordeal. Then it only remained to dispose of the king.

Edward, under arrest, had been taken to Kenilworth Castle. Now a gutted ruin, it had not at that time achieved the grandeur which John of Gaunt was to give it with its great hall and magnificent environs; the principal offices of the castle were contained in a massive structure called Caesar's Tower. Here the king was housed; and here a deputation from the queen and the prince came to visit him. Once more the unforeseen had happened, and the boy, showing an unexpected strength of character, firmly refused to depose his father—the only solution, then, was for the father to make a voluntary abdication.

The deputies arrived at Kenilworth late on a gray and freezing January afternoon, their horses stumbling wearily through the snow, their noses pinched and frostbitten, the flowing cloaks wrapped tightly around them for warmth. They were admitted to the courtyard, dismounted on the icy cobblestones, beating their arms to improve their circulation, their breath hanging white in the cold air, and were ushered solemnly into the tower to the chamber where the audience would be held. Inside those thick walls the cold was less penetrating. Rushes covered the paved floor, and a fire crackled in the huge stone cavern of the fireplace. The company headed by the king's old enemy, the Bishop of Hereford, heavy of jowl and oysterish of eye from too much food and too many rages, began throwing back hoods, discarding cloaks; the party clustered into smaller groups, speaking in low voices; and at last the door at the far end of the apartment was timidly opened, and the wretched captive shuffled into the presence of his lords.

His head was sunk forward, and his shoulders were hunched beneath the dismal folds of a cheap black robe, showing a rusty patina of dirt in the wavering torchlight. There were gray strands among his blond hair; and his eyes, too, seemed to have lost their color as they roamed hopelessly from one hard face to the next. The hostility in the air was almost tangible. The bishop moved ponderously forward, and in a shrill voice oddly at variance with the overflowing splendor of his appearance he began to harangue his former sovereign with a flood of angry insults and invective. That penetrating voice, almost a scream, echoing back from the stone walls, washed over the king. He had already a dreary pallor, but now it was seen that the pallor was acquiring a weirdly blue cast. His once muscular body began to tremble convulsively, his knees buckled beneath him, and before anyone could move to his assistance he pitched forward onto the floor among the dry rushes in a dead faint.

The bishop's voice halted. Two gentlemen stepped forward and raised the king to his feet, standing beside him to support him so that, only half conscious, with his head lolling, he was forced to listen to that vicious voice starting up again and continuing with the interminable, cruel tongue-lashing. As he revived somewhat, tears began to course down his gray face. All the men eyed him narrowly. At last the bishop finished, and an ominous silence descended on the room, broken only by the spitting of the fire, the rustle of damp garments, and the distant screaming of the winter wind outside as night began to fall.

The king said weakly: "I am in your hands. Do what seems right."

This constituted the abdication upon which the young prince had insisted. The bishop and the other lords were grimly pleased; the tension broke a little; feet stirred among the rushes. Sir William Trussel, the man who had sentenced the young Despenser to his awful death, now came briskly toward the king, his eyes glittering evilly, and in an inhuman, sneering voice pronounced the declaration which broke the oath of loyalty: "I do make this protestation in the name of all those who will not, for the future, be in your fealty or allegiance, nor claim to hold anything of you as king, but account you as a private person, without any manner of royal dignity." An incredible degree of scorn was injected into the words. The gentlemen shuffled and coughed smugly. The fire popped. The torches flared up orange.

The ex-king, still shaking horribly, went on standing there. His humiliation was not finished.

Sir Thomas Blount, the steward of the royal household, now marched forward through the crowd to the center of the room, the focus of all eyes, and with a single violent gesture he broke his white wand of office in two. It was the final act of renunciation, a thing which was only done at the death of a king.

Edward seemed to shrivel inside his fusty black robe. The shuffling stopped and the silence descended again. Everyone stared at him intently, waiting for him to make one final statement; and in a lifeless voice he managed to force out these words: "I am aware that for my many sins I am thus punished. Have compassion on me. Much as I grieve at having incurred the ill will of the people, I am glad they have chosen my son to be their king."

With all his spirit now totally crushed, he turned in his shambling way, deeply bowed inside his threadbare robe, and with slow and faltering steps withdrew from the cheerless, firelit hall, watched out of sight by all those narrow, pitiless, unrelenting eyes, no longer a king. Dickens, pithy as usual, describes the scene in brief: "Being asked in this pressing manner what he thought of resigning, the king said he thought it would be the best thing he could do. So he did it, and they proclaimed his son the next day."

Berkeley Castle stands upon the bank of the River Severn, where tower and battlement and column-shaped chimney oversee the verdure of meadows and trees, the tranquillity of flowing water far removed from the titanic struggles and noisy warfare of medieval England. The castle is a monument of gothic architecture: the hive of antiquaries, the barrow of historians; and as well it is a visual account of England's past.

The drawing rooms present an engaging mixture of periods and centuries. Upon ancient stone walls, dotted with carved stone doorways and cavelike window embrasures, hang great suites of Flemish tapestries in all their baroque opulence; and the rooms are furnished with eighteenth-century gilt gesso chairs and tables and benches of the choicest quality. Lord Thomas Berkeley's Great Hall is dominated by the elaborate Tudor screen of oak across one entire end, shimmering in the peaceful English sunlight as it filters through the stained-glass windows. And everywhere are paintings, more than two hundred altogether, from the hands of many of the greatest masters.

Naturally enough, portraits constitute the larger number of the paintings, portraits of the Berkeleys themselves, and these are found throughout the rooms. But many pictures only indirectly related to the annals of the family may be seen in the Picture Gallery; and in the room known as the King's Gallery there is a gathering of portraits of the kings and queens of England.

This room, irregular in shape and full of juts and corners, is the first room visitors enter. It contains at one end a staircase at the foot of which lie widespread the dining room, the great fourteenth-century kitchen, buttery, household offices, and finally, far along, the Great Hall. Then the King's Gallery contains as well an ornate flight of stairs leading upward, massively neweled and heavily decorated, more conspicuous than the descending stairs; and in the triangular, plastered wall below these ascending ones a stone-framed, iron-grilled opening some three feet above the floor gives view into a tiny guardroom set within the crook of the angle under the stairs. Its furnishings are grim and severe: a straight chair of sixteenth-century design, a sparsely carved table supporting a religious figure; its walls are of bare stone, its windows undraped. It was in this dreary hole that Edward II was most foully murdered.

In the year 1327 Berkeley Castle was not the showplace it has later become. Then there were no baroque tapestries, no suites of gilt furniture, scarcely any pictures. Primarily a fortification for defense, the castle served first the purpose for which it was built. Secondly it was also a residence for the warlike Berkeley lords; then it was a center for the feudal life of the neighborhood, a post for barter, a battle shelter for peasants and livestock alike; and, of course, it was a prison. As such it received the deposed king.

Maurice, the seventh Lord Berkeley, had fought against the grasping rule of the Despensers; for his efforts they imprisoned him, and in prison he died the year before Edward's downfall. His son, Thomas, also in prison, was released by Isabella in her conquering march across the country. Naturally enough, there was no doubt as to which side he would choose; and when it was

decided that a new jailer was needed for the former king, Thomas
of Berkeley was the logical choice for the post.

Kenilworth would no longer suffice for Edward's detention.
A backswing had taken place. In practice, if not in name, the
country was entirely in the hands of the besotted Isabella and
the greedy, scowling Mortimer, and they were making the most
of their opportunities: Mortimer had raised his barony to an earl-
dom, granted himself the justiceship of Wales for life, taken
over the bulk of the Despensers' property, and dealt himself
many other honors and riches. It was becoming plain to the
country at large that he and Isabella were worse than the Despensers or Gaveston had ever been; and accordingly there were
those who began to think that it would be at least a slight im-
provement to see Edward II back on the throne again. And
Kenilworth Castle, where the deputation had forced him to ab-
dicate, was at the heart of a neighborhood which was conspiring
and plotting to obtain his release.

Apparently the plotting was not especially secret. It came to
the attention of Mortimer and the queen; and since Isabella had
already considered moving Edward on the grounds that he was
unduly pampered at Kenilworth (and it does seem to be true
that after his abdication the treatment accorded him improved
somewhat, and those around him behaved toward him with at
least token respect), the time for making the move had obviously
come.

The king, in the midst of his guards and jailers, was removed
from Kenilworth at night; they penetrated the ring of the royal
partisans, and made their way to Corfe Castle in Devon, whose
bare, buttressed ruins may still be seen upon their high hilltop,
like the stumps of so many teeth. At Corfe, too, sentiment ran
in Edward's favor, and the sojourn there was, of necessity, brief.
Another plot was afoot. The company moved on to the town of
Bristol, but here the situation was even more desperate; the
citizens of the town were actually banding together to ensure the
release of the royal captive. And so, at last, they came to
Berkeley Castle.

All this journeying had, for Edward, been accompanied by the

greatest privations and the most humiliating of indignities. Isabella no longer had reason to think him pampered. After the
scene of his abdication where he had fainted and his tears displayed his weakness, his health must have improved; otherwise he could not have withstood the rigors to which he was
subjected. The journeying was done almost exclusively at night,
and his captors found a maniacal pleasure in forcing him to
travel only in the thinnest of clothing through the chilly dampness of the early spring dark. Then, also, his captors perversely
and with barbaric malice kept him awake as much of the time
as possible, depriving him of sleep on one excuse or another between the rounds of traveling. In the spirit of mockery he was
crowned with straw: the niggling irritations must have rankled
almost as sorely as the more serious miseries. Edward had customarily worn a beard; but now he was forced to shave—partly
as an insult to his dignity, but partly, too, for the more practical
purpose of changing his appearance so that should he be met by
any of his partisans during the journeys he would be less easily
recognized by them. Even the simple act of shaving, however,
was callously designed to reduce him to the limit of endurable
degradation. It took place in an open field under the sullen glare
of his brutal escort, where cold and muddy water was slopped up
and brought to him in one of the soldiers' helmets from where it
stood, stagnant, in a brackish ditch; and with that negligible assistance the royal face was barbered.

But here, at last, he was roused to assert his kingship, however
futilely, and he shouted passionately, pointing to the tears of
rage, hot on his face: "In spite of you, I shall be shaved with
warm water!"

Berkeley Castle, finally reached, gave him sanctuary of a sort.
Thomas of Berkeley had married one of Mortimer's daughters;
but notwithstanding this connection, he treated Edward with
more civility than had been shown him in many months. An allowance of five pounds a day had been granted for his care, and
altogether he had, no doubt, cause to feel that his situation was
decidedly bettered. Lord Thomas was one of the less warlike
Berkeleys.

Meantime the plotters on the outside were gathering their forces and achieving a considerable strength. The ringleaders from the vicinity of Kenilworth now appeared at Berkeley; an active conspiracy developed in southern Wales, not very far away; and the priests in their handsome gothic pulpits waxed loud in Edward's favor. Finally he actually did escape from Berkeley Castle. That fact alone is known, without details or embellishments, brought to light in a letter of the period. But however the conspirators had contrived to pull off so grand an accomplishment, it all came to nothing; Edward must have been recaptured almost immediately, and he was never more to leave the castle alive.

There was only one thing to be done. Where the first escape had been very nearly successful, the second might be completely so. The queen and Mortimer had rewarded their old friend, the Bishop of Hereford, the same one who had connived at Mortimer's escape from the tower, and harangued Edward at Kenilworth, by placing him high in their confidence: it was he who dispatched the death sentence to Berkeley in one or the other of two lines of Latin:

Edwardum occidere nolite timere, bonum est.
Edwardum occidere nolite, timere bonum est.

The comma is all-important. It is the sort of line which appeals to historian and grammarian alike, for its meaning could be drastically altered by the arrangement of punctuation. In translation the first line reads: "Do not fear to kill Edward, it is good," whereas the second line reads: "Do not kill Edward, it is good to fear." The jailers chose to take the first meaning, and the king was doomed.

The old charge that he was being pampered once more put in an appearance, leveled this time at Thomas of Berkeley himself, and he was ordered out of his own castle. Lord Thomas took a respectful leave of the prisoner, telling him that although he regretted such a necessity, he was forced to be absent for some time on affairs of his own, but that he would return as soon as possible. Edward clung pathetically to his hand, and must have realized that all hope was now lost to him. Berkeley retired in angry disgust to his manor at Bradley, powerless to interfere.

And so began the approach to the end.

At the time of the king's removal to Berkeley Castle, Lord Thomas had been provided with the aid of a co-jailer, a gentleman with whom he was to divide the responsibility for Edward's safety and his care: this was a member of a wealthy Dorsetshire family, and Thomas's own brother-in-law, Sir John de Maltravers. A third man, Sir Edward de Gurney, was also introduced into the castle with orders to share in the problems and difficulties attendant on the incarceration of a former king; but so long as Lord Thomas remained at the castle, his was the dominant voice of the three since the castle itself was his, and since his position commanded the respect of the other two men.

At about the time that Edward's fate was decided, however, still another jailer was sent to Berkeley, presumably by no less a personage than the now-great Mortimer, for this new man was one of Mortimer's dependents. His name was William Ogle, and he was quite evidently a professional tough (had Dickens indeed devised these characters from his own brain, rather than retelling their histories, even he could scarcely have arrived at three names more appropriate for such villains than Maltravers, Gurney, and Ogle, for as villains they were quickly to show themshelves).

It remains to the credit of the Berkeleys that they had no part in the ensuing events. During the period when Berkeley himself was in command of the castle, the king was treated with at least a certain degree of courtesy; his keeper undoubtedly possessed a genuine sympathy for the royal prisoner, and did whatever lay within his power to lighten the king's suffering. But it is scarcely credible that, as the queen maintained, Edward was pampered, at Berkeley or elsewhere. With the dismissal of Lord Thomas, however, the tolerable was rendered intolerable. Such superficial regard as had been offered the kingly rank was now flatly dropped. No protection stood between the king and Gurney, Maltravers, and Ogle.

At first the persecutions took a casual if unpleasant turn.

The prisoner was brought garbage to eat, instead of the regular castle fare, and often it was so nauseous that he could not stomach it. The degradation of shaving in cold water was repeated regularly, the water now being lugged up from the moat which surrounded the castle. Orders were barked at him, and rough hands laid upon his person. His health began, little by little, to fail.

This was, of course, the first intention of his keepers. In a current phrase which had originated in a letter sent to Mortimer by his appointed deputy in Wales, the death of Edward II was straightforwardly referred to as "a suitable remedy" for the situation which had developed; and for some while now the manner and occasion of that remedy had been the objects of thought, planning, and decisions in high places. Obviously if he could be hounded to death that would be preferable to the outright committing of murder; but if he could not be induced to die of his own accord, then instead he must be done to death.

The sinister appearance of the man Ogle upon the scene must have suggested to Edward the direction which matters were to take. Ogle's presence was grimly accepted by the staff of the castle, although at no point does he seem to have specified the reason for which he had been sent there. The first scheme for the murder was subtle and oblique. Edward was moved out of the quarters which had been assigned to him by Lord Thomas, and in which he had, up to this time, lived in reasonable comfort, if not in luxury; and he was put into a dark and tiny cell in the dungeon tower. He was to be allowed every facility which his jailers could devise for dying a natural death.

The carrion bodies of dead animals, already stinking with putrefaction as they moldered under the late summer sun, were spread about below his cell. Flies buzzed round the slimy stones, and the awful odor penetrated the cell to the point of suffocation. The custodians must have reasoned that a man of declining strength would quickly be carried off by the horrors of this charnel house, or that if the mere sights and smells were not too much for him, he would at last succumb to the infections which the rot and decay so fruitfully produced and which were being funneled into his cell.

But he did not succumb to the infections. Even after all he had been through, there was astonishing strength left in his constitution, and the malodorous hole of his confinement was insufficient to bring about his immediate destruction. Yet the destruction had to be immediate. Delay was impossible. The priests in their pulpits were growing daily more eloquent on his behalf. As his bodily reserves slowly dwindled, the reserves of his partisans outside the castle increased rapidly. The murderers could no longer bide their time and wait for diseases to take him off. The murder must now be committed outright.

And on the night of September 21, 1327, all the inmates of Berkeley Castle—servants, maids, cooks, grooms, men-at-arms—were sharply wakened from their sleep by screams of pain and agony so horrible that none dared venture out or attempt to interfere. The screams were, indeed, so fearful that they carried even through the thick castle walls to the huts and houses of the village nearby; and the villagers drew their heads down in fright under their bedclothes. On the wave of these screams "many a man awoke and prayed to God for the harmless soul which was that night departing in torture." As the screams ceased all knew that Edward II, King of England, was no more.

When his body was publicly displayed on the following day, there was nowhere any mark of violence upon it. Had it not been for the screams, it might have been supposed that the foul infections had, indeed, brought him low: but the once-handsome features of his face were so violently contorted in a grimace of pain and intense suffering that it was impossible to smooth them down or in any way give them an appearance of tranquillity. That imprint of anguish told the amount he had endured as clearly as any visible wounds could have done.

His three murderers had waited until all the castle, including the wretched king, was asleep; and then they crept stealthily into his fetid room, one of them carrying a brazier of glowing charcoal, and imbedded in it an iron bar or poker, pulsing with the heat. The captive slept so soundly that he did not instantly wake, and when he did it was too late for him to defend himself. He had been lying prone on his stomach upon his miserable bed;

and while the man who was carrying the brazier set it down on the floor and busied himself over his tools, the other two picked up a table, flung it upside down on the king's back, and bore upon it there so that, twist and writhe as he might, he could not get loose. The long nightgown in which he had been sleeping was hoisted up so that below the waist he was naked. The man with the brazier stepped forward and produced a horn, open at the narrow as well as the broader end, which he forced into the thrashing body. Then taking care not to burn himself, he withdrew the red-hot poker from the coals, and while the other two held the table firmly in place, he slid the poker through the horn and into the king's body, burning out his innards to the accompaniment of those frightful screams, but leaving no mark on the body's surface, going about his labors with expressionless and unemotional cruelty until the spasms of agony slackened, the screams died away, the scrambling arms and legs hung limp. The new smell of burning flesh mingled with the older smell of rotted animal bodies rising from below. The poker, no longer red-hot, was taken out and laid in the coals once more; the horn was removed; silently the table was set back on the floor in its proper place. The brazier was picked up, and the three black figures stole out of the cell into the terrified, waiting, listening midnight darkness of the castle.

A wave of shock swept across all England. The king who, in his life, had been mocked, reviled, and deposed, was regarded in his death as a martyr and almost a saint. It was believed by many persons that when the Abbot of Gloucester was removing his body from Berkeley Castle to Gloucester Cathedral, four wild harts emerged tamely from the forest to draw the bier; and his tomb became a popular shrine where it was thought that by his intercession in heaven miracles were brought to pass.

Then, too, there were also and inevitably rumors that the king was not dead, but that he lived on in hiding. A man who called himself Edward II appeared at the papal court in Avignon, and upon examination was acknowledged to be the dead king. He had come to France from Ireland, and from France he went through

Germany to Italy where he was granted asylum at a castle which belonged to the diocese of Milan. He stayed in this place for two and a half years, at last moving to another Milanese castle where he lived out the final two years of his life. But the curious point in this story, the point which sets it aside from other stories of impersonation, is that this man, even after he was formally recognized and acknowledged to be the true Edward II, made no attempt to capture the British throne. Perhaps he realized that Edward would be venerated by his subjects only if he were dead, and that already history had, like a fast-moving current, swept the life and times of that unhappy king into the disappearing past.

In England, at the time of his father's murder, the young king, Edward III, was only fifteen years old; and the actual powers of the monarchy and of dispensing justice lay not in his hands, but in those of his mother and the ferocious Mortimer, so for a period he was powerless to avenge his father's murder. Little by little, though, he gained strength, and at the end of the first seven years of his reign the matter had been fully dealt with.

Seven years marked the end of the trial of Thomas de Berkeley. It had lasted so long partly because of interruptions and diversions, but partly also because the young king, a statesman to the bone, was approaching the situation cautiously, taking suitable care as to how much of the scandal should really be given the light and how much, as in the interests of saving his mother's reputation, should be eliminated and ignored. Even in his youth Edward III was notably a fine diplomat. At the end of the seven years, then, he declared himself quite satisfied with the evidence of Berkeley's innocence, and all charges against this lord were dismissed.

Berkeley, however, was the only member of the group to be judged blameless. Gurney and Ogle both fled to the continent in desperate haste. Ogle's fate is not precisely known, but it is believed that he died shortly afterward of natural causes. Gurney took refuge first with the King of Castile, and then his flight carried him on to Naples where he was captured by an English knight sent out for that purpose; he was taken aboard ship to return to England, there supposedly to be tried and punished for the murder; but at sea during the voyage he was summarily beheaded. It was thought that this action had taken place at the king's order, and was designed to protect his mother's name, for her vital part in the conspiracy would inevitably and fully have been revealed had a trial taken place.

Of the three men who had actually committed the murder, Maltravers alone remained. Perhaps because of his connection with Lord Thomas, and through him with the great Mortimer, he appears to have felt himself secure, and he stayed on at Berkeley Castle for some time. He possessed a certain strain of glibness, and this enabled him to whitewash himself and present a face as blameless as Lord Thomas's own, implying that Gurney and Ogle had been the sole murderers, and himself as misled as everyone else. Eventually, however, the young king found time for dealing with him. Maltravers was sentenced to death; but before the sentence could be carried out he escaped to Flanders, where he held large properties.

A curious transformation now took place. This convicted multiple murderer—for not only was his reputation originally in sad repair, but on top of assisting in the murder of Edward II, he was also hopelessly implicated in the killing of that king's brother, the Earl of Kent, during Mortimer's reign of terror—this undoubted scoundrel became abruptly the best and most law-abiding of subjects to the crown when he had no longer a reason even to appear to be such. His particular field of usefulness lay in supporting happy feelings between Flanders and England, a sort of primitive public relations man; and here his skill was applied with such advantage and profit to England that in the end even the murdered king's vengeful son was obliged to look upon the villain favorably, he was allowed to return to his estates in Dorset, and he died there in his bed in a reasonable state of grace, if not quite a national hero in his old age.

So there remain only the two chief instigators of the crime: Mortimer and Isabella.

Upon the official abdication of Edward II at Kenilworth, a

council of regency (which included neither Mortimer nor the queen) had been formed to look after both the kingdom and the young king. But this in no way deterred the grasping pair. The council was composed of weak and vacillating men who could scarcely enforce their directives in the face of Isabella's beauty and popularity (for she continued popular beyond the time of the murder), young Edward's loyalty to his mother, and the harsh blast of Mortimer's will. The upshot was that the boy was a virtual prisoner of the dowager queen and her paramour.

He was, to be sure, allowed to wage a little war against the Scots (which he lost ignominiously) and to get married (to a girl of Isabella's choice), but in a thousand ways, large and small, he was made to feel that he owed his kingdom and his life to Mortimer's sneering benevolence. The king, chosen of God, scion of the Plantagenets and the Capets, was forced to rise and stand respectfully when Mortimer entered a room; Mortimer's train of knights and men-at-arms and courtiers was the largest in the land; haughty Mortimer walked step by step beside the king in processions, rather than behind him as any other subject was required to do. But most humiliating of all must have been the knowledge which Edward was forced to accept at such close quarters, that his mother and the murderer of his father were living as if married in everything but name.

Discreetly and little by little young Edward began gathering his forces. He was strangely mature in his judgments for a youth not yet twenty. His life had taught him the value of biding his time, of choosing the proper moment for action, and this moment came when, some three years after the murder, Mortimer and the queen removed with their following to Nottingham Castle for the convening of parliament, taking the young king with them, carelessly, as if he were merely another member of their huge suite of attendants. In the midst of all their glory, the king himself was allowed only four attendants; and no single point could be more microcosmic, focusing the entire situation, than the fact that every night after each entrance to the castle had been locked, the keys were brought to Isabella's room, and she slept with them under her pillow. Of course the castle bristled with guards, and no one was allowed an audience with the king unless first approved by Mortimer or Isabella.

There was no conceivable possibility that so great a fortress as Nottingham Castle could be stormed and taken by the king's forces, with the king himself a hostage on the inside, even had there been any sizable force at the king's command. But there was yet another and a better way. He had prudently struck up a friendship with the castellan of the place, and from him an important fact came to light: there existed, although neither the queen nor Mortimer knew about it, a secret passage of ancient date which ran down from the castle's keep, underground, and emerged at some little distance on the outside of the formidable walls in the shelter of a natural cave hidden in a grove of trees. It had been constructed as a possible means of escape for the castle's occupants when, many generations earlier, there had been fear of Danish invasions. Edward, however, intended to use it as an entrance rather than an exit.

The means by which he got word to his supporters on the outside is not known, but somehow he managed it. The attack was planned for the night of October 19, when his most loyal young baron, William de Montacute, was to lead a body of well-armed men through the secret passage from the cave in the woods, and meet the king inside the castle, there to take Mortimer prisoner and secure the garrison in the king's interest.

The great night arrived without the plans having been discovered by Mortimer or his henchmen. Edward, pretending to be sleepy, withdrew to his room where without undressing he must have paced the floor, distracted with apprehension, for upon this night's work his future would depend. At long last the bustling life of the castle grew still, and the hour appointed for the rendezvous arrived. He let himself out and made his stealthy way down through the labyrinth of the castle's halls and corridors, passing the door of Mortimer's room on his way, hearing from behind its closed panels the favorite's voice in conversation with a group of friends, and knowing that just beyond, with a connecting door between, lay his mother's room. Reaching the secret opening of the passage in the castle's rocky foundations he could hear sounds of movement from far below, and could make out a distant flicker of torchlight as his helpers crawled the length of the cobwebby, bat- and mouse-infested tunnel.

Montacute emerged first, his face set with resolution, and the others scrambled out at his heels. Edward held up his hand to keep them absolutely silent; and then, cautiously watching and listening, he led the way up into the keep, easily avoiding the sentries in the darkness, and hurrying soundlessly up the narrow stone stairways until they came to the hall outside Mortimer's door. The voices were still raised within.

At a gesture from the king, but without a spoken word, the men threw themselves upon the door, and with a great clamor burst it inward, hurtling through the opening and in upon Mortimer where he sat with four of his friends, deep in discussion. They were hopelessly outnumbered by the king's men, and taken altogether by surprise. They sprang at once to their feet, drawing their swords as the attacking knights fell upon them, and with a great clash of arms and suddenly raised voices the fray was engaged. But there was from the outset no question as to the direction it would take. It was as brief as it was bitter: two of Mortimer's adherents were instantly slain, and over their fallen bodies Montacute and his men drove the others back the length of the chamber. Mortimer, himself, snarling savagely while he hacked at the force of opposition, did manage to mortally wound one of Edward's men; but the rest, leaping over their dying comrade, quickly disarmed him and bound his hands together behind his back.

There now occurred an interruption, not of the castle guards rushing in to Mortimer's defense, but coming instead from the adjoining bedroom. The door was flung open, and in it, as in a niche, appeared the queen's beautiful figure. Obviously she had been in bed, and had arisen and dashed to her lover without thought of her appearance, for her hair hung loose and disheveled about her shoulders, and she wore only a light robe through which the charms of her person were clearly evident.

A glance was sufficient to show that matters had progressed beyond the point where she could halt them by a show of her own authority. The young king, all this while, had not entered into the fracas, but had remained silently in the corridor outside, for he had foreseen that his mother would have to be considered before the affair was finished, and he was sufficiently dutiful that he had no desire to cause her unnecessary pain. Nevertheless she sensed his presence, even though she could not see him, and above the last sounds of the scuffle she called out in desperate appeal: "Fair son! My fair son! Have pity on gentle Mortimer!"

He neither answered her nor entered the room.

All eyes were on her in her gorgeous state of undress: Mortimer's full of black hope, his two friends' full of fear, while Montacute and the knights holding out their bleeding swords stared at her with faces made as expressionless as possible, but still frankly curious at the sight of a queen who was also acknowledged to be a very great beauty awaiting, semi-nude, the lover whom they had just taken captive.

When there was only silence in answer to her appeal she understood that her son had no intention of having pity on Mortimer now that the tables were turned. Advancing a step farther into the room, unaware of her appearance so great was her distress, she cried imploringly to Montacute: "Do no harm to the person of Mortimer, for he is a worthy knight, my dear friend, and well-loved cousin!"

As if her presence had held the scene paralyzed for a moment, and her words then released it, it came abruptly to life once more. Montacute moved sternly away from her, motioning that Mortimer was to be dragged out into the corridor. The noise of the encounter had waked the castle, and a crowd was gathering. Rough hands were laid upon the body of the man so suddenly brought low, and no attempt was made to stand by him or rescue him. The keys of the castle were removed from under the queen's pillow. Mortimer, loaded with chains, was thrown into a dungeon under the heaviest guard. Without qualification that night belonged to the king.

England went nearly mad for joy at the fall of the wicked queen and her even more wicked lover, and the triumph of the handsome and virtuous young king. The memory of Edward II and Berkeley Castle was avenged; the ghost of that poor, unfortunate creature was laid to rest at last. In the town of Notingham the rejoicing was so tremendous that nobles and peasants danced together in the streets. Mortimer was quickly removed to the Tower of London from which he had once so spectacularly escaped, and in London stood trial for, among other counts, alienating the affections of mother and son. Edward III was far too shrewd a young man to allow the subject of his father's murder to get full billing in the courts lest his mother should be implicated, or, in the opposite direction to sentence his arch-enemy out of hand and thus place himself in the position of a tyrannical monarch without regard for due process of law. When he chose to commit a murder he did it more skillfully and more legally than his mother had ever done. However, among the charges was also the one that Mortimer had instigated the murder of Edward II; yet when a full—and possibly truthful—version of the whole story was volunteered by some of Mortimer's cohorts, they were hastily hanged to silence their tongues.

Mortimer, of course, was condemned to die. At this point poetic justice entered upon the scene. The perfection of this would have been to see Mortimer die, as Edward II had died, with his intestines singed out; but since this was hardly a practical sentence, he was condemned instead to the grisly death which the younger Despenser had suffered: he was dressed in a similar black gown, and endured the awful agonies of being dragged at horses' hoofs, the partial hanging, the disemboweling, the beheading, and finally the chopping to pieces. Justice had been served.

But there was still the beautiful Isabella.

Her fate seems very gentle indeed. She surrendered her large holdings to the crown in the person of her son; she was granted in their place an allowance of royal proportions for herself and her numerous attendants, and she and they were shut away in a castle in the loneliest district of Norfolk. On ceremonial occasions, such as a religious pilgrimage to a holy shrine, or the spending of Christmas with her son, daughter-in-law, and grandchildren at Windsor, she was permitted to leave her enforced retirement. Toward the end of her long life the spirit of sanctity overtook her, and she joined the lay branch of the Sisters of Santa Clara, the Poor Clares, as they were called. But this was only toward the end. Her comfortable but nevertheless rigid incarceration lasted for thirty-eight years; and through much of that time she was in a state of raving insanity. It was reported that upon hearing of her beloved Mortimer's end she had gone altogether out of her mind, and that while her senses did return to her intermittently, such an event took place only at irregular intervals and at periods impossible to predict.

PART 4

Catherine de' Medici and Her Sons

Catherine de' Medici and Her Sons

Henry II, King of France, was a dull, unhappy, and inarticulate man. Perhaps he was inarticulate simply because he had nothing to say, no force of personality to express through the conveyance of words; and if this was the case, it would account for his appearance of dullness. On the other hand, it is also possible that he merely appeared dull by contrast with the dazzling figure of his father, Francis I, prototype of the Renaissance prince: patron of the arts, great lover, warrior, pleasure-seeker, builder of palaces, and embellisher of kingdoms. Following in the traces of a father so brilliant in all the ways of the world, Henry II's dreariness would naturally appear to be accentuated; he was sober and retiring by disposition; he preferred the tranquil atmosphere of a few close personal relationships to the grandeur of show that had made his father's name synonymous with ostentation across the earth; he disliked bother and pressure and turmoil to such a degree that when he died at the age of forty after a reign of twelve years' length, it seemed almost as if those twelve years had been no more than an interregnum between the death of his father and the delivery of power into the hands of his widow, so little did Henry himself obtrude upon the scenes of history.

The heavy, silent side of his character being taken thus into account, his particular unhappiness remains to be explored. Its sources were two in number, one public, the other private. The public cause for misery and grief to this king was the fact that after some fifteen hundred years in which Christianity had managed to retain a semblance of unity throughout western Europe, a host of splits and divisions and cracks had at last become visible on the stately façade of the Church, and now with a terrible upheaval its body broke and crumbled into smaller,

fiercely independent groups whose members, because they pro-
tested the abuses of the papacy, were called Protestants. These
divisions came into being everywhere, as a part of the enlighten-
ment of the Renaissance; but the farther away from Rome
they occurred, the more healthily they seemed to flourish. Scan-
dinavia, Germany, the Lowlands, and England and Scotland all
broke more or less completely with the Church of Rome. It was
by no means a painless process, but in the end it was achieved.
In the other direction, Portugal, Spain, and naturally enough
Italy, since it was the seat of the Church, remained for the most
part faithful. Unfortunate France was trapped between these two
immense opposing forces, and in this way became for many years
the bloodiest of European battlegrounds where the new beliefs
laid siege to the old. The French Protestants were known as the
Huguenots.

While Henry II was publicly plagued with the blossoming of
the religious wars, his private life was also torn apart by two
women, one of whom he loved, the other of whom he did not.
As a youth he had become infatuated with Diane de Poitiers, a
French noblewoman more nearly his father's age than his own;
and this passion persisted as both his personal development and
his royal consequence increased, to such a point that even at the
very hour of his death, when matters of a more spiritual character might appropriately have occupied his mind, his love
showed not the slightest sign of dissipating itself, and his chief
concern was for the future of his beloved.

The other woman of importance in his life was his wife, the
queen, Catherine de' Medici, for whom he had neither love nor
affection. Catherine was proud and cold and inflexible and surrounded by hostility which was due in equal parts to the hate-
fulness of her own nature and to a reflection of her husband's
dislike for her. But hateful as she was, he nevertheless caused
her to suffer a needless amount of pain and humiliation, and
this background of her life was eventually to transform her into
a creature as monstrous as any woman of her time. Contrasted
with the evil queen, Diane in spite of her advancing age was
womanly (with all this implies), so that predictably she could

not resist flaunting before Catherine her position as the king's mistress, tormenting her with the fact of it, which she did even to the extent of persuading the king that the royal children—offsprings of his loveless marriage to Catherine—should be brought up under her own tutelage rather than their mother's. As Catherine suffered more, she grew in strength of will and in odiousness; and Henry, wrenched by the warring personalities of these two overpowering women between whom he hung like a surveyor's plumb, seems to have existed only as a shadowy, speechless, and accidentally handsome figure.

In this triangular situation, Henry's unexpected death came about as the result of a wound unintentionally inflicted in the play of a tournament. He was not killed outright, but continued the process of dying in his bed, to which he was carried with the stump of a broken lance protruding from one eye; and when Catherine saw that his end was upon him, she seemed of a sudden to become possessed of an energy on her own behalf such as she had never before permitted herself to demonstrate, but which was all the same no more than the first mild indication of a savagery that would, in time, embrace the whole of France. Although it could afterward be seen that having once seized the initiative she was never again to let it go, still her first step in this new direction was tentative: she wrote a formal note to Diane charging her with the return of the crown jewels which had for years been in her keeping. Diane replied loftily that the king was not yet dead, implying that her career, also, was not yet finished. Immediately, however, Henry did die; and the jewels were prudently returned without comment.

Suddenly it lay within Catherine's ability to persecute Diane to whatever extent she chose; Diane could be imprisoned or especially murdered, now that her royal lover no longer lived to protect her, and no reprisal could be visited on Catherine for her vengeful actions. Yet she was too subtle to embark so abruptly on a course of violence, and instead of offering Diane up to prison or death, Catherine merely and humanely forced her to abandon the court once and forever, and to forego hereafter all the luxuries and pleasures of position, immunity, and respect to which she had until now been accustomed (although Catherine did allow herself the minor gratification of inflicting upon her enemy an additional number of petty but galling insults).

There is no doubt that Catherine wished her restraint in this business to bolster the frail myth of her openheartedness and generosity; and besides, she was still only trying her wings, discovering lap by lap how far her new freedom of action might be stretched, and to what extent she might indulge her native savagery, a quality which, through her subsequent acts, was increasingly to present itself as an irresistible murderousness of temperament. She was to survive her husband and to rule after him (in every way except by title) for another thirty years, and through that time she was to manifest in a variety of ways both vast and minute her singular ferocity. In the same motion, then, with which Diane de Poitier's life could be seen falling away to nothingness, it could at last be observed that the life of the hitherto oppressed queen was emerging from its obscurity of so many years. For the first time she had now to be regarded as a mighty force in France, and so for the first time it was necessary to consider her not only as the symbol of a crown, but also as a person, a being with a history and a present, with motives and desires, an article of flesh which gradually and awesomely allowed itself to be discovered, seen, and known as a very secret, very complex woman.

In her generation Catherine de' Medici was the most precious flower of the celebrated Florentine family of ducal bankers which, more than any other single family of the Renaissance, came to reflect the image of that period, echoing its greatness in their own persons, its nobility in their grandeur, its baseness in their wickedness, its originality in the splendor of their minds. The greatness of the Medici came not only from the tremendous wealth of the house, nor only from the distinction of producing two Popes, two queens of France, and a horde of lesser dignitaries from among its ranks, but also from the fact (which was as true of Catherine as it was of others of her blood) that these persons were significant humanists, liberal supporters of the arts and sciences, their courts centers of learning, themselves often immensely cultivated and sometimes even actively creative. Catherine herself was the most energetic and ardent supporter of the burgeoning French Renaissance; and under her patronage and direction this era in French history produced such writers as Ronsard and Montaigne, such painters as the Clouets, such architects as Lescot, father of the modern Louvre, and such great codifiers as du Bellay, who organized the beautiful language of France. Under the influence of Catherine's frankly irreproachable taste such objects as carpets and curtains and tapestries entered the realm of household usage; she was, herself, a collector of the first importance, and owned 129 tapestries, 44 oriental rugs, 476 paintings, 259 enamels of all kinds, 4500 books, 776 ancient manuscripts, as well as rare porcelains, jewels, and gold and silver plate to an almost incalculable quantity.

Yet hand in hand with the intellectual attainments of this cultured, literate woman there ran throughout her whole character a strain of the most utter viciousness and moral depravity. Although a relative of Popes and cardinals, she was known to celebrate the black mass when it suited her purpose; and in many other ways, as well, she took few pains to hide those faults of personality to which the wickedness of her character and the exaltedness of her position allowed her to give free rein. This exaltedness of position had, however, to be earned by her; the house of Medici was, at best, of no more than semi-royal lineage, so that to advance from this relative eminence to the ultimate one of an actual throne represented a hard-won change of altitudes and stations for the young Catherine.

The betterment of the fortunes of its members was, of course, a constant ambition of the House of Medici, so that while Catherine might by no other means have been able to marry into the proud House of Valois, the royal house of France, it happened that at this time a cousin of Catherine's was Pope Clement VII, whose aid in the invasion of Milan was urgently required by her future father-in-law, Francis I, the bird of gorgeous plumage; so after suitable negotiations an agreement satisfactory to both parties was reached. The Pope's assistance could be guaranteed through the bonds of marriage, and accordingly Catherine voyaged to France and the wedding took place with appropriate pomp.

But the mere fact of this wedding could not fully change Catherine's status by itself. She was not the daughter of a king, but only the daughter of a noble banker, and as such (no matter how urgent it might be to secure the Pope's good will) her blood did not rank with the blood of kings, and it was not even suggested that she should properly marry Francis I's eldest son, the heir to the throne. Instead she married his second son, Henry, and it was not supposed that either of them would ever come any nearer to the crown than they now were. But here Catherine's ambition had not been sufficiently allowed for. The present situation being disadvantageous to her interests, she quickly set it right.

In a short time Henry's elder brother died, unexpectedly and inexplicably. Catherine was then a young woman of presumed virtue, so at the time she was not accused of murder, and it became afterward impossible to establish absolutely the fact that she had poisoned her brother-in-law. But such an action was not at odds with her character, and certainly she derived great benefit from the young prince's death. (And there is also no question but that she introduced the elaborate Italian art of poisoning into France: among the maids and wardrobe mistresses and pages who accompanied her on her bridal journey, there were also two professional poisoners whom she had attached to her service in Florence, and who were nominally protected by the somewhat transparent fiction that they were actually pharmacists.)

At any rate, as a result of the death of Henry's elder brother, Henry became heir to the throne; then upon the death of his father he became king, and Catherine became queen; and when in the course of time, after long years of patience and scheming and jealousy, Henry II died, she found herself in the position to which she had so long aspired. The entire land lay wholly in her power, and power was the one possession above any other which she coveted and loved.

In the kingdom of France the survival of the ancient Salic

Law, which had originally forbidden women to own land, was now interpreted to mean that a woman could not rule the land in her own name; but this law failed to daunt Catherine. What she could not do in her own name, she could do instead behind the cloak of guile, and since she was fully able to bend her children to the purpose of her own steely will, she reigned in fact through the minds and persons of a series of junior figurehead kings. The first of these, her eldest son, Francis II, was a sickly and somewhat feebleminded child. He came to his crown at the age of fifteen, and died after reigning a single year. He was married to that widely admired martyr, Mary Queen of Scots, who, after his death, returned to her native Scotland where her more popular adventures took place.

Catherine's second son became Charles IX, and it was during his reign that the religious troubles swelled to their grossest proportions in France. Once more Catherine took good care to see that she obtained total ascendancy over her puppet son, and had herself named regent. However her third son, another Henry, had always been her favorite, and in due time Charles died and Henry III succeeded his two older brothers as king; everyone believed that when Charles had served his mother's purpose she poisoned him; it had not been necessary to poison Francis—he was, as events demonstrated, at death's door in any case.

These murders within the family were in the best Italian tradition, dating back to the days of the Caesars. But Catherine had other and more specifically French problems with which to cope. First there were the religious wars, with the constant intrigue they made necessary. And second there was the fact against which she had always to battle, that the French people absolutely detested her. All her life in France she was known as "the Italian woman," than which nothing nastier could have been said about her. (This nationalistic slight was visited upon many unpopular queens: Isabella-the-beautiful had been known in England as "the French woman," and an equally unpopular queen of France many years later, Marie Antoinette, was to be known as "the Austrian woman.") More familiarly Catherine was also called Madame Serpent.

Without a doubt her mind had a serpentine twist to it; but the analogy was less successful when applied to her appearance. There was nothing sinuous or slithery about her. She was a very corpulent woman, with pendulous double chins, and a vast, matronly bust. Her coloring was swarthy—muddy, in fact—and from under heavily folded eyelids her eyes, ominously glassy, bulged with goiterous protuberance. Briefly, she bore a close resemblance to a gigantic, inert toad. For the last half of her life she never dressed in any other color than black, austere as an executioner's garb, thus contributing greatly to the fearful atmosphere she generated; and the seal was set upon this by the irresistible, almost hypnotic weight of her murderous personality. This, then, was the woman who ruled France, controlling the balance of power, and plucking profits for herself at the cost of her bleeding country.

At this time there were in the kingdom, aside from the king's own followers, two major political groups possessing tremendous force and influence. One of these consisted of the Huguenots, to which a part not only of the peasantry and the growing middle class was attached, but to which also belonged some of the greatest nobles in the land under whose protection the new beliefs were able to prosper as actively as they did. On the other hand—and literally pressing upon the king's other hand—was the extreme Catholic party, supported by more commons and equally great nobles, and by the huge body of the established Church. In addition, the Catholics were supported by the menace of the Pope and of the Spanish king to the south. But here, too, the Huguenots had a counterbalance in the German princes, the Netherlands Protestants, and the imposing Tudor kings and queens of England.

At the head of each of these religious parties, two mighty families, almost equal in grandeur, were contending for the actual rule of the kingdom. The three last weak Valois kings were no match for the wits of these professionals, and the aging queen mother, with all the depth and guile of her wicked mind, alone supported the sagging royal family. On the side of the Huguenots stood the House of Bourbon, which was to be the next royal house of France. Opposing the Bourbons, as leaders of the rigid Catholics, were the ambitious members of the house of Guise, dukes and cardinals stemming from the princely family of Lorraine, who made their names and fortunes at the court— and at the expense—of wretched France. Here, then, was the cast: the drama had only to follow.

At an early stage in the religious wars, the two most prominent Huguenot leaders, the Prince of Conde and King Antoine of Navarre, were killed; and into their shoes, as head of the Protestants, stepped yet another of France's greatest nobles, the Admiral de Coligny. This gentleman was a Huguenot by conversion, and therefore particularly ardent. His presence was magnetic, and his character, no matter how unscrupulous he might be, was of a sort which drew devotion to him involuntarily. His lineage was among the highest in the land, stemming from the great house of Chatillon which, unluckily for France, was the hereditary foe of the house of Guise. He was, in a word, the perfect leader for the Huguenots.

On the opposite side, the Guises were no less capable. They were equally brilliant, resourceful, and unscrupulous men. They understood their goal—explicitly, power—and they never deviated from the pursuit of it. They were, as well, highly successful. And they were no more barbarians than Coligny was: they were wholly acclimated to the intellectual atmosphere of the Renaissance.

In the middle of this conflict the flimsy royal government was experiencing greater and greater difficulties. The civil wars exhausted the kingdom; the land lay unworked; no taxes were being paid; the treasury was bankrupt. Plainly something had to be done, and at this point sly old Catherine was willing to perform any trick to protect her position and her influence. Events had finally passed so far that the extreme Catholics had managed a decisive victory over the Huguenots in pitched battle, but neither they nor the government had the wherewithal to enforce the victory. Money, as such, was no longer available.

The Huguenots having been defeated on the battlefield, the Catholics were in turn defeated across the conference tables; and as a guarantee for the good intentions of the paralyzed Catholics, the young King Charles IX's sister, Marguerite, was pledged to marry the new head of the House of Bourbon, the Huguenot Henry of Navarre.

All should have been well, but it was decidedly not. Nine years earlier Duke Francis of Guise had been shot to death while riding round his encampment where he was besieging the Protestants. The assassin had been captured, but nothing of importance had been elicited from him, even under torture. There was no direct connection with the Protestant Admiral de Coligny, but it was widely believed that he had instigated the shooting. The duke had, himself, upon his deathbed, named the admiral as his murderer. When the admiral was confronted with the accusation he denied it, but so arrogantly as to cancel any effect of innocence he could have produced. It was natural that Duke Henry of Guise, son of the murdered Duke Francis, swore to revenge himself upon his father's killers.

This vengeance was not immediately carried out, and the young duke's thirst for blood grew stronger and stronger. It took on the semblance of an obsession when the Catholic party under his patronage, having defeated the Huguenots in war, was now obliged to submit to them in diplomacy—and particularly when the king actually appointed Coligny his chief minister and head of the government. Coligny's purposeful charm had served him handsomely once more. It could now only appear to the Guises and to the entire Catholic world that the admiral, with the Huguenots firmly behind him, was taking over the full running of the kingdom.

On August 18, 1572, the peak of the Protestant triumph was achieved. The Huguenot Henry of Navarre and the Catholic Marguerite of Valois were married, in the presence of a stupendous throng, and in the brilliance of the morning sunlight, on a platform set up outside the portico of the Cathedral of Notre Dame in Paris. The capital city was the Catholic stronghold of the nation, but notwithstanding, great numbers of the Protestant nobility had flocked to the wedding, and to witness the week-long festivities which accompanied it—festivities which, no doubt, they saw as the visual expression of the Protestant ascendancy. The Guises and all the royal family except the king and the new bride were on the most extreme edge of despair and excitability.

And on August 22, four days after the wedding, while Paris was stuffed and overflowing with his followers, Admiral de Coligny was shot.

Since he was a man of methodical nature, it was possible to predict the hour at which various of his activities would take place. It was his custom to spend a part of his mornings at the palace of the Louvre, returning to his own house almost instantly at ten o'clock; and on this particular morning his schedule was followed as usual. His house stood in the street which is now known as the Rue de Rivoli, only a few minutes' walk from the Louvre along a route which never varied. As he strolled forth now, accompanied by a dozen or so of his friends and adherents, he was occupying his time in glancing through a petition which had been handed to him. The company was on the point of turning into the Rue de Bethisy (as the Rue de Rivoli was then called), having passed the cloisters of Saint-Germain-l'Auxerrois, when one of the admiral's large and elaborate slippers came undone. And he was just starting to bend over it, motioning one of his servants to his assistance, when two shots rang out from a small, curtained window of a house bordering the street.

Both the bullets found their target, but neither wound was mortal. The first bullet shot off the tip of the index finger on the admiral's right hand; the second entered his left forearm, ripping upward and shattering his elbow. He staggered, but did not fall, crying out in an awful voice: "This is how honest men are treated in France!"

His attendants closed about him, supporting him, for he was in great pain, while blood poured down his arm and out of his finger, spattering all their clothing. He was, however, able to rally sufficiently to point out to them the window from which the shots had come, its curtains still billowing in the warm morning air. While two or three of his gentlemen stayed with him, the rest burst into the house, forcing the door and rushing through the rooms in search of the attacker. The place was empty except for two servants who watched, agape. In the upper room, the room behind the little latticed window, they found an harquebus still smoking from the shots, even loaded with a third bullet, where it had hastily been thrown down as the attacker fled—and, indeed, they had at the first moment of entry distantly heard the rattle of his horse's hoofs galloping away in the next street.

Emerging from the house once more, they found that the admiral had been able to proceed to his house, half led, half carried, and they followed him there. A pastor and a surgeon were summoned. With great difficulty the bullet was extracted from his elbow, with all the horrors of surgery in that period, using dirty instruments, and without the benefit of anesthetics; the arm was dreadfully mangled in the course of the operation; but at the end of it the doctor could assure those who were waiting for news that the admiral's life was out of danger.

Word of the attack spread rapidly through Paris, and within only hours through all of France. The initial shock to the Huguenots was quickly succeeded by furious indignation, and a great Huguenot threat, almost a battle cry, was heard: "That arm shall cost thirty thousand other arms!" The king was playing tennis when the news reached him. He flung down his racket in a fury, shouting: "Am I never to have any peace?" and stalked into the Louvre.

Of course an inquiry was at once set in motion, and a search made for the attacker. The inquiry revealed that the house of attack belonged to the Guises, that the horse on which the villain made his escape was from the Guise stables, and that the villain himself was one of the lesser members of their suite, a man by the name of Maurevert, an acknowledged professional murderer. The search had little difficulty in tracking him to the country estate of a steward of the royal household. For obvious reasons it was here abruptly brought to a halt, for the connection with the royal family was unmistakable. The attack had taken place under direct orders from the great, black toad-queen.

It could have been taken for granted that not even the mighty Catholic Duke of Guise would undertake the murder of his Protestant rival without some guarantee of protection, some assistance from above. And the truth was this: Coligny, at the head of the government and in continual association with the young king, had deliberately set out to alienate him from his mother, subtly leading him to think that he was no more than a tool in her hands (which was perfectly true) and in this manner arousing a rebellious spirit which was intended to bring about her downfall.

Catherine, watching him slyly with her motionless, bulging eyes, knew all along what he was attempting. He must be put out of the way, and murder was of course the immediate solution. It was a stroke of ill luck that the first attack on the admiral failed, because Catherine played with lives as other women play with their household utensils.

The king's first reaction of peevishness upon hearing of the attack was soon replaced by a genuine dismay, and on the afternoon of the same day he and his mother and his younger brother, Henry, went ceremoniously to the admiral's house to see for themselves the degree of his recovery. Once there, however, he and the admiral were closeted together for some time while Catherine and her younger son waited in furious impatience. When the king returned to them, she demanded angrily to know what the admiral had said to him, and the king, equally angry at her interference, replied that he had been told (once more) that the affairs of the kingdom had subtly slipped into his mother's and brother's hands, and that he should be on his guard against this doing great injury to the whole kingdom, adding: "By God, since you wanted to know, that is what the admiral told me!" and stomping back to the palace while the other two put their evil heads together.

For twenty-four hours the plotting and scheming and bristling continued; but then, on the following day, a convenient happening took place which provided Catherine with an excuse for direct action. In the late afternoon a gentleman arrived at the palace, panting from the haste with which he had come from Coligny's house, and spluttered that a *coup d'état* was being planned for the next day: the Huguenots intended to storm the palace, and there was to be no question of merely holding the royal family as hostages: all its members, along with the Guises, were to be put to the sword without mercy.

Twice before the Huguenots had threatened the royal house— once during the reign of the short-lived Francis II, and once before during Charles IX's reign. Since the beginnings of civilization three has been a magical number. Twice Catherine de' Medici had known herself and her family in danger at the hands of the Huguenots, and twice she had restrained her murderous disposition, and had simply stored up the memory of these indignities in that implacable mind of hers, which never forgave nor forgot an offense, against the day when they could more practically be avenged. That day had now arrived. The Huguenots were to feel her claws. It only remained to convince the king —for however great the dreaded queen mother's power might be, she was not in the last analysis the ruler of the country; if the admiral were to be killed openly, since the time for an unofficial murder was now past, such an order could officially come only from the king, and from no one else. A scene of the most awesome proportions now ensued. Catherine, with her younger son, Henry, and various of the nobles who supported her policy, descended upon the unstable king with the firm resolve that he should uphold them in ordering Coligny's execution.

All the intensity of Catherine's will, all the smothering force of her powerful personality, all the decisiveness of her character and the strangling weight of her domination speedily quelled the frail king and demolished his good intentions. At the end of two hours, reduced to quivering agony, he gave way altogether. Pacing the floor in a frenzy of rage and frustration, he screamed: "By God, since you want the admiral to be killed, I consent. But then every Huguenot in France must also die, so that not a single one may be left to reproach me!" And he rushed out of the room like a wild beast, foaming at the mouth.

The important men of the city were summoned to the palace. The city gates were closed and locked; no one was either to leave or to enter; the boats on the river were chained to shut this avenue of escape. The militia was ordered out. The Duke of

Guise was called to the palace as the evening wore on, and the actual killing of the admiral was entrusted to him. It was evident that all this activity was not alone necessary for the dispatching of one man who was already confined to his bed.

At nightfall a friend of the admiral's arrived from the Rue de Bethisy with word that the city was rising, and requested a guard for the admiral's house. Henry of Navarre, Catherine's new Protestant son-in-law, had already lent Coligny five of his own Swiss guards, who were stationed in the courtyard of the house. The king's countermove was swift and effective; he sent fifty of the royal guard under one of his most loyal captains to the admiral's house—ostensibly to safeguard the invalid, but actually to assist the Guises when the time for the murder arrived. It was at once clear to the admiral's friends what was taking place, but they were powerless. One of them urged him to escape from Paris while it might yet be possible, but he refused to stir, for he believed that his influence over the king was still intact.

At the Louvre the king retired early to his private apartments to pass away the evening with a few intimate friends. When after midnight the last of these friends had left him, the queen mother descended upon him once again. She was afraid that at the final instant he might relent and change the orders. After a little while her younger son also arrived to stiffen the king's morale. They hectored him unmercifully while he paced the floor in the candlelight, torn between the blast of their lectures and the slight hold which his own beliefs still had upon him, until enough time had passed that it was no longer possible for him to rescind the orders. What they had begun must be seen through to the finish.

It was well past midnight now, a hot night in the confines of the city. This new day just being entered was August 24, the feast of St. Bartholomew. The early summer dawn had not yet broken, but the skies were beginning faintly to silver themselves in the east. With the gross black figure of the queen mother waddling in the lead, the king and his brother followed her down the long corridors and galleries of the Louvre to a room in a far corner whose windows commanded a view in the direction of the admiral's house. The house itself was not visible, being blocked from sight by a row of nearer houses, and the church of Saint-Germain-l'Auxerrois. With narrowed eyes they could imagine the scene which was taking place in the Rue de Bethisy, as they stood at that graying window, waiting and waiting.

In the failing darkness the Duke of Guise arrived at Coligny's house on horseback with a crowd of his followers. The king's fifty guards were waiting for them. The captain of the guards pounded loudly on the door which led into the courtyard, demanding admittance in the king's name; one of the admiral's servants unbolted the door, and the captain stabbed the man with a single stroke, pushing around his fallen body into the courtyard with the soldiers at his heels, and the duke and his adherents just behind them. A sudden beam of light appeared in one of the windows looking down on them; it was the admiral's bedroom. The five Swiss guards, taken unawares, sprang up to defend the household; one of them was instantly shot, and the other four, turning tail, dashed to the stairway leading upward, closed and locked the door at the foot of it, and began barricading it from the inside.

The admiral, asleep, had been roused by the noise of the troops in the street outside. With the aid of a servant he hoisted himself up out of bed and got a dressing gown around him; then he dropped to his knees and began to pray. After only a moment, however, the prayers were interrupted. One of his admirers who had been staying in the house now burst into the room, shouting that the barricade at the foot of the stairs was being broken through. The noise of a shot from the depths of the house told them that another of the Swiss guards had met his end. The admiral ordered all his retainers to escape immediately over the roof under cover of what little darkness was still left; and such was his authority, even in this crisis, that most of them obeyed him. One servant alone remained with him.

From below they could hear the splintering of wood, loud voices, and then the clatter and clanging as the soldiers climbed up the stairway over the barricade of crates and furniture which the Swiss guards had thrown down there. The banging, crashing footsteps reached the head of the stairs, advanced along the corridor, and the door of the bedroom was thrown open. In it stood one of the servants of the Guises, a German soldier named Besme. Breathing hard through clenched teeth, he said: "Are you the admiral?"

Coligny, holding himself very erect, said: "I am. You should respect my age and my weakness. But you will not make my life any shorter." And then, as the soldier, sword in hand, came toward him: "If only a man had killed me, and not this scum!"

Besme ran his sword into the admiral's chest, then pulled it cleanly out again, and while his victim swayed there, not yet fallen, he slashed him across the face. Other soldiers had run into the room; they surrounded the admiral and, as Besme stepped back, they in turn fell upon him. Outside in the courtyard the Duke of Guise had not dismounted from his horse; and now, straining with impatience, he shouted up: "Besme, have you finished?"

Besme went to the open window and called down: "It is done."

The duke's bearded face stared up at him, white against the surrounding gloom. Gesturing to one of his companions, he called back: "Monsieur le Chevalier will not believe it unless he sees it with his own eyes. Throw him out the window to us."

Besme turned again into the room. The soldiers had moved away from that inert form lying on the floor covered with blood, but now two of them came forward, bent over it, clutching at the least bloody spots they could find on the clothing, and dragged it across the floor, hoisted it up, and pitched it out over the window ledge. But even with all this, the admiral was not dead yet. There was still strength left in the battered husk of his body, and he caught with his hands at the sill as he was tossed over it and dangled outside there, swinging in space and dripping gore on the stones below him. His grasp had such strength, even though one finger had been shot off, and one arm was a mangled wreck from the first attack and the operation, that the soldiers had to pry and hack him loose before he fell to the pavement below with an awful, wet, crunching thud.

The duke got leisurely down off his horse. The admiral's face was so covered with blood that it was unrecognizable, and producing a handkerchief from some recess of his doublet, the duke bent over and fastidiously wiped away enough of the blood to make the identification. The admiral, still not quite dead, fixed his eyes malevolently on the duke's. The duke straightened, lifted his booted foot, and dealt the dying man a savage, bone-shattering kick in the face to speed the final journey. Then, still leisurely, he remounted his horse, and wheeled out of the courtyard into the street. The dawn was appearing in all its summer glory.

For many minutes there had been a great clamor in the silvery air. The bells of Saint-Germain-l'Auxerrois were tolling heavily, and in the distance there could now be heard a bell ringing from the palace. These bells were a signal to waiting Catholics throughout the locked city of Paris, a signal for the beginning of the most discreditable event in French history, the Massacre of St. Bartholomew's Day. The Admiral de Coligny had merely been the first to go: thirty thousand other Huguenots, in Paris and the provinces, were slaughtered in the days which immediately followed, while Catherine de' Medici and the Duke of Guise bestrode the land in triumph.

At the *Musée Cantonal des Beaux Arts* in Lausanne there is a painting which portrays in the most graphic detail the massacre of the Huguenots. From a technical viewpoint the picture is somewhat primitive, but this only serves to intensify the scene: crowds of figures, buildings, horses, a canal or moat to one side, a castle besieged in the background, a gallows from which two bodies dangle, and a litter of corpses everywhere, dispensing rivulets of blood which drain away out of sight behind the frame. From an upper window of the most prominent building a dead body wilts halfway over the sill. On the ground below a man is attacking a kneeling priest; another man is hurrying off the scene bearing on his shoulders a huge sack which could, from its outlines, only contain a body. In the left foreground another man is dragging his victim away by means of a rope tied round his neck. There are duels and cudgelings and horsemen running down those on foot. There are several dogs which appear to be highly excited. Toward the rear a naked woman is plainly ill-fated in the determined grip of two soldiers. Behind these a pile of corpses is rapidly mounting; and near the front the bodies of two children lie forgotten.

But not even this painting fully reveals the extent of the horrors. Children were not only killed by adults, but were hideously tortured and murdered by other children. A pregnant woman, trying to escape across the rooftops, was shot, and when she fell to the gutter below she was disemboweled and the fetus battered to a pulp. Groups of Huguenots were chained together and pitched into the Seine to drown; and other corpses, after being stripped of their clothes and jewelry, were loaded onto tumbrels and dumped in the river to clear the ground for further action. The body of the Admiral de Coligny was left lying in the courtyard of his house where he had fallen, the blood baking and the flies buzzing. Then the head was chopped off, and for a while the rest of the body remained there. Finally a band of dusty children dragged the headless torso out through the streets, cut off the hands and genitals to sell as souvenirs, and at last what remained of the great admiral was hung up on a public gibbet by the feet, there being no other part of the body by which it could be attached to the scaffolding.

In Paris the massacre lasted for three days, and inevitably what had begun as an organized attack on a political party degenerated utterly. Looting was commonplace, and it was even recorded matter-of-factly that the royal guards broke into houses and stole whatever of value they could find, staggering out under the burden of gold and silver plate, or leading away horses from private stables. Without doubt personal vengeance accounted for a number of the deaths, and a much greater number may be set down to the simple, senseless, motiveless lust to kill. As if ironically, the summer weather continued beautiful throughout.

The reactions of the world were almost as striking as the massacre itself. In the Louvre the queen mother and her sons moved from one window to another, watching the carnage with grim satisfaction. It was even said that the king and his brother carried harquebuses around the palace, and took potshots with them into the crowds below. In England the great Elizabeth and her court went into mourning for the Protestant cause, as if a member of the royal family had died. But the Catholic monarchs were as jubilant as if they had been presented with an heir. Philip II of Spain wrote: "This has given me one of the greatest joys of my life!" And in Rome Pope Gregory XIII ordered a thanksgiving celebration, and commissioned the striking of a medal to commemorate the event.

From such a high peak of historical drama, from a situation so heavy with emotion, the relatively swift transition back to the normal pace of life was almost startling; yet there was such a transition; even to the most murderously minded the joy of killing must dull after a time; the thirty thousand dead could scarcely dent a population as thick as that of the Kingdom of France, and that population had to go on existing, eating, drinking, working for a livelihood, pursuing agriculture and commerce and industry and the arts and the sciences and diplomacy and government and all the other strands of occupation with which the kingdom was rooted together. As they had arisen, the horrors now subsided. Life went on.

The infuriated nations to the north and east did not invade France (as they had threatened to do). The excitement of Spain and the papacy waned with time. Catherine de' Medici and the House of Guise had accomplished what they desired to accomplish; the religious tide had been turned once and for all, and from this time forth the Huguenots, either as a religious or a political group, ceased to grow and expand; the general population of the country, having grievously wronged the Huguenots, now justified itself (precisely as individuals, finding themselves in the wrong, might do) by becoming more stanchly Catholic than ever. The burden of this stupendous crime rested upon the shoulders of one man.

The weak Charles IX, having allowed his mother and brother to browbeat him into giving the fatal order, realized too late the enormity of his action. It drove him to his grave. He had once been strong and athletic, but now he went almost immediately into a steep decline, from which there was no recovery. Fevers devoured him; he grew thin to the point of transparency; and less than two years after the massacre he died. All this, at least, was the official story, the one which the ambassadors accepted at its face value and conveyed to their various governments. But there was also another story currently circulating.

It is undoubtedly true that the wretched king received an awful shock when, after the massacre, he understood what he had done in permitting it; but was this enough to account for his suddenly failing health and his death? There were many who did not believe it was, and their eyes turned unhesitatingly toward the queen mother. This formidable woman had never been hampered by the possession of scruples. Charles IX had not been one of her favorite children; her next son, Henry, on the other hand, was her most favored. She had used Charles as a tool, and his usefulness was now exhausted. It was fully in keeping with her character that she should murder her second son in order to make her third son king. Even the details of the murder were thought to be known. Charles had been poisoned, of course, slowly and systematically. One of his mother's poisoners had, at her order, smeared the leaves of the king's hunting book with arsenic so that, when he licked his thumb to turn the pages, he absorbed the poison insensibly, and was thus killed. The last word he spoke was: ". . . mother . . ."

The third son upon whom the queen bent the fullest force of her domineering affection now ascended the throne as Henry III. Even before this time, his mother had done everything which lay in her power to advance his fortunes; and through numerous and complex intrigues she had managed to have him elected King of Poland. But Poland was not France, and Henry had not been happy on the Polish throne. He set off for his new kingdom through the Protestant German principalities, where he was insulted and reviled for his part in the massacre—the Elector Palatine rudely showed him a portrait of Coligny hanging in his palace at Heidelberg, and asked him if he recognized the man— and once he reached Poland he was even more miserable. He neither understood the Polish temperament nor spoke the Polish language; nor, indeed, did he speak Latin, the diplomatic tongue of the period. He spent six months huddled shivering in the private apartments of his palace in Cracow, scribbling his memoirs while homesickness gnawed at his vitals; and when word reached him that Charles IX was dead and that he was, himself, King of France, he leapt onto the back of the first horse he could lay hands upon and, without providing for the governing of Poland or even for the transportation of his suite back to Paris, he galloped off alone, hardly stopping for food or rest for three days and nights, and finally riding the poor horse to death.

This time he did not go through Germany. He took, instead, a southerly route through Vienna and Venice, in both of which Catholic cities he was magnificently received, feted in the handsomest style, and accorded the treatment due his position. It was a sad change of atmosphere to move from these felicities to the ravaged air of France where his throne awaited him in a land laid waste and cowering under the shadow of the evil queen, a shadow which covered the entire kingdom with a thunderous, twilit gloom.

For Henry this contrast of atmospheres was a particular jolt. He was the sort of man to whom the delighting of the senses was especially important—a dandy, a wit, a dilettante, frivolous, utterly unstable, and no more capable than a small child of taking upon his shoulders the heavy duties of kingship. Like so many weak persons in positions of responsibility, he substituted cruelty for the strength he did not possess. He had inherited his mother's bloodthirstiness. Unfortunately, however, he had not inherited her qualities of statesmanship, and it was under his direction that the House of Valois came to its end.

Once established upon his throne he surrounded himself with silky little lapdogs and even silkier favorites—not singly, one at a time, but in chattering, swaggering droves, jeweled, painted, and posturing; the little lapdogs scampered in and out among the favorites' legs, yapping in voices almost as high as the favorites' own, and the air was musky with gossip and backbiting. The black queen, fiercely as she adored her son, nearly suffocated in the atmosphere of his new court. Finally, angry and embittered, she moved out of the Louvre altogether, and set up her own household. It was a happier arrangement for everyone.

The king proceeded to revel away the months with his gay court, dressing more extravagantly each day, giving banquets where the young ladies of the court were subjected to the indignity of being costumed as footmen and attending the guests, or masked balls where he, himself, appeared in the garb of a woman of fashion, complete with décolletage and strings of pearls. His extravagance was catastrophic to a government already financially ruined.

For there had been no recovery from the bankruptcy which had occurred before the massacre. The court was barely holding itself together on a series of tiny loans—no more than a few hundred crowns at a time—and matters had actually arrived at the incredible point where it was necessary, in order to get any loans at all, even to pawn the crown jewels. The king, as might have been expected, refused to trouble his head with such affairs, prancing gaily on through his lighthearted existence; but the situation could not be glossed over. One thing, and only one, could save the royal house. A really permanent peace had to be established, and the Huguenots and the Catholics must somehow learn to live together in what would later become known as peaceful coexistence.

So the king, pushed from behind by the full-blown black figure of his mother, set the wheels in motion. The Huguenots were offered absolute religious tolerance. At this they were exultant, of course; but the Catholics now turned rebellious—and their rebellion took the shape of a famous and extraordinary institution known as the Holy League.

The League was, in fact, a banding together of the solidly Catholic villages, towns, manors, and communities of every sort under the patronage of all the Catholic nobles, and under the supreme leadership of the Duke of Guise, who accepted this post with the readiest enthusiasm. An indication of the future could not have been clearer. The League was nothing less than a state within a state; and the Duke of Guise, the second most important man in the kingdom, was rapidly becoming even more important than the king. At the same time the movement spread so rapidly, and included such a large portion of the population of France, that the king was powerless to resist it. He was, after all, a Catholic himself; the queen mother was a Catholic; the two avowed purposes of the League were to defend the Catholic religion, and to support the power of the throne. The throne had no choice but to accept all this—and even if there were a strong desire on Henry's part to resist, there was no money in the treasury for the raising of an army to suppress the rebellious Catholics.

A genealogist of the period estimated that Henry III and Duke Henry of Guise were twenty-second cousins (if so remote a connection could be said to exist at all), and this tenuous relationship was, from the Guises' point of view, much strengthened by the marriage of a cousin with a princess of France, one of Catherine's daughters, a sister of the king. The House of Guise was not at all concerned with the future of the House of Valois, but it was very much concerned with the occupancy of the French throne, and the succession was a matter of the most vital interest to all Europe. Henry III did not have, and was not expected to have, any children. Therefore the crown would go to some other branch of the family upon Henry's death.

The most logical heir by right of blood relationship was Henry of Navarre—but he was a Protestant; France was now an almost wholly Catholic country, and he showed no inclination to change his religion in order to further his political career.

The next most likely heir, although the blood relationship was so thin as to be virtually nonexistent, was the Duke of Guise, a Catholic hero with his handsome, scarred visage (for a gun had blown up in his face), his haughty bearing, his long, inscrutable sloe-eyes (all the Guises had these sinister eyes), and the full weight of the League at his back. Philip of Spain, fanatic that he was, was prepared to uphold the Guise claim with arms, men, and money for the assurance that France would be as totally Catholic as Spain. The Huguenots, beaten and bowed, were in no state to jockey Henry of Navarre into a better position. And in the midst of this imbroglio the king was barely keeping afloat, even with the queen supporting him by all her iniquitous powers.

Indeed, with the passage of time, the duke's ever-increasing strength led him to feel that he was literally on the steps of the throne. Henry III was so negligible as to be dismissed with a wave of the hand, and the duke began to act as if the crown were already his. He quarreled with the king by letter, and immediately in his rage advanced upon Paris.

He came, full of bravado, but with only a small band of followers, without an army, and the city welcomed him hysterically. He was not so sure of himself, however, that he could ignore the queen mother (to whatever extent he might choose to ignore the king), and so he went quickly to see her where, still awesome but now aged and ailing toward the end of her life, she lived in her own establishment outside the palace. He asked her if she would go to the Louvre with him to confront the king; and she agreed, partly because she was so long accustomed to the dealings of state that she saw herself as necessary to them, but partly also because she saw that she might be able to soothe for the moment the embattled personalities of her son and the duke, and she knew that open conflict would be fatal to her son.

At the palace, however (to which she had to be carried in her litter), the king was found to be curt, rigid, furious, and unwilling to enter discussion. Her presence saved for the moment an open breach; but the duke imagined himself so nearly the victor that he dared to leave the audience and depart the Louvre through a cheering throng. The king had already said of Guise's entrance into Paris: "He shall die for it!"

On the following morning the duke again came to the palace, this time accompanied by a retinue of some size, and again fell into altercation with the king. Henry now saw himself as occupying a stronger position than before, for he had summoned to the city troops loyal to him, and he hoped by this means to restrain the power of the duke. But the presence of these troops soon gave birth to the popular rumor that another, a reverse massacre of St. Bartholomew's Day was about to take place—that the Catholics were now to be slaughtered as the Huguenots had been slaughtered previously—and in response to the presence of this soldiery, the city of Paris itself now rose in arms.

Short of a civil war, affairs could scarcely have been more criti-
cal. Again the black queen mother exerted herself to dominate
the scene, and setting forth in her litter once more, this time
had herself borne at night through tortuous side streets to the
mansion of the Guises where, confronting the duke with her
customary and commanding authority, she required from him an
immediate explanation of his recent and current activities. The
duke, without being quite rude to her (for she had been so long
established in her power and was a figure of such legendary
stature that one could no more be rude to her than to a stone
monument), was also not quite as cowed by her as her children
habitually were; and although he paced the floor while he talked
to her, and in this way as well as in other ways revealed the agitation of his spirits, he nevertheless answered her frankly and
uncompromisingly. For himself, he wished to be appointed
Lieutenant-General of the kingdom. Then he demanded assurance that all the provincial governships would be given to ranking members of the League. And as well, he made various other
demands to which Catherine listened.

At the end, having anyway discovered the ambitions of the
man even if she had accomplished nothing else, she departed
through the night without making any promises or definitely
committing herself. In fact, the situation had already gone beyond the point where, by the wielding of her personality or the
manipulation of her diplomatic skills, she could possibly set it
straight; action had unmistakably passed out of her hands and
into those only of the duke and the king.

The king, himself, was badly frightened by the seriousness of
the situation, and his fright entered the region of panic when, as
a result of the presence of the troops which he had poured into
the city, the fury of the Parisians was expressed in a gesture of
open rebellion: barricades which consisted of stretched chains,
rows of barrels, wooden beams, piled furniture, and virtually any
other objects which came readily to hand were built across the
streets leading to the palace, so that while the troops were stationed outside the palace for the king's defense, they and he and
the rest of the court were, in effect, imprisoned within this cor-

don. The demoralization of the royal house at this point became complete.

Even at this juncture the queen mother was trailing out bait for appeasement. She sent a message to the Duke of Guise inviting him, under her auspices, to the Louvre so that he might undertake further conference with the king; but the duke declined this invitation with ironic caution, saying that he dared not offer himself up in such a manner. At the same time, matters in the city were becoming more ominous hour by hour. Riots took place at the barricades; here and there persons were killed; portions of the royal troops laid down their arms; and it was said on every hand that the palace itself was on the verge of being stormed by the mob. It seemed to the king that there was now only one thing to do, and that was to run away. The palace of the Louvre abutted on the palace of the Tuilleries which, in turn, gave access to one of the city gates beyond the barricade. Without loss of time Henry went casually for a stroll, came to the palace stables, sprang onto a horse, and galloped off. The court followed immediately after him, although with some difficulty amid volleys of bombardment. The city of Paris, the heart of France, was unreservedly in the duke's hands, and the anointed king scarcely more than a fugitive in his own kingdom.

He fled first to the cathedral town of Chartres, and from there on to the royal château of Blois in the Touraine. And here the king and the League at last came together once more. For upon the king's flight a rush of alarm had passed over the League. What was it doing? Had it not, perhaps, gone too far? It was, after all, a royalist as well as a religious organization. It began at once to put out feelers for conciliation; and the king, quite naturally, was ready to go halfway toward any arrangement which might somehow stabilize his tottery position.

So it was agreed, after months of parleying, that the States-General—the governing body of the kingdom, principally in the hands of the League—should meet at Blois to discuss with the king the terms of an amnesty to everyone's benefit. But it should be remembered that although the frightened king had apparently welcomed the rebels to his sanctuary, matters had gone too far to be so easily adjusted; the House of Guise was as ambitious as ever, the League as strong, and the duke as determined to become king. Whatever recess might be created in the active hostilities, it was clear that sooner or later either the king or the duke would have to give way.

It had already been intimated on all sides that the king's death would be met with unreserved joy; and it was by no means impossible that his natural death should be precipitated somewhat by human agencies. A crazy resolve was forming in Henry's foolish, effervescent brain: if the Duke of Guise wanted to murder him, he would murder the duke instead. There was, except for defeat, no other way out of this tangle. By the murder of Coligny and the Massacre of St. Bartholomew's Day he and his mother had destroyed the balance of power in France; and in the swamping of the Huguenots, the royal house was swamping as well. Therefore, logically, if one murder had upset the balance, another murder might restore it. Would the League not, as the Huguenots had done, crumble without a leader? From Henry III's point of view, at least, there was no other possible course to be followed.

On October 16, 1588, the meeting of the States-General was opened at Blois. The king presided from his throne in the great hall of the château; but the Duke of Guise, as Grand Master of the assembly, sat only one step lower, and it was perfectly plain which of them controlled the gathering. Henry began in his mind to lay more concrete plans for the murder. There was no hurry about carrying it out, for it soon became evident that a great deal of time would be required before the king and the States could come to any workable agreement, and so long as the States remained in session, the duke would stay at Blois. Accordingly the king had an abundance of time in which to lay his plans and lure the victim into his trap; and for once he behaved with better judgment than was his custom, for he allowed more than two months to elapse after the opening of the assembly before he set his trap, and thus the duke's caution was somewhat relaxed. At the same time an extraordinary change had come over the king: he had decided to perform the first major act of his life without consulting his mother. Old Catherine, of course, was at Blois; she had followed from Paris trailing political demands and enticements to be near the center of action; but now in her very teeth, as it were, without announcing intentions or seeking advice, Henry was determined to stage the first real expression of his individuality and his kingship. Its date was to be December 23, 1588.

Preparing for that fatal day, the king had called a meeting of his council for six o'clock in the morning, to which he summoned both the duke and his brother, the Cardinal of Guise. On the evening before, Henry had given orders to the Captain of the guard that at seven o'clock on the following morning soldiers were to be stationed along the grand staircase, and that after the duke arrived for the council meeting, the soldiers were to prevent anyone either from leaving or entering until further notice.

Henry went to bed at midnight; and at four o'clock in the morning his valet, following instructions, rapped at the door of the royal chamber to waken him. A servant inside the room called softly, without opening the door: "Who is there?"

"Tell the king it is four o'clock."

"The king is asleep."

"Then wake him! He told me to call him."

But Henry, his thoughts awash with the murder, was not asleep. He sat up, swinging his skinny legs over the edge of the bed, and calling for his robe and a candle. The robe and the candle and a pair of slippers were brought to him, and he went out into his study which flanked the state bedroom on one side; the council chamber lay on its other side, the three rooms strung out in a row.

Here he was brought a bite to eat, and he conversed briefly with his valet and others who were privy to the plot. Ten of the stoutest and least-principled men from his personal bodyguard had been selected to carry out the actual killing, although not even they had been told precisely what they were expected to do, partly for fear word of it should reach the duke, but even more for fear word should reach the queen mother and she would commence her inevitable meddling and rearranging; so now surreptitiously, one by one lest they should attract attention to their movements, the guards began to arrive, gathering silently in the state bedroom. When all ten were assembled the king went in to them there and, by candlelight, led them up a secret stairway concealed inside the wall to the floor above where they could remain hidden until the time for the murder arrived. Everything had to be carried out amid the deepest hush because the queen mother's apartments were directly below the king's, and her sleep, peacefully unaware of what was going on, must on no account be disturbed until the murder was finished.

It was now six o'clock. The gray winter dawn had broken, and rain was falling outside. All the members of the council except the duke, his brother the cardinal, and another bishop, arrived and took their places in the council chamber. The king waited until the noise of their movements, chairs scraping, voices, the rustle of their clothes, and the rattling of the rain against the windows would hide more distant and softer sounds; and then he brought the ten guards back down the secret stairway and dispersed them about the state bedroom, as if they were merely waiting there, off-duty, reminding them again to keep silence. Then he went on into the council chamber.

The members were awaiting him without the slightest apprehension, or the least idea of what he might be about; and he took quick advantage of their lack of suspicion. He had no sooner settled in his chair at the head of the table than he launched into a speech, so intense, so bitter, and so thick with emotion that his listeners could only follow it aghast. The purpose of the speech was to recount everything the duke (still absent from the group) had done against the person and will of his king for years past. As the list mounted, so did the passion of the speaker until at last, leaning forward on the council table, he screamed wildly: "And now, as a result of his limitless ambition, he is on the point of attempting to take not only my crown, but even my life; and he has reduced me to such an extremity that either *I* must die or *he* must die!" In the deadly quiet, only broken by the sound of the rain, Henry added almost as an afterthought that he intended to execute the duke at once.

The council was taken so violently by surprise and struck so dumb that its collective reasoning power deserted it. It agreed to the murder tamely and without any real attempt to divert him from it.

The king stood up, signifying that they might resign the rest of the affair to him, and left them, returning to his bullies in the state bedroom next door, where he made another speech telling them that he counted on their loyalty to him, reminding them of the many favors he had granted them, and finally asking with a burst of nervous energy if they would kill his enemy for him. Even though they had not, up to this time, known precisely what was expected of them, without hesitation they vowed fervently to obey him, and he hustled on into his study, the third room of the suite, where in solitude he paced the floor feverishly, waiting in a state of the most extreme agitation for the blow to be struck.

At eight o'clock (an insulting tardiness which in no way embarrassed him) the duke arrived at the château and swaggered up the grand staircase to the council chamber, while the soldiers on duty closed the exit behind him. If he noticed this action, he considered it of slight importance. No longer ago than the previous evening he had received an anonymous note warning him that his murder was being plotted. But with typical bravado he had scrawled across the corner of the paper the words "He would not dare" and had thrown it aside. He had then proceeded to revel away the night with feasting and carousal and had not gone to bed until three o'clock in the morning, just an hour before the king was roused by his valet; this accounted for the lateness of his arrival.

He had dressed himself spendidly in a suit of gray satin which nicely matched the weeping heavens outside and the frozen state of the council within. Upon his entrance into the council chamber there was some hollow show of discussing a taxation problem. The duke, who was insensitive to atmosphere, and who was anyway in a good mood this morning, blithely ignored the tension in the room, spoke cheerfully to the members as he came in, and said that he had given orders that the fire on the hearth should be built up to warm the cold dampness of the apartment.

Then, taking his seat at the table, he said that he would like something to eat. He had risen so late that he had not had time for breakfast.

A dish of plums was brought to him, and he began immediately to munch; but before more than a very few minutes had passed a gentleman of the royal household entered the room, approached the duke's seat, and whispered in his ear that the king wished to see him in his study. The other members of the council noticed the pallor on the messenger's face, and themselves grew ashen.

The duke was holding the dish of plums, selecting one from it; he set it down on the table, saying in his confident way: "Who would like some?" and passing his glance quickly over the councilors. No one answered him. He slid back his chair, stood up, and slinging his cloak over his left shoulder with a swishing swirl of the fabric, picked his gray gloves off the table where he had laid them. "Farewell, gentlemen!"

The man who had brought the message had, by now, backed discreetly away. An usher of the household was opening the door into the state bedroom with its great bed and its tapestry-hung walls. The duke went through the open door without a backward glance at the council, and the usher followed him and locked the door from the inside. Once again, if the duke noticed this odd gesture of imprisonment—coming even more oddly upon the example of the soldiers below barring the staircase behind him—his manner showed nothing. His military sense of danger was highly developed, and it must certainly have told him that there was danger here; but he walked steadily down the length of the room toward the door at the far end, half hidden behind a drape of tapestry, which led into the king's study.

The rain continued to dash and whip at the stone-mullioned windows. The ten trusty guards—nine of them with daggers, the tenth with a sword—had been lolling informally about the room; but at the duke's entrance all ten sprang at the same time to their feet, as if in deference to him. Each one bowed as he passed, and the duke courteously returned the bows as he progressed down the room. But then, with an unmistakably ominous movement, the men began to draw in, closing upon him as he neared the end of the apartment.

He had not looked back or hesitated; but now, only a step or two from the study door, he stopped. He had one hand lifted to stroke his small, pointed beard as he turned to see what the men circling behind him wanted. But before he could speak, one of them lunged at him and sank his dagger through the shining gray satin into the duke's chest. He gave a great, hoarse, surprised bellow of rage and pain, and jerked backward away from his assailant, pulling the blade loose by his movement. In spite of that wound he would have broken through the ranks which surrounded him had one of the men not made a flying, leaping dive and tackled him at the thighs.

Even the force of this tackle did not bear him to the ground, but for a moment he was halted where he stood by the weight of the tackler's body; and in that moment the remaining eight of the evil crew fell upon him with their blades, plunging them into his body from every angle and aimed toward every part of his anatomy. He was a man of extraordinary strength and endurance, and as one of the daggers pierced his loins he cried out in a terrible voice, as if he were a general on the field of battle rallying his forces: "My friends! My friends!" But there were no friends to come to his aid.

Still he would not relinquish his hold on life. Punctured with wounds, and with his assassins yet raining more assaults upon him, he managed—forcing them aside with the thrust of his unprotected arms, the satin of his sleeves now knifed to shreds—to drag himself and the ten murderers clustering round his person, like a pack of hounds with their teeth sunk into a wild animal's flesh, away from the study door, back in the direction of the council room where, he knew, there was at least one of his supporters, his brother, the Cardinal of Guise. But that scrambling, scuffling group of eleven went its crooked, zigzag way down the paving of the floor for only a short distance. The duke was bleeding heavily, staggering under the blows, recovering, crying out: ". . . Treachery! . . . Treachery! . . . Oh, my God! Have mercy! Have mercy!"

In the council room the cardinal, white to the lips, started from his chair at the first roar of his brother's voice. He had arrived at the meeting too late to hear the king's speech; and now, in an agony of frustration, he shouted: "They are killing my brother!" But before he could rush away from the table or make any attempt to interfere, another member of the council drew his sword, pointed it at the cardinal's heart, and said softly: "Do not move! The king will deal with you." And the threat was, indeed, carried out. Within hours the cardinal was imprisoned, and on the following day he, too, was done to death.

But while the maddened prelate, at sword's point in the council chamber, was protesting his brother's assassination, in the room beyond the locked door the dying duke was still hauling his pack of murderers forward, not so much by the strength left in his body now as by the strength of his will. Before him, with its head against one wall, stood the great bed of state, the king's bed. Surging forward, leaving a smeared trail on the floor, he made blindly for the bed. His legs gave out beneath him. He slumped to his knees, the red blood of Lorraine coursing down over the slashed satin, but then he reared forward one last time and grasped at the edge of the bed. With his head and shoulders on the mattress, his arms widespread, his torso and legs dangling out like uprooted weeds across the cold floor, he collapsed for the last time. The clinging assassins stood clear, realizing that there was nothing more they could do to him. That scarred, excited, bearded face which had called up to Besme from the courtyard of Coligny's house sixteen years earlier now, though not yet quite dead, contemplated the picture of its own immediate extinction.

The king, waiting in a frenzy of excitement behind the door of his study, burst forth. The drape set in front of the door was torn aside; and the majesty of France appeared, prancing gleefully forward to join and congratulate the ten bullies who had carried out his orders so satisfactorily. His first command was that the duke's clothing should be searched without delay for any evidence which might further incriminate him and justify the murder. The proud duke, still barely alive, gasping out his last breath, was tumbled to the floor, and rough hands pawed at the satin doublet. An unfinished letter was discovered, and one of the guards, rocking back on his heels, handed it up to the king: "In order to sustain the civil war in France 700,000 livres each month will be needed . . ." The body lay sprawled on an uneven hump in the paving of the floor, so that although a rug was hurriedly thrown down over it as soon as the search was finished, and the king had looked his fill at his vanquished enemy, still the blood of the gory corpse ran out from under the rug and formed a little pool on either side, so that it stained the paving stones of the state bedroom floor; and when the rug was lifted and the duke's body removed, it was found that the blood had so penetrated the stones that, resisting every scrubbing and scouring, it was impossible to wash it away.

So fell the House of Guise as the House of Chatillon had fallen. The circle of the tragedy had been completed: Duke Francis of Guise murdered by Coligny—Coligny murdered by Duke Henry of Guise—and Duke Henry now murdered by the king. To fulfill the ultimate tragedy and decimate the entire cast it remained only to destroy the king and the dowager queen.

In a condition of almost insane jubilation and triumph the king went to the rooms on the floor below where his mother, just rising from her night's rest, ancient, obese, and rotten with gout, was in consultation with her doctor. Deliberately avoiding any preamble, the king announced joyously that the Duke of Guise was no more. Catherine heard the news in ominous silence, her sick, bulging, expressionless eyes never leaving his face. She knew that this murder could only spell disaster. Out of that heavy mouth, between clamped jaws, she said grimly: "God grant you may benefit by it." The king, untouched by her pessimism, went his way with the air of a man who has had a decade added to his life.

Through all Catherine de' Medici's existence, acid and spleen, bitterness and hatred had been storing up inside her toad's body. But this was the final dose of gall, the one she could not survive. During the reigns of two of her sons, she alone had kept them on the throne amid all the troubles; and this third son had been placed on the throne by her efforts. But in return for these efforts he had now served her with the final humiliation, had treacherously cast her out of the seat of power. From her, who had supervised the running of this kingdom for almost thirty years, he had failed to seek advice or counsel; he had not even troubled to notify her of his plans. That stabbing in the state bedchamber killed her as surely as it killed the Duke of Guise, for her hatred burst the casing of her gross form, and less than two weeks after the murder the abominated queen, herself, was dead.

On January 1, 1589 she was heard to say harshly: "I cannot bear it any longer!" She took to her bed for the last time. On the morning of the fifth, apparently knowing her end to be at hand, she dictated her will; almost immediately she lapsed into a coma; and at one-thirty in the afternoon, quietly, she died. After a lifetime of such storm and thunder, her ending was so muted that it went almost unnoticed in the holocaust of events whirling about the throne.

The cast of characters had now been reduced to one: the foolish, pathetic Henry III. It only remained for him, too, to be murdered; and then upon the scene of this grisly drama the curtain could once and forever fall.

The great, black queen was dead, and France was at war with herself once more. Paris, Lyons, Marseilles, Toulouse, Rheims, Chartres, Amiens, nearly all the principal cities of the kingdom denied the king; the League arose in all its might to strike down forever "Henry of Valois, sometime King of France," and like a tidal wave crashing upon a coast, the Catholic forces burst across the land. The *coup de théâtre* was administered by Pope Sixtus V in a bull which demanded that the fallen king present himself at Rome for trial within ten days, or suffer excommunication. The ten days passed, and the king's soul was formally lost to a state of grace. Such were the consequences of the murder of the Duke of Guise.

But there was still one truly noble figure left: Henry of Navarre, the king's Protestant brother-in-law. There was no one else to whom the king might turn, no other group than the Protestants, so long scorned, to which he might look for help. Instead of the League being crushed by the murder of its leader, it was at last rearing to its full and awful height, and before the blast of its fury, any backing was a gift from fate. Henry of Navarre offered the helping hand, a treaty of coalition was signed, and four months after the duke's murder—helter-skelter months for the king—the two sovereigns, doomed French and heroic Navarrese, met, embraced, wept, and joined forces.

Matters were now to be seen in a different perspective. Not only was Henry of Navarre a distinguished prince in his own right, a man of known valor and high principle, but he was as well the heir apparent to the throne of France as the scion of the House of Bourbon; and in addition he was married to Marguerite de Valois, the king's sister, by that same wedding which had been celebrated only days before the massacre.

Now others rallied to the cause of the two kings. All the Protestant troops were at the command of Navarre, and their numbers were swelled by levies from Germany and Switzerland. The course decided upon was to march against Paris and, by capturing the heart of the nation, to compel the submission of its other parts. Toward the end of July 1589 the march was begun with the vigorous Henry of Navarre at its head, and as if the current of fortune had changed at last, towns fell to the oncoming hordes, skirmishes were won, and troops which had until now remained neutral, joined the royal forces. On July 29 the army, grown to enormous proportions, encamped outside Paris. Plans were made to attack the city on August 2, and it was generally believed by both sides that the attack could be carried off successfully.

The Catholic partisans were in a condition of panic. Better, they thought, that they should venture forth to do battle with the heretics outside the walls than that they should remain solidly within to be surrounded, cut off, and eventually conquered. The plans, then, were all set; the tacticians had drawn up their charts of campaign; the decisive struggle was finally to be engaged when, on August 1, the single piece of news which could halt every movement and stop every maneuver broke upon the world. Henry III had been murdered.

After so much drama already past, it was the culminating dramatic act; and yet, perhaps because so many murders had already been committed that one more could hardly top them all, there was something almost commonplace about it. A little Dominican monk had stabbed the king, and had himself been stabbed to death by the lords in attendance.

His name was Clement; he was twenty-eight years old, a bug of a man with an absolutely literal mind and very small personal experience in the world. With this cloisteral background, he took in and absorbed all the imprecations being hurled at the king by his Catholic subjects; and because his mind was so empty of imagination, he presumed that the imprecations were literally true, and that the king was a monster bent on the entire destruction of the Church. Clement, in his foursquare craziness, somehow forgot that the French can be a volatile people with a leaning toward exaggeration.

He began to see himself as the hero of the hour (Navarre, the real hero, was of course the anti-Christ, being a Huguenot) and to make his preparations for the murder. He was so firm in his intention that he was prepared to act without regard for the consequences, and perfectly willing to lose his own life in such endeavor; but the monkish cast was thoroughly enough engrained in him that he was much disturbed by the prospect of risking his soul. He required some reassurance on this point.

Accordingly, with all the rational guile of the purposefully insane, he consulted the greatest available authorities on divine matters and Church procedure. What he wanted to discover from these learned doctors was whether—the question had, he told them, been put to him by an anonymous third party, and was entirely theoretical, like the arguments about how many angels could dance on a pin's head—whether, then, if a pious man were to kill the monstrous king and were, himself, to be killed on the spot, he would be able to enter heaven having not submitted the question of his possible guilt to his confessor.

The learned doctors gave the matter their consideration, and finally arrived at an answer which was a neat piece of sophistry, but which suited Clement to perfection. They told him that in their opinion anyone who committed such an act of regicide with any selfish interest whatever would not, presuming he died immediately, go to heaven. But if, on the other hand, he did it wholly in the interests of country and Church, then he would win eternal bliss. They may have felt that not even this simple monk could be quite that disinterested.

Clement, however, saw himself differently. He was to be the savior of France. So he took himself off to get his soul in order; he fasted; he prayed for guidance, although he was in no way susceptible to having his stubborn mind changed at this late hour, even by the intervention of Providence; and finally, resolutely, he received the sacrament and went to work.

The pathetic king, who hid in cellars whenever there was a thunderstorm, was temporarily settled at St. Cloud in a building called the Red House, among all the bustle and confusion, the noise and color and dust and smells of an army bivouacking; and there Clement presented himself. From a royalist prisoner in Paris he had managed to obtain a letter of introduction, and this he had shown to one of the royal aides with a request that he might be presented to the king. His story was that he possessed information about a secret group in the city which was prepared to open one of the gates to the royal forces. With the assault drawing so close, there was the bare possibility that the story might be true—and who could suspect the veracity of this plain, bun-faced monk?—so the audience was arranged.

Clement arrived at the Red House early on the morning of August 1. The king had not yet risen, so he was obliged to wait for an hour. The courtiers surrounding the king at his levee pressed him to deny the interview; the subject of murder was never very far from anyone's mind in these days; but the king, after considering the matter, said that he thought it would produce an adverse impression if he turned the monk away now, and so, at eight o'clock, he was summoned and admitted to the royal presence.

Robed in the white habit of his order, Clement shuffled into the room and made a deep obeisance before the king, the long sleeves of his garment concealing his hands. At this point Henry had only put on his breeches, with a long dressing gown hanging from his shoulders; and thus informally garbed he approached the monk through the milling, watching members of his entourage who were in attendance this morning, bright peacock shapes in silk and brocade, with here and there a more soberly arrayed figure from among Navarre's retainers.

Clement, flat-faced as ever, lifted himself somewhat from his deep bow, and withdrawing one hand from the capacious folds of its sleeve, held it out toward the king with the letter of introduction.

The king took it from him, opened it, and began to read it; and while he was thus engaged, his eyes off his visitor for a moment, the visitor rummaged in the depths of his other sleeve as if to produce a second document, and produced instead—with a miraculous swiftness, as in a sleight-of-hand trick—a little knife which had been hidden there, and with a continuing movement of that flashing quickness plunged it straight into the king's abdomen.

But not all the king's attention had been focused on the letter. Some shadow of the courtiers' apprehension had stayed in his mind, and even as Clement struck, his victim, bending double, arms outthrust, tried to parry the blow. Yet the knife blade entered his body; and he cried out: "The wretch has killed me! Kill *him!*"

The courtiers, surging together as on the crest of a wave, fell upon the white-robed figure. The stamping crowd moved off toward one corner of the room, its center invisible among flailing arms and tramping legs; and when, after a minute, the tight knot of men dissolved itself and moved away from that corner, Clement's body lay dead on the floor, the robe heavily dabbled with blood from a dozen sword thrusts.

The king's slumped figure was lifted and carried to the bed, trailing blood over the long dressing gown and the sheets. Physicians were called, and the wound was dressed. The king, suffering very little pain, was assured that his hurt was trivial, that—

thanks be to heaven—the dodge of his arms had saved his life. All was well. The loyal might rest easy.

But the doom which pursued the House of Valois was not to be evaded. By evening the wound had become inflamed. It was no longer possible for the doctors to deceive either themselves or their patient; his pain became much more intense, and a fever developed. Yet somehow this man, whose entire life had been so hectic, became tranquil as the end of it approached. Henry of Navarre was at the bedside. He kissed the king's limp hand, his eyes overflowing; and the king said wearily: "The crown is yours." At midnight he became unconscious, and at three o'clock in the morning he died.

The fate of the House of Valois had been fulfilled; its doom had been met; and in the destruction of the houses of Guise and Chatillon, in the wreckage of the Kingdom of France which it contrived, it designed as well its own extinction. From among all its numerous members there was not, at the death of Henry III, a single male still living. Henry of Navarre, for that reason, became Henry IV of France, and by changing his religion from Protestant to Catholic, at last united the kingdom under his sway.

PART 5

Ivan the Terrible

Ivan the Terrible

When, in the year 1453, the final remnant of the Roman Empire at Constantinople fell to the Turks, the last thread connecting the beginning of modern times with the classical age was snapped; and as if this thread were the mooring rope with which the balloon of civilization was tethered to its anchorage, by its snapping the Renaissance was set loose to ascend into regions of altitude which had never up to this time been explored by the human mind.

The facts of information, knowledge, and even wisdom which had been stored in the repository of Constantinople for the better part of a millennium were now scattered across Europe, like embers collapsing in the heat of a fire, and wherever one of these live coals settled it ignited a new flame so that before long the whole of this continent was ablaze. But Europe alone was not the sole beneficiary of Constantinople's fall. The last of the Roman emperors, Constantine XI, died in the futile defense of his capital against the Turks; but that was not altogether the end of his house, for as Europe garnered the cultural treasures released by his death, so that heritage which constituted the crown of the Caesars extended beyond him into the frozen north through the person of his niece who, as the last important member of her line, married the Grand Prince of Muscovy.

To the medieval Russians, Constantinople had been called *Czargrad*, Caesar's city; but now Caesar's city became Moscow, whose rulers could legally press their claims as direct heirs of the emperors, and could oppose the much less legal claim of the Turkish sultans who strutted presumptuously about the usurped capital calling themselves Kaiser-i-Rum (or Caesar of Rome). The family into which the last emperor's niece married, the

House of Rurik, was one of the great families of Russia, but even
so it was only princely, hardly ranking above a score of other
comparable houses, savage and half wild. But as if the Byzantine princess had brought the spirit of all the empire's pomp and
consequence with her, in only a short time the men of her new
family began denying the near equality of the other princes, taking
the title of czar to themselves and with it the eminence which
that title proclaimed, surrounding themselves with every available evidence of power and royal ease. What her husband started
in this way, her son and grandson continued and amplified, themselves growing always loftier, more independent, and more
autocratic, so that within three generations after the fall of Constantinople this suddenly self-conscious new empire was so well
established that all the dignity which had attended the reigning
of the Caesars at Rome and Constantinople now embellished
also the czars at Moscow.

It was a peculiar demonstration of this spirit of empire which
the Byzantine princess was able to pass from her blood into the
blood of her descendants that in hardly more than a century the
uncivilized land to which she came as a bride (overrun by conquering Tartars, inhabited by a backward and subservient people
dwelling wretchedly in mud houses behind wooden palisades)
should undergo such a dramatic process of sophistication that
the physical treasures of its current czar, only three generations
removed from absolute barbarity, could be described by one
European ambassador in terms almost delirious with admiration: "Never in my life have I seen things more precious or more
beautiful. Last year I saw the crowns and miters of our Holiest
Father in the Castel Sant' Angelo. I have seen the crown and all
the clothing worn by the Catholic kings, as well as the Grand
Prince of Tuscany. I have seen many decorations of French
kings, and His Majesty, the Hungarian king. I have been to
Bohemia and many other places. Do believe me that all these
things cannot be compared in any way with those which I saw
here."

But if the circumstances and trappings of the Muscovite
princes had changed, the ferocious dispositions of the rulers

themselves remained the same. This incalculable, more-than-royal treasure belonged to the Byzantine princess's grandson, Ivan IV, surnamed "the Terrible," in whose mighty person were combined elements of such alarming type that he was not only manifestly the natural heir of the most eccentric of the Caesars in spirit as well as in fact, but in his own day of mad monarchs as well there was no other able to compare with him in the breadth of his aberrations or the wickedness of his individuality.

Quite naturally a man of such complexity as Ivan the Terrible could not avoid exposing by certain external signs the tugs and skirmishes of madness ranging within him; and it happened, in his case as in the cases of so many other devils in human form, that he experienced great difficulty in sleeping at night. Having accepted this fact about himself at a fairly early stage of his life, he was then able to find a practical way of passing the small hours: sleepless and with burning eyes he would descend the endless, icy, torchlit stone stairways of the Kremlin at midnight to the dungeons in the deepest cellars where he was able somewhat to relax the tension of his nerves among the awful sights and sounds and smells and heat of the torture chamber.

It was Ivan's fortune to found on the unshakable rock of his cruelty a career which, without that cruelty to reinforce it, would soon have been tumbled. Yet Ivan's activities were not altogether destructive; he was an empire-builder, the first ancestor of the mighty Russia which exists in modern times; and if he was to become, in his own time, an unprecedented phenomenon of wickedness, this event was not entirely without logical causes. Even before his birth prophesies concerning him were spread like carpets, and in one instance the Patriarch of Jerusalem warned his father: "You will have a wicked son. Terror will ravage your estate. Rivers of blood will flow. The heads of the mighty shall be laid low. Your cities shall be devoured by fire." In the midst of such supernatural fanfare as this, Ivan the Terrible arrived on earth.

When he was three years old his father died, and his mother and her lover together assumed the regency. It was their pleasure to imprison and kill both his uncles, as well as the mother's uncle, too, who had been up to this time her colleague and mentor. Shortly afterward, however, she herself was fatally poisoned by a group of ambitious nobles who coveted her power, and her lover was imprisoned and starved to death; thus at the age of four Ivan was well acquainted with the uses of violence.

In later years he described the woeful childhood he shared with his younger brother, Yuri: "On the death of our mother . . . we became orphans in the fullest sense. Our subjects only furthered their own desires, finding the country to be without a ruler. They ceased to regard us . . . strove only for wealth and glory . . . and quarreled among one another. They seized my mother's treasury, and trampled on her goods . . . They treated us as foreigners, or even as beggars. We lacked food and clothing, our wills counted for nothing, and no one was found to provide for us . . . The children of the boyars took away our father's gold and silver plate, and wrote their own parents' names upon it . . ."

A fundamental root of Ivan's character manifested itself in whining of this sort; in the midst of committing his most frightful atrocities it never struck this madman that such deeds on his part might not be perfectly justified, for he sincerely believed every period of his life to be encircled with exactly the same amount of hostility as his childhood had been, and thus, with a strength of conviction compulsive to the point of paranoia, he could righteously proceed with his chastisement of the whole world since the world had (to his satisfaction) proved itself a threatening menace to him. Compassion was not to exist in his mind or in his heart.

Even as a child Ivan's instincts were neither gentle nor kindly. One of his favorite pastimes involved carrying dogs up to the top of the Kremlin walls and dropping them to their deaths. It might be supposed that the dogs' masters, the keepers of the palace kennels, would object to this brutality; but in fact, the dog keepers were among Ivan's firmest friends; and when he required a group of followers to perform a service for him, it was to them that he turned. At the age of thirteen he resolved that he had suffered insult enough at the hands of his overbearing nobles. The

time had arrived for him to assert himself. He organized the loyal
dog keepers, and sent their militant little band out on a destructive mission. The leader of the usurping nobles was to be found
and murdered. This act was carried through with efficiency and
speed; the man was strangled; and on this note Ivan's reign officially began.

At sixteen years he felt that he had come to a marriageable age,
and accordingly began to cast about in search of a bride. The
rulers of other countries reacted unenthusiastically to his pro-
posals that they should send daughters or sisters to far-off Russia,
so a suitable native bride had instead to be found. And in order
that this might be done, an ancient custom was now unearthed:
eligible girls from all over the empire were commanded to assemble at Moscow so that Ivan could look them over, like so
many cattle at a fair, and take his pick.

It was a fairy-tale beauty contest to which two thousand girls
came with their ambitious, jockeying relatives, readily offering
themselves for inspection. Ivan worked his way through this
enormous number, reducing it to a relatively few girls, and then
to one, a regal, charming, and virtuous creature named Anastasia. They were married, and everything went well for them.
Anastasia produced an heir to the throne, a young Ivan, and
contentment reigned in the imperial household. This was the
decent period of Ivan's life; but after thirteen years of tranquillity, Anastasia died.

Ivan was not the sort of man to live alone. The eligible girls
were called to the palace once more, a fresh crop this time which
had grown up since the previous concourse. The new winner was
a Circassian maiden of great beauty, great vulgarity, and a Mo-
hammedan, as well. She was rapidly converted to Russian Ortho-
doxy, and the second wedding took place. This marriage lasted
for eight years. Toward the end of that time Ivan began courting
Queen Elizabeth of England (there was something about the
English which attracted him all his life); and since the presence
of a wife at his bed and board was something of a hindrance to
this new project, he discreetly poisoned the Circassian to leave
the field open. He had grown tired of her vulgarity, in any case.

Then presently, when it became evident that Queen Elizabeth was not going to marry him, invitations went out for a third rally. The girls poured in again. By this time young Ivan, the czarevitch, was old enough to marry also, so two brides were chosen, one for the father and one for the son. Both ladies were commoners; but by this point in the reign domestic matters had become weird enough, disheveled enough, and crazy enough that it made no difference. The terrible czar was so grossly depraved in his sexual appetites that within two weeks after the wedding he had simply worn his poor new wife to death.

A fourth bride was needed. This time there was no bother about calling up the ranks; he had already selected the wife of his choice, an out-and-out prostitute, so he married her. This union lasted for four years, and when he grew tired of it, he shut the woman up in a convent, and was ready for a fifth try.

Here, however, matters became more complex, for he married not one, but two new wives at about the same time, and lived with them both. For this reason, the second of the two is not generally accepted as being bound to him in marriage. By and by these ladies also were set aside, and a sixth (or seventh) bride put in an appearance.

She was the daughter of a court official, and reasonably acceptable so far as position went. But now there was trouble from another quarter. According to the dogma of the Russian Orthodox Church, no man might marry more than four times, and the czar had already greatly exceeded that number. The Church stood firm, so Ivan and Maria Nagaya (meaning Maria the Naked) had to make do without a trip to the altar. Still, she was treated as his wife, and was shown the respect due an empress. But eventually he decided to be rid of her, too. She had borne him a son, Dimitri; but in the meantime, unable to keep his wandering eye off the English, and having failed to woo their virgin queen, Ivan had resolved upon marrying a kinswoman of Elizabeth's, Lady Mary Hastings. Neither Lady Mary nor Elizabeth was at all in favor of this match, nor did Maria Nagaya wish to unloose her position and see her son declared illegitimate; but before the whole tangle could be settled, the czar handily died.

While many of these events were taking place, however, the czarevitch had also managed to marry three wives of his own; and the question as to which woman really belonged to which man in the family was somewhat complicated by the domestic procedure, agreed upon between father and son, of periodically although irregularly trading wives back and forth between themselves. All else aside, it placed a strain on the manners of the court.

At this time there lived also in the imperial household Ivan's younger brother, Yuri, with his wife. Yuri was a feeble-minded person, of gentle disposition, who never troubled or worried Ivan, and to whom Ivan seemed genuinely attached. His wife, the product of yet another of the convocations of girls, was named Ulyana; strangely enough she was virtuous and faithful to her husband; and she managed adroitly to hold herself above entanglement with the trading and wife-shifting which took place inside the family. Ivan was fond of her because she was kind to Yuri.

But then, unhappily, Yuri died. The czar was stunned with grief. The court went into a state of mourning in which the ceremonies of the state funeral trailed on for days, the Kremlin churches were filled with chanting priests, and the palaces subdued with the howling and wailing of mourners. Ulyana was beside herself in her sorrow, and when she could speak she announced her intention to relinquish the world and retire to a nunnery.

It was by no means an unusual event for the ladies of the imperial house to do this; rather the unusual lay in that Ulyana was doing it of her own free will; she was not being incarcerated as a matter of convenience to the czar. Had this been the case, no privation would have been too great for her in his eyes, no humiliation too profound, no austerity too sharp. But since she, his own sister-in-law, the chaste widow of his beloved brother, was doing it voluntarily, it came into his head that he might render the conventual life somewhat pleasanter for her in the way of earthly comforts; and with this intention he dispatched to the convent not only furniture and rich hangings and gold and silver plate, but also a large retinue of servants and companions and ladies-in-waiting so that Ulyana the nun would be living on almost precisely the same lavish scale as Ulyana the princess had done, holding court and leading a life of the most extreme elegance.

But it so happened that Ulyana was perfectly sincere in her desire to renounce the world. If she had wanted to go on being pampered and honored she need never have left the palace in the first place. The retirement, in brief, was not merely a gesture; she had genuinely been taken with religion. So the furniture and the hangings and the gold and silver plate were packed up, and the retinue sent back to the czar with her thanks, but explaining the situation.

Now here Ivan the Terrible enters the scene in the place of Ivan the bereaved brother. Ulyana or no Ulyana, he was not accustomed to having his wishes thwarted or his gifts returned. He flew into a fearful rage. Whom did this woman imagine she was, to thwart him thus? She should pay for her impudence. His rage, of course, took its customary turn; and without delay the unhappy widow was murdered in her convent cell.

Allowing for the varied influences which colored different periods of Ivan's life, the violence of his nature had always been visible (whatever portion of it might be temporarily submerged), and so it was always to remain. It was reported that at the age of seventeen, when a delegation from the city of Pskov approached him with petitions, he poured hot vodka on their hair and beards, and stalked among them with a taper, setting them on fire. This early era of cruelty came to an end for a time with his first marriage, but easily reappeared in his grief at the death of Anastasia. This queenly creature managed during her lifetime to keep his behavior within bounds, and it was actually believed that he would continue to be a just and honorable ruler; but anyone who had troubled to study his personal appearance would quickly have been undeceived.

Ivan was tall, lean, straight, and awe-inspiring. His deep-set eyes appeared to glow red, as if from furnaces inside him. His nose was long and hooked; and a long, shaggy, reddish beard—graying with the years—flowed from his chin. But there was an odd fact about this beard: it seemed, somehow, to come and go, and the reason for this was that in his fits of rage he was given to jerking out great handfuls of it and also of the hair on his head, so that his aspect was that of one who has been gnawed by rats. It considerably enhanced the ghastliness of his looks, a ghastliness which was conspicuous even in a nation and an age as fierce as this.

For while Ivan had inherited the empire of the Caesars, and appreciated in himself and his court all the grandeur of that inheritance, still the country over which he ruled continued to maintain much of its age-old barbarity, having no pride in culture, a minimum of development in native art forms, and neither scientific nor technical achievements such as were appearing in more southern nations during the high Renaissance. For a brief period during Ivan's reign one single printing press was in operation in Russia, and for the rest of this period no printing whatever was being done. Naturally, against such a background as this, the highest stratum of his subjects was composed of blood-thirsty, free-ranging men with all the peculiar exultations and depressions of the classic Russian spirit, excitable men, as savage in appearance as in the lives they led: these were his nobles and warriors. The vast bulk of his people were slaves or peasants; and the Church constituted the remaining segment of the population. The country was studded, as with jewels, with great monasteries, convents, churches, cathedrals, abbeys, and religious institutions of every sort, their saints and ikons and treasuries glowing through the ceaseless gloom of primitive Russia. The Church was incredibly wealthy; but no one except Ivan ever thought of pillaging it, and he only thought of it when he had gone altogether insane. The country as a whole was fervently religious.

Ivan, at the head of the country, was the most intensely and superstitiously religious of all. He saw himself as a bridge between his subjects and heaven; and when some disaster fell upon his kingdom, a plague or a famine or the burning of Moscow, he regarded it as the punishment for his own sins. Just before his death, possibly as a sort of sop to the Almighty, he prepared a list of some three thousand persons whom he had done to death over the years (although that number could scarcely begin to cover his actual deeds), and gave orders that the monks of the monastery of St. Cyril should pray for his victims' souls; in this way he hoped to advance his own spiritual progress.

But intensely religious as he was, Ivan was not a fanatic; and the most scandalous religious murder since the killing of Thomas à Becket at the altar of Canterbury Cathedral in 1170 was the murder by Ivan of Philip, Metropolitan (or Archbishop) of Moscow and chief prelate of the Russian Church, some four hundred years after the English affair. Philip, like Thomas à Becket, was a popular hero; and, again like Becket, he was canonized after his murder. This gesture was virtually unnecessary, however, for the Russian people already believed him to be a saint in human guise.

But he was, as well, a man of considerable good sense. As Abbot of the monastery of Solovetsk on the White Sea, an isolated, lonely, and self-sufficient establishment, he not only prayed, but also cleared forests and drained swamps, and built roads and fleets of fishing vessels and even a reindeer farm. He was, then, prepared by experience for the post to which Ivan summoned him.

At first, after his consecration as Metropolitan, all went well. He told Ivan what faults he found with the government, and particularly with its czar; and meekly Ivan listened. But a meek Ivan ran contrary to nature, and in a short time the more familiar figure began to assert itself once more, and this familiar Ivan was of a suspicious character and imagined plots against himself wherever he looked. One of the foremost plotters he imagined was Philip, since Philip was now one of the first men in the empire.

Matters came to a head one day when, with several members of his party, all of them drunk, Ivan staggered into the Cathedral of the Assumption where Philip was conducting Divine Services. In his sodden way, he demanded to be blessed. Philip ignored him and proceeded with the service. Ivan approached him again, and again was rebuffed. The third time this occurred, Ivan's drunken companions began to insult and threaten Philip, and at this point Philip sternly discontinued the service, turned from the altar, and gave the czar a thorough and meticulous tongue-lashing. In return Ivan pounded wildly on the floor, shouted back at Philip, and stomped out with his friends around him. Philip's doom was sealed at this moment.

Even for a man in Ivan's unassailable position, however, it was not as simple to bring the head of the Church crashing down as it was to dispose of ordinary persons; and since he could not immediately lay hands on Philip, his ire fell instead on lesser members of the clergy whom he arrested, tortured, and killed in wholesale lots. Meantime, while he was diverting himself in this way, he was also busy framing a set of false charges against Philip.

Upon his elevation as Metropolitan, Philip had been succeeded as Abbot of Solovetsk by an ambitious churchman named Paisy, who was now persuaded, by the hope of advancement in the Church, to endanger his soul by accusing Philip of numerous crimes. Paisy was brought to Moscow to be close at hand; and on the feast of the Archangel Michael, while Philip, surrounded by priests and bishops, aglow with the pomp and splendor of jewels and vestments, was celebrating the service, a band of Ivan's friends burst into the cathedral, bounded to the altar, set upon the saintly Metropolitan, tore the vestments and clothes off his back until he was revealed to his thunderstruck congregation almost naked, then hurriedly wrapped him in a sheet and hustled him off to prison. The crowd poured out of the cathedral at the soldiers' heels, and rushed along in the wake of the crude sleigh upon which Philip had been unceremoniously dumped, to see what inconceivable event might next take place.

On the following day Philip was delivered up for trial, convicted of practicing black magic, and sentenced to imprisonment for the rest of his life.

But matters were not to be settled so easily. Ivan had, to some small extent, to consider public opinion, and this was now very strongly on Philip's side. Huge crowds of the faithful gathered outside the prison and stood there, silent and unmoving, for the single purpose of being near the sainted Metropolitan in his cell. It was plain that this situation had still to be corrected. But Ivan was in no position to forbid his subjects the following of their religious devotions; everyone knew of Philip's holiness, and understood exactly how unjust was the black magic charge. The only choice open to Ivan, then, seemed to be Philip's removal to a different prison.

This failed of its objective, however, because at the new prison a new crowd gathered, and the situation was in no way improved. At this point a certain lack of inventiveness seems to have come upon Ivan (who was generally inventive to a fault); the only device which presented itself to his mind was to continue moving Philip from one place to another; but at each of the places to which he was moved a new crowd appeared, so that before long the whole business took on something of the aspect of a game or a race, each side trying to outrun and outguess the other.

But in the mere fact of holding Philip prisoner, Ivan possessed the upper hand. If the imprisonment was a failure, there remained only one last alternative. There was, in Ivan's group of favorites and murderers and drinking companions, a certain man of crude and brutal disposition named Skuratov, who was to play the role of Philip's executioner. This decision was reached when Ivan was on one of his cross-country journeys, on which Skuratov chanced to be attending him. It happened conveniently that they passed close by the spot where Philip was imprisoned at that time, and it was arranged that Skuratov should visit him and ask for his blessing. From the manner in which Philip had acted, even when he was still the practicing Metropolitan, it could be foreseen with reasonable accuracy that he would decline to give his blessing to one of Ivan's cohorts; and that was precisely what happened.

Skuratov was shown into the cell. Philip looked at him critically as he knelt and asked for the blessing; and then he said sharply: "I bless the good, or those trying to do good. I cannot bless you."

This was exactly what Skuratov was waiting to hear. He

sprang to his feet, and flung himself upon the frail bundle of the Metropolitan. The old man could not begin to defend himself; Skuratov's hands were about his throat, bearing him back and down; when the hands were released, the murdered body toppled into a heap, strangled to death. With Philip dead a new Metropolitan was appointed, one more subservient to the desires of the czar, and the Russian people could do nothing but mourn their lost saint. They had no defense against the terrors of the reign.

And among such terrors, death by strangulation was one of the mildest. In this instance it was not the fact of the murder which was so shocking—murders of more dreadful violence were constantly being perpetrated on every side—as much as the identity of the victim. Ivan had not really extended himself to provide a colorful death for Philip. As a rule his methods were a great deal more picturesque.

One example, in particular, illuminates the darkness of his mind. Two of his minions had been sent to destroy all the members of a certain family upon which his anger had fallen. It was, of course, impossible to resist the czar's anger; if one's life were marked down, it was better to die calmly than to put up a useless and humiliating fight. So the head of the family and his wife were murdered. The sons and daughters were murdered, too, as were all other members of the household until, suddenly, breaking into a distant room of the place, the men came upon a baby lying in his crib, smiling innocently and cooing to himself. In spite of their orders, the men took pity on the child. They lifted it out of its crib, carried it gently back to the czar, and placed it in his arms. It seemed as if, for a moment, the sun had broken through the everlasting clouds. The baby smiled up enchantingly into the great, ravaged, bearded face; and in response the awful, rat-chewed beard parted in an unaccustomed smile. As the court watched incredulously, the czar bent over and kissed the rosy, dimpled face. No one dared to breathe. It was as if a miracle were taking place before their eyes. Without losing his tender expression, the czar rose from his throne, carrying the baby. He walked slowly across the room, and without a second's hesitation hurled it savagely through a window to be eaten by a pack of bears below. The two soldiers who had dared to disobey his orders in sparing a member of the family were also killed.

Ivan felt a great affinity for bears, not only because they symbolized the Russia which was *his* Russia, but also because he sensed, beneath the surface, a kinship with their shaggy, shambling destructiveness. He always kept a few bears in captivity to use as instruments of torture or death.

On one occasion he released a bunch of them in the market place of Moscow to have the pleasure of watching them maul and kill his subjects. On another occasion he had a certain bishop sewn up inside a bearskin, and threw him to the bear-hounds, who quickly tore him to pieces and devoured him. A third bear game, the punishment for some monks who would not reveal the extent of their treasure, is described in a contemporary source: "The Emperor commanded his great bears, wild, fierce, and hungry, to be brought out of their dark caves and cages, kept on purpose for such delights and pastimes . . . into a spacious place, highwalled. About seven of those principal, rebellious, big, fat friars were brought forth, one after another, with his cross and beads in his hands, and, through the Emperor's great favor, a boar spear of five foot in length in the other hand for his defense, and a wild bear was let loose, ranging and roaring up against the walls with open mouth, scenting the friar by his fat garments, made more mad with the cry and shouting of the people, runs fiercely at him, catches and crushes his head, body, bowels, legs, and arms, as a cat doth a mouse, tears his weeds in pieces till he came to his flesh, blood, and bones, and so devours his first friar for his prey. The bear was also shot and killed with pieces by the gunners pellmell. And so another friar and a fresh bear were singly hand to hand, brought forth, till they were all seven devoured in manner as the first was; saving one friar, more cunning than the rest, bestirred his spear so nimbly, setting the end thereof in the ground, guiding it to the breast of the bear that ran himself through upon it, and yet not escaped devouring, after the bear was hurt, both dying in the place. This friar was canonized for a valiant saint by the rest of his living brothers at the Troitsky monastery . . . whereof seven more were promised to be burned."

Ivan was just as fond of burning people as he was of giving them to his bears. He not only burned them at the stake in the commonplace fashion, and set fire to their hair and beards and clothes himself, but he thought up numerous refinements, as well.

His personal astrologer (for he was by no means so pious as to overlook the actions of the stars) fell from favor, and was delivered to a fearful end: first he was stretched on the rack—a sort of limbering-up process—where his arms and legs were disjointed, and where he was nearly flayed alive with wire whips; then he was taken down and bound to a pole or spit which was slung over a fire and slowly turned, so that he was roasted like an animal being prepared for eating.

Indeed, Ivan seemed fascinated beyond the power to surfeit by the semi-cannibalistic notion of cooking people. They were not, of course, actually eaten once they had been cooked; but the process of cooking them afforded him infinite pleasure. The ultimate refinement of the cooking process was the invention and use of an enormous frying pan which was suspended over a roaring fire. The victim was then plopped into it, and literally fried to death. This fiendish device was first used on a certain Prince Shchenatov in his prison cell, but by and by Ivan was to expand the idea to much more colossal proportions.

Meantime, however, the murders mounted up in all their wide variety. In addition to burning and cooking and strangling and the bears—and, naturally, the deaths which resulted from the midnight torture orgies—there were drownings, to which he was much addicted, and ordinary stabbings and impalings. These last were grisly affairs, imported from the Turks to the south of Russia. The victim, stripped of his clothes, was thrust upright onto the sharpened point of a long pole stuck in the ground; at first there was relatively little pain, but the shaft continued to press farther and farther upward into his body, for he was suspended upon it above the ground. The harder he struggled against it, the faster and more painful it was, and there was no way of stopping it, for his own weight was pulling him down and down on the pole. At last it had penetrated the entire length of his body, piercing the organs through which it had passed, and if he had not already bled to death by this time, he was finally killed by the point entering his brain just as his feet touched the ground. The process of impaling often required hours to complete, and was regarded as something of a circus: spectators came and watched and brought their lunches.

But on top of the deaths which Ivan enjoyed merely as an observer, he also enjoyed killing with his own hands, and one particular method appealed to him most of all. It lacked the picturesqueness of some of his wilder ventures, but it had the virtues of being practical, quick, and relatively clean. Early in his reign he took to carrying a staff some four feet in length; it was handsomely carved and decorated, and the only really unusual thing about it was that the bottom of it, instead of terminating as a regular cane would, held a sharp steel point, like the point of a spear.

He carried this instrument with him always, and was thus able to deal out death whenever the notion took him, which was very frequently. On one occasion he poured hot soup over one of his courtiers, and the man cried out in pain. Since this constituted an insult to the czar, the steel-tipped staff was raised, and he was run through with it. Or again, as a great jest in front of the whole court, Ivan abdicated in favor of a certain feeble old prince, gave him the crown and the imperial mantle, and taking him by his trembling hand, led him to the throne. When the old prince was seated there, and the prolonged laughter at this jape had died away, Ivan lifted his voice: "I had the power to make you czar, and I have the power to unmake you again"; then he pointed his staff at the old man and stabbed him through the chest. He gave a weak little cry, fell backward off the throne, dead, and rolled out of sight behind the platform. It was this same staff with which Ivan banged on the cathedral floor during his fight with the Metropolitan Philip. In fact it was useful for a large number of purposes—as, for instance, when a messenger arrived at the Kremlin bearing a letter which irritated the czar, he placed the point of the staff on top of the messenger's foot, leaned forward, and nailed the wretched creature to the floor. The murders committed with it are almost countless; anyone who displeased the czar, whether slave or great noble, might expect at any moment to be done in.

The mystery of the entire situation was that the Russian people, never a very passive race, should permit such calculated brutality and bestial savagery to go unchecked. Allowing that Ivan was no crueler than a Nero or a Caligula, both those emperors were overthrown by their people. But Ivan was not. To some extent this may be accounted for by the sheer fright which he engendered in his entire country. But beyond that, he was sly enough to perform one clever and crafty act which was designed to ensure his safety for life.

To be certain, there had been a period in his life, early in his career of cruelty, when his subjects, and particularly the Church, felt called upon to criticize his actions. Ivan was, at this stage, still desirous of retaining the Church's favor—almost as desirous of this as he was of getting his own way; but plainly these two objectives were mutually exclusive. It appeared that the Church would have to be brought to terms. So he did a very curious thing.

On the morning of Sunday, December 3, 1564, a vast number of sleighs with horses and drivers assembled on the brilliant, frozen snow in the Kremlin square. There was a great bustling, a rush of activity to be seen on every hand. Porters and servants dashed in and out of the palace; voices chattered in the cold air; the horses pawed the snow and breathed fog in the winter sunshine. No one outside the imperial family except those closest to it had the slightest notion as to what might be taking place.

Such of the nobles as were astir at this early hour watched with astonishment. There had been no announcement about the court moving from the Kremlin, and yet that must surely be what was happening. Servants were carrying out the gold plate, the jewels and most precious ikons, and packing them onto the sleighs. And meanwhile in the nearby cathedral a service of leave-taking was under way, although the elderly Metropolitan (this was before Philip's day) knew no more about all this than the nobles did.

Finally the czar came out of the cathedral, stopped at the entrance to receive the Metropolitan's blessing, and climbed into one of the sleighs. The current czarina, his second wife, the beautiful, vulgar Circassian, got in after him. All the packing and loading was now finished. A cavalry escort was prancing impatiently about on the snow. Ivan's children appeared and got into a second sleigh. A few of his favorites got into sleighs of their own. The top court officials and functionaries, looking smug and pompous, got into *their* sleighs; and then the whole huge procession drove off without so much as a word to anyone or a hint of its destination.

News of the imminent departure had burst upon the city, and as the procession passed out of the Kremlin gates there was to be seen a large number of nobles and merchants kneeling on the frozen ground, their robes wrapped around them for warmth, waiting to kiss the czar's gloved hands and wish him Godspeed. This ceremony was conducted with dispatch; and the procession moved away once more, gliding out of the city and across the countryside, disappearing into the frozen wastes. The entire affair was utterly mystifying—it was almost as if Ivan were simply wandering away, without any destination at all—and that is, in fact, precisely what he was doing.

The city had a vague feeling of apprehension and misgiving. What was the terrible czar up to this time? And before the unease could turn to panic, a message came back from Ivan on his journey: "Since I am unable to stand the treachery by which I am surrounded, I have forsaken the state, and am taking my way wherever God shall direct."

He had merely walked off and left the whole country to its own devices, and the news was nothing less than a bombshell. Here his craftiness may be seen. He understood perfectly that his people might fear him—or even hate him—but that in their eyes he was still the representative of heaven, the anointed of God, and that when he left them he was taking with him God's favor and abandoning them, in a word, to the powers of darkness. Moscow went utterly to pieces when the picture became clear. Trade ground to a standstill; all the shops were closed; the people only left their homes to go to the churches. It was a national disaster.

The Metropolitan and the great nobles met and conferred as to what should be done. Ivan had to be enticed back to his capital city. It was decided that all the bishops should form a pilgrimage to follow him and beg for his return. Accordingly the plans went forward. But the pilgrimage turned into a sort of exodus. No one dared to stay behind in Moscow lest it appear that he was not eager for the czar's return—this, of course, would be construed as treachery—so the pilgrimage of bishops developed into a vast assemblage of churchmen, nobles, courtiers, government officials, and commoners which wended its slow and ponderous way out across the snowy countryside, following Ivan's trail.

He, meantime, had roosted on his journey in the little town of Alexandrof, a hundred miles from Moscow (far enough away, presumably, that his flight would appear to be in earnest, but close enough that his subjects could get in touch with him whenever they chose), and here he set up temporary headquarters. On January 5, 1565, a little more than a month after he wandered away from the Kremlin, the pilgrimage straggled into view, wailing and moaning and beseeching him with prayers. The bishops poured all their eloquence upon him: he could abandon the state if he chose, but how could he think of abandoning the Holy Church? He should remember the saints and the relics in Moscow, and particularly he should remember the millions of souls whose only safeguard against eternal damnation lay in him.

The petitioners got down on their knees in the snow; he alone stood, towering over them, and delivered himself of a lengthy harangue, ending with these significant words: "I do agree to take back the throne, but on the following conditions—that I shall be free to execute whatever traitors I desire, and free to visit my displeasure anywhere, whether by death or arrest or the confiscation of estates, without incurring any criticism or objections on the part of the clergy." This was the point of the whole gigantic maneuver: he was to be declared positively above and outside the law. And he had judged the situation correctly. Russia would take him back at his own price, however dear it might be.

Having achieved his objective, however, he did not choose to rush at once back to the deserted capital city; another month passed before he made his triumphal return. Everybody knelt in the snow once again. All the bells of the city rang joyously. But the czar was not quite as festive-looking as the occasion warranted; large tufts of his beard had been plucked out, and his head had been snatched nearly bald; the expression on his face was nothing short of maniacal—squinting, brooding, and vengeful. His people were soon to feel the weight of his oppression, but the promise of the Church that he might do as he pleased without interference had been given, and could not be taken back.

A reign of terror began at once. Executions and tortures were carried out on a stupendous scale. But at the same time, something even more important was happening. Ivan had decided to build an organization around himself of a sort which had never before been seen. He called it the *Oprichina*—a name which he had coined, and which, approximately translated, meant "the Surrounding." This *Oprichina* was to consist of a thousand young men, all eager to serve the czar in his bloodiest enterprises. Most of them were drawn from the nobility, and in their ranks two classic functions were combined: they represented not only the idea of a group of courtiers with which the ruler could surround himself, and in whose company he could spend his leisure hours, but they were also very frankly a band of soldiers, an enormous, salaried bodyguard.

The advantage which accrued to the members of the *Oprichina* was, first, the close companionship of the czar. They became his bosom friends, carousing with him, participating in his orgies, and reaping many benefits from the work they did on his behalf. But beyond this there was an even greater advantage—they, as his servants, shared the immunity which he had wrested from the Church; they were no more subject to the law than he was; indeed, as matters now stood, they *were* the law.

Upon their enrolling, they were required to swear a powerful oath renouncing their families and rendering all their allegiance to the czar. Then they were given houses, money, and arms, and set loose on the innocent population. Ivan was so pleased with the results that he raised the enrollment of the band from one to six thousand. Its members were allowed to make arrests at their own discretion, to confiscate any property they fancied, and even torture and murder without the least fear of reprisal.

But the *Oprichina's* doings were not all in the nature of willful vandalism and crime; it was a closely knit organization which accompanied the czar on his travels, saw to his wishes being satisfied, and carried out his murderous orders. Even in the midst of this band, though, Ivan had not felt at home in Moscow since his return; he sensed the ghosts of his ancestors watching him with disapproval. So he and the *Oprichina* moved back to the little village of Alexandrof once again. A palace was built for him, and houses for the band, and churches and shrines. And when the whole job of construction was done, Ivan decided that it should be consecrated as a monastery, that his company of cutthroats should be the monks, and he himself the abbot. It made no difference that he was married, and his wife living there in the "monastery" with him, nor that many of the "monks" had one or more ladies in attendance.

The rules for the new order were drawn up, and everybody fell in with the silly scheme. And the life did have its religious side: everybody got up at four o'clock in the morning to go to church and pray for two or three hours. After the early services there followed immediately the regular matins which lasted until ten o'clock, and only then was breakfast served. Later Ivan spent the whole afternoon torturing prisoners, which put him in a cheerful mood for the evening.

The religious costume of the order of the *Oprichina* was equally clownish: the outer layer was a regulation black monk's robe with a cowl about the head, but underneath were cloth-of-gold robes with sable trim. The monks carried brooms to symbolize that it was their mission to sweep the dirt out of Russia; and under their black cowls they wore masks formed in the shape of dogs' heads—for the quaint purpose of biting the enemies of the czar.

Ivan, all this time, was becoming madder and madder. He did away with a goodly lot of his associates, including the second czarina. But no matter how many people were killed outright by the operations of the *Oprichina*, nor how many were brought in to die in the dungeons and torture chambers, where he had thought he saw one foe, one threat, one piece of treachery before, in his imagination two now sprang up in their stead. These alarms and betrayals existed almost entirely in his mind: his subjects were too desperately afraid of him to meditate seriously the chances of treachery or rebellion. Still, he imagined that these things existed, and they were not restricted to attempts upon his life (none of which actually occurred), but went on to encompass the alienation of his subjects' affections, which if it had not already happened by this time was clearly impossible to accomplish; and finally his worries settled on the chance that the mythical traitors were selling him out to his arch-enemy, the neighboring King of Poland.

To deal with this problem, he committed the grandest and most magnificent of all his many acts of cruelty, the subjugation of the entire city of Novgorod the Great. This city was one of the oldest and proudest and most independent in the empire— old enough, indeed, that it regarded Moscow as somewhat newly risen, crass, and bumptious. Still, it was abjectly loyal to the czar, being ground under the weight of the *Oprichina*, and nothing could have been less true than the rumor that Novgorod was on the point of transferring its allegiance to the King of Poland.

This Pole was also a madman, although by no means as mad as Ivan, and for some time there had existed running warfare between the two countries, as well as considerable hatred between the rulers. Quite a number of persecuted Russians had fled to Poland for sanctuary, which infuriated Ivan more than anything else—especially when, from their position of safety, they wrote him long, accusing letters, spotlighting all his faults, and he was unable to punish the writers. Neither side was really winning the war, for it was the sort of back-and-forth affair which could drag on indefinitely; but of the two sides, Ivan's was slightly the stronger and more forceful. The Polish king truly had his hands full, and was in no state to offer Novgorod any protection, even if its citizens had thought of going over into his camp.

They had no such thought, of course; but still there was that disquieting rumor (and the same thing was being said about the city of Pskov, near Novgorod), so Ivan resolved that this fictional treachery must be stamped out, and he acted accordingly. At first five hundred families were brought from Pskov, and 150 from Novgorod to Moscow to be held as hostages for the good behavior of those cities. But everyone could see that this, by itself, was not going to content Ivan for long, even though some of the families did get shuffled off to prisons and torture chambers.

Around him at the "monastery" of Alexandrof the czar assembled a large group of which the *Oprichina* was the core, but which also included many independent nobles with their armed troops, as well as young Ivan, the czarevitch, who was at the age of fifteen fully his father's equal in brutality and crime. With this horde at his command, the czar set off on his expedition against Novgorod across the winter countryside.

First the great marauding company came to the town of Klin, where there occurred a pause while the soldiers with their doghead masks killed all the inhabitants with much raping and looting and setting of fires. The streets were littered with bodies, and blood ran in the gutters. Unfortunate Klin had been innocent of any misdemeanor, merely being unlucky enough to find itself in Ivan's path. When Klin was thoroughly wiped out, the party moved on. The next stop was the city of Tver, a spot as blameless as Klin: for five days the soldiers slaughtered the citizens, until those left alive were too few for consideration. Then the throng moved forward once more. The horrors of Klin and Tver were repeated in every city, village, and town which lay in the soldiers' road; everyone was put to the sword, so that a perfect swath of destruction was unrolled across the land. Even in the open country, farms were laid waste and their occupants killed; and travelers who were so unlucky as to meet the oncoming forces were slaughtered at once. The butchery was so terrible that some excuse for it had to be found, so it was given out that the campaign against Novgorod was intended to be a secret, and that therefore it had been strategically necessary to dispose of anyone who gained knowledge of it, as everyone along the way had naturally done.

At last the horde arrived at Novgorod. As an opening maneuver in the business of punishing the entire city, care was taken that none of the inhabitants should escape: a high stockade was built all around the walls so that no one could get out. Then the city was entered by the czar and his forces, and they went about their preparations in a methodical, businesslike way, while a deathly quiet hung over the old streets and houses and church domes. All the markets and shops were closed. All the monasteries and convents and churches were evacuated and sealed up, so that no one should be able to find refuge in them. The wealthy merchants were locked in their houses; and all the city officials and clergymen were rounded up and tied together.

But before the slaughter commenced, there was something Ivan wanted to get out of the city: its valuables. And most of the valuables were in the hands of the Church. Within the city there were, however, some thousands of priests and monks, and Ivan conceived the idea that each of these holy men should pay a fine of twenty rubles, which would total up to roughly the extent of the ecclesiastical treasure. What he neglected to consider was that most of the simple monks and priests had no connection with the administration of Church property, and had no money of their own since they had renounced worldly goods, and were totally unable to help him, no matter how willing they might be.

If they couldn't pay, they must be punished; so they were stripped naked, lashed to posts all over the city, and flogged without mercy from dawn to dark. Innumerable churchmen perished in this holocaust. Ivan's notion was that it would look better if he could induce the Church to turn over its valuables to him (even if he forced the issue by extortion) than if he allowed his dog-faced soldiers to rifle the churches and holy buildings, carrying away candlesticks and ikons and relics as the fruits of pillage.

But he intended to lay hands upon the treasure, no matter how he had to do it; and when the flogging of the priests and monks produced no advantage for him, he proceeded to sanction the outright sacking of the churches. At this point the Archbishop of Novgorod (whom Ivan believed to be at the head of the non-existent plot) came forward in an attempt to propitiate the czar's wrath. Ivan shouted him down for several minutes, and refused to accept the blessing which he offered; but then, contradictorily, he decided to go to church, where he listened with great piety and attention while the archbishop conducted the service; and when it was over, the entire crowd, including Ivan and his followers, progressed to the archbishop's palace for dinner, as if they were on the most amiable of terms. In the middle of the meal, however, Ivan gave a loud and unexpected yelp of rage—apparently just recollecting where he was, and in whose company—and thereupon the soldiers bound up the archbishop, hustled him off to prison, and despoiled the palace of everything of worth. Then, this recess being over, Ivan returned to the table and finished his food.

On the day after this he made perfectly plain his intention to punish the whole population of the city. Every day a thousand citizens were to be rounded up and tortured to death in his presence. The *Oprichina* busied itself carrying out these orders, and thereafter each day for five incredible weeks the carnage continued before the czar's thirst for blood was temporarily slaked. During those five weeks every conceivable refinement of torture was brought into play. Husbands and wives, parents and children, were torn apart and tortured before one another's eyes, while the czar and the young czarevitch watched hungrily. And not only were the old torture instruments brought into use—the rack and the knout and the impaling stake and many others—but two new devices for mass murder were introduced, as well. One of these was the frying pan which had killed Prince Shchenatof in his prison cell, now greatly enlarged. It was possible, on this new scale, to pitch a large number of persons at the same time into a frying pan of absolutely stupendous proportions. The smell of their frying was indescribable.

The second mass-murder device was quicker and cleaner. Below the city ran a river which now, in the depths of the winter, had a thick layer of ice frozen across its surface. A hole was hacked in this ice near the bank by soldiers, and a sort of trough or track was made in the snow, rising from the edge of the hole to the top of the slope above the river. Then, while the spectators gathered eagerly at the hilltop, a sled was loaded with victims, and given a push. It shot down the sloping path in the snow, through the hole, and into the water under the ice, carrying its load of passengers with it, where they drowned in the freezing water, unable to fight their way up through the thick ice to the air. The watchers above were able to distinguish their shapes through the ice, flopping and floundering like trapped, panic-stricken mermaids.

But at the end of five weeks the czar had grown tired of watching his subjects die. The monotony of those weeks had been varied now and again by excursions out from the city to wreck and pillage the surrounding towns and farms, but even with this, his interest flagged. It was estimated that he had murdered some sixty thousand persons, fifteen thousand alone on the worst single day. So now, gray-faced, dull-eyed, and glutted for the moment, he called together the terrified remnants of the once-great city, told them that their punishment was at an end, and virtuously instructed them to pray for him after he was gone. Then he gathered his forces together and started off.

He was not altogether finished, however. There was still Pskov, the second city which he had imagined was rebelling; so it was in that direction that the great horde took its way. The inhabitants of Pskov had, of course, heard of the fate of Novgorod, and, quaking with fear, they forsook all the customary occupations of life and spent day and night in prayer. Continuous services took place in the churches, and the bells of the city rang incessantly, for everyone knew that nothing short of the intervention of heaven could save the city from the czar's wrath.

With his big army, Ivan arrived outside Pskov as evening was falling, and stopped to spend the night at a monastery beyond the walls. But his rest was disturbed and uneasy because the bells and the wailing, praying, beseeching people of the city were raising such a noise that he could not sleep through it; and during those wakeful hours the thought came to him that there was still one final indulgence which he could allow himself, one further pleasure on top of all the other pleasures he had recently enjoyed. He could actually relent and spare the people of Pskov. The truth was that he found their fear of him gratifying: it was just the emotion he wished to arouse in them. And in addition, he was experiencing a certain caution: the clergy—in spite of the bargain at Alexandrof—was once more taking up its muttering; a local prophet said that his horse would drop dead under him if he tried to remove the famous bell from Pskov Cathedral.

So he decided to spare the population. They met him kneeling the next morning, and his entrance into the city was everything he could have wished. His kindliness shone like the sun. But no matter how many lives he had decided to spare, he was still not going to spare any treasure he could find (he was even more avaricious than he was cruel) so, without killing people, he simply started robbing the churches and private houses. Among the spoils was, of course, the bell of the cathedral; and as it was being lowered, Ivan's horse *did* drop dead under him. Plainly it was time for him to stage a calculated retreat.

But this was not yet quite the end of the affair, for he had not killed every one of his victims in Novgorod, but was taking some of them home with him as prisoners, including the unfortunate archbishop. Ivan had the foresight to anticipate that while he might be weary of torture for the moment, his hunger was by no means permanently satisfied. The prisoners would provide excellent material for the torture chambers when his appetite revived.

So he withdrew from the conquered cities and led his army back to the "monastery" at Alexandrof where he rested for a little while and commenced to plan his next bit of mischief. This was still to be connected with the Novgorod-Pskov conspiracy. It now occurred to him that these cities would never have dared to consider rebelling against him unless they received a promise of assistance from some of the more important figures at Moscow;

so now the problem was to discover who these new conspirators were.

The obvious method of doing this was to hand the prisoners over for torture (although not to kill them: their lives were being saved for the grand finale to these goings-on), so the questionings began. But the prisoners, even at this desperate pitch, were able to take a small revenge on him. When placed on the rack or subjected to other dreadful treatments, the people they named as their cohorts and accomplices in the supposed conspiracy were his favorites, the heads of the *Oprichina*, his most intimate companions; and when Ivan was frightened, the ties of friendship meant nothing to him. So as soon as a man's name was mentioned in connection with the plot he was automatically either murdered with his entire family, or locked in a cell for future handling. In this way the czar's immediate circle was greatly reduced in numbers, and the wretched prisoners had at least the satisfaction of throwing some of their misery back upon their persecutors.

At last all the evidences of treason were gathered to Ivan's satisfaction. He was ready to emerge from his hermitage at Alexandrof and, taking his prisoners with him, to descend upon Moscow for a great mass execution. It was midsummer by now; the snow had melted and the ice had thawed; and the Muscovites had been quivering with fright for months, wondering what the infernal monster would do next. Novgorod was gone. Why shouldn't the capital city follow the same route?

In advance of his arrival, a great marketplace was selected as the site for the executions, and among the booths and stalls a variety of torture instruments was set up, including the odorous frying pans, cauldrons of water over fires for boiling the victims to death, pens of bears and gallows and so forth. But while this activity of construction was afoot, no one had thought to tell the people of Moscow explicitly who was going to be tortured and killed here, and quite understandably they got it into their heads that the mad czar was coming to kill *them*. So on the lovely summer day which had been set for the executions, there was no one to watch them, no audience. Moscow was silent, the streets and marketplace deserted; all its inhabitants had slunk away into hiding.

Ivan was greatly annoyed. He had arranged what he thought was a beautiful spectacle to be enjoyed by his Muscovite subjects, and they repaid his thoughtfulness and generosity by running away. The fact that Moscow had already been considerably oppressed by the *Oprichina* and had no reason to guess that the fate which had been Novgorod's would not be its own next, apparently slipped his mind. He was determined that the entertainment should be carried out as he had planned it, and for that he needed an audience.

The executions were temporarily postponed, although the prisoners were ready, the cauldrons boiling, and the frying pans sizzling. A number of the soldiers were told to go out into the city and recruit an audience. This was accomplished in the most forthright way by the soldiers proceeding from street to street and square to square, breaking into houses and dragging their occupants forth from basements and closets and wherever else they might have chosen to hide, and marching them back to the marketplace. At the same time Ivan himself was riding about the city on his horse, beaming with false benevolence and calling out in a cheery voice: "Come along, good people. There is nothing to be afraid of. No harm is going to befall you."

In this way a reluctant audience was finally gathered together, so that even the roofs of houses neighboring on the marketplace were crammed with unwilling spectators, all pale of face and trembling of limb. Then the executions were, at long last, ready to go forward. Affairs of this kind were commonplace in Ivan's career, but the watchers were not accustomed to such brutality, such a carnival of bloodshed and death, and it was almost too much when the czar himself actually condescended to kill one of the prisoners with his own steel-tipped staff. All the contrivances of torture were put to work—the marketplace was a kind of outdoor death factory; and as a special plum in the pudding of the entertainment, the chief prisoner—an absolutely innocent man, not even one of the fallen favorites, but an honest member of the council of nobles—was hung up by his heels and sliced to death. The killing, although paltry by the standard of Novgorod, lasted for four hours.

This chief prisoner, now dead after incredible agony, had been imprisoned without (astonishingly) any harm touching his family; but this had only been another example of Ivan's prudence in saving up pleasures against another time when they might be more urgently needed. He now concluded that the time had come when he needed this prince's family. When the executions were finished, he and the young Ivan set out for the late prince's home where, finding the ladies of the house assembled to mourn, their arms about one another, huddled in grief, they rapidly injected a note of vivacity into the domestic picture. Ivan raped the new widow, while his son raped the eldest daughter of the family.

This example was being followed all over the great city. Soldiers were raping any of the wives and sisters and daughters of the dead prisoners who were still to be found. When this tremendous orgy had at last reached an end, all the widows and sisters and daughters, all the crazed victims of the rape, were dragged off to the banks of the river, pitched in, and drowned there to complete the punishment. It only remained now to dispose of the mutilated bodies in the marketplace. For some days they lay moldering and decaying in the July sunshine; and finally, overreaching even his own prior ingenuity, the czar ordered the *Oprichina* out with their long, sharp swords to hack up the corpses into small bits. When this had been done, all the dogs of Moscow converged in that locale and occupied themselves in gnawing the human flesh off the bones, until those bones, clean and drying in the sunshine, were forgotten by the Muscovites, who kicked them off the streets as they walked to and from the reinstated market stalls once more, conducting their daily business.

The destruction of Novgorod took place when the czar was nearing the age of forty. His years and his depravity were beginning to tell on him. He had not lost his erect and awe-inspiring carriage, but he was growing heavier from a terrible gluttony, and such beard as he had left was gray. He was still fourteen years from the end of his life, however; and although the Novgorod affair was the high point of cruelty in his entire career (indeed, there was nowhere to go from here: having crushed a full province of his empire, the only thing he could do on a yet larger scale was destroy the *whole* empire, but even to him this scarcely seemed a profitable action), he nevertheless continued all his life the policy of torturing and murdering whomever he chose.

And inevitably, toward the end of his life, there was one single murder which was so dreadful as to cast even Novgorod somewhat in the shadow. That was the murder of his beloved son.

It was not a premeditated murder, as all the others were, nor was there any torture involved in it. It was an accidental murder —which is not to say that it was an accident; it was distinctly a murder; he struck the young man dead with his own hand—but the mere, paradoxical fact of an accidental murder makes it both the worst and the rarest form of that crime. And in Ivan's case it is ironically appropriate that the hobby which all his life he had pursued with such assiduity should, in the fullness of time, recoil on him so that by the very habit of murdering indiscriminately and without thought, he committed one murder too many, one more than he had ever intended.

The young Ivan was now a man in his middle twenties, married to his third wife; and inadvertently this wife contributed to the situation which brought about the murder. It happened in the retreat at Alexandrof. At this particular moment in the relationship of father and son, it chanced that the czar was living with his own wife, and young Ivan with his; but on this special morning, as if acting upon impulse, the czar chose to assault his daughter-in-law.

Of course, she should not only have been accustomed to this —she had been through it all to its conclusion before—but even have been expecting it. It happened, however, that the princess was pregnant, and feeling squeamish. Ivan, with his increasing corpulence, his scraggly beard, and his mad, roving eyes was hardly a figure to call forth romance from a lady's heart, and the princess rebuffed him. A graceless and uncouth tussle ensued, in the course of which the czar made a startling discovery. His daughter-in-law was wearing only two petticoats, instead of the three which were considered to be an absolute minimum for decency. In one part of his mind he was an awful prig—certainly where the behavior of others was concerned—and he was flabbergasted by this discovery. Even though the girl had been to bed with him, and he expected that she would come there again, he had no difficulty in overlooking the laxness of her actual conduct while being profoundly shocked by the symbolic number of her petticoats.

He was the representative of heaven. He loosed the wrath of the righteous on the unlucky girl, and began to beat her with heavy blows, belaboring her roundly. She could not defend herself beyond covering her head with her arms; but she cried out loudly for help, half-hysterical with fear, expecting at any moment to be struck dead as she cowered in front of him.

Before any serious harm was done her, however, the czarevitch rushed into the room. He saw at a glance what was happening. His temper being as violent as his father's, he did not hesitate to throw himself into the fray, and was able forcibly to drag the two of them apart and haul the czar out of the girl's immediate vicinity so that he could no longer continue to beat her, at least. But this intervention was, by itself, sufficient to protect her, for the czar's fury was now turned upon his son instead.

This would have been a perfectly logical moment for his murderous instinct to assert itself, to cause him to kill the young man, as he might swat an insect, without a thought of the consequences. But the deed was not to be done yet. The two of them stood there, hurling angry words back and forth at one another. The czar flung in his son's face the immodesty of his pregnant wife; and the czarevitch retorted that his father had ruined his happiness in his first two marriages, and was now trying to spoil this one as well.

But it was not the first quarrel they had ever had, for their temperaments were each as savage as the other; and like their previous quarrels, this one appeared to blow over after a bit. By dinnertime amity had been restored. The atmosphere of the imperial household was always strung high with emotion, in any case, so there was no reason for anyone to suppose that this quarrel had more significance than any other. Father and son dined side by side, drank together, and appeared to be in a state of normal concord—insofar as real concord ever existed between them except as rivals in sadism or in the eccentricities of the alcove. Over his food the czar grew drunk and boastful; the czarevitch grew drunk and silent.

Finally, having retired from the table together, Ivan began to brag to his son about his wealth, the treasures he possessed. The boy was not as impressed as he should have been. Ivan became plaintive and sentimental. He bragged on lengthily about how happy he was to be able to provide so well for his son, to know that he would inherit all this; he was, by his own statement, a marvelous father; the more he ranted about this, the sourer the czarevitch grew. At last he broke in sneeringly: "Valor is better than wealth!"

Ivan's mad red eyes bugged incredulously.

The czarevitch went on to drive his point home: "Valor such as the King of Poland possesses is worth more than wealth. What good is wealth if you are not strong enough to keep it?"

The czar was seized with such rage that he was inarticulate; a bellow of anger shook the walls, but no words came forth.

The czarevitch could not stop himself from going on: "Why not let *me* lead an army against our enemy, and win back what we have lost?"

A fury of such strength as he had never before experienced swept over the aging czar. He trembled violently, and his face took on an evil purple cast, while his arrogant son stood facing him scornfully. Ivan had no idea what he was doing. His terrible steel-tipped staff, always in his hand, was there now. He brandished it menacingly for a second; and then, because he was so completely accustomed to striking out heedlessly with it, he extended his arm and lunged forward. Blindly he struck at his son's figure with that fearful point, which pierced the white cloth of the tunic and entered the living flesh; he struck again and again, and then, the violence of his rage still mounting, he reversed his grip on the staff, and began mercilessly to beat his son over the head with its weighted handle.

One of the favorites who was present during this scene now leapt forward and tried with his bare hands to intercept the hail of blows. But it was useless. The czarevitch slumped bloodily to his knees, then sagged to the floor. And suddenly, all in an instant, the czar regained his senses; his sight returned to him, and he saw what he had done. He stared, frozen in speechless horror, at the red, dripping staff in his hand, and down at his son's body lying sprawled at his feet, gore welling darkly from the wounds which the staff had inflicted.

Sobbing convulsively, his mouth opened wide in soundless anguish, he dropped to the floor beside that grisly body in the awful, overwhelming grip of repentance. He swept the limp body into his arms, hugging it to his chest, and at last began screaming aloud to heaven for succor. There was a deep wound in the side of the body from which the blood coursed out in a thick stream, and futilely he cupped his hand over that wound, trying to stop the flow. Howling like an animal, he kissed his son's pale, battered face, kissed it over and over, until anxious courtiers took the body from his arms, and he struggled to his feet, not knowing what he did, still shrieking his grief so that the halls of the palace trembled with his voice.

The czarevitch was unconscious and mortally wounded; but he was not yet dead. Doctors and priests were summoned, but the primitive medicine of the times was powerless against those wounds. Consciousness returned briefly, and out of that clotted mouth a faint, almost inaudible voice spoke words of forgiveness. In a short time he died.

The czar was prostrated with sorrow. All the empire went into deepest mourning, but the mourning of millions was as nothing to the abysses of grief into which was plunged this most wretched of men, the father who had murdered his own son. The earliest grief of Ivan's existence had been the death of his first wife, Anastasia, from which he had gone into his great period of debauchery. And now the son of that same Anastasia, to him most precious of all flesh, had perished by his uncontrollable hand. The last years of his life were lived out in that black shadow. He wandered his palaces blankly, like a sleepwalker, as if haunted; and often he was found in the morning by his servants huddled, unconscious, in a damp corner or at the base of a cold column where he had apparently fallen in his tracks. His appearance reached the extreme limit of wildness and disorder.

But it was too late for him to change his mode of existence entirely. The uses of cruelty were so deeply rooted in him that it was impossible for him to tear them out, although he never again reached the heights of wickedness which had characterized the most violent period of his reign. On the strength of a momentary whim the *Oprichina* had already been disbanded, and the old procedures of government revived. Torture and sudden death were served up as before, but on a moderated and less enthusiastic scale. He had lost the energy and incentive required to produce great evil. Toward the end he drew up the famous list of his victims, and sent it to the monks of St. Cyril for prayer. Less than three years after the murder of his son, he died. Clothed in a loose gown, he had been playing chess with one of his few remaining favorites when he fell limply back in his chair, fainting, and within minutes his life was gone. The Metropolitan, summoned in all haste, pronounced over his body the ritual for the renunciation of the throne, and Ivan the Terrible went to his maker as Johan, a simple monk severed from all earthly attachments.

It was typical of the Russia of that day that the passing of a czar who had held his subjects in the most abject terror for almost half a century should be met with the gravest mourning. His death marked the end of an era; and because he was so completely the spirit of that era, it seemed to his subjects that he took something of it with him when he died. He had been the greatest political figure thus far in the history of Russia. He had more than tripled the size of his inheritance, and had elevated his country from the status of a mere kingdom to the dignity of that empire whose spirit his grandmother had brought with her from Constantinople a hundred years earlier. For better or for worse, his like was not to be seen again.

PART 6

~~~~~~

Pope Alexander VI
and His Children

Pope Alexander VI and His Children

The moral laxity of many of the Renaissance Popes is a fact so well established that it can no longer command, on the one hand, doubt, or on the other astonishment. The great papal families of the period—Medici, Piccolomini, della Rovere, Cibo, Colonna, Farnese, and others of such distinction—consistently practiced the most blatant nepotism for the advancement and enriching of their members; personal avarice was accepted naturally as the strongest motivating force for a Pope; the chair of St. Peter floundered in a wash of voluptuousness and perversion; one Holy Father after another surrounded himself with his illegitimate offspring (Pope Innocent VIII was credited by Marullo, a humanist of the time, with fathering sixteen children); papal elections swung by bribery were commonplace (after the election of Sixtus IV his friends felt it necessary to excuse his generosity toward those cardinals whose votes he had bought by saying that he was inexperienced, and thus failed to anticipate the adverse construction which might be put upon his simple openhandedness); and altogether the level of the Popes and their families had, on a basis of personal behavior, become so consistently low that it is surprising, in the general sordidness of the era, to consider one family, the Borgias, as conspicuously worse than any of the others.

The truth is that the Borgias' reputation for wickedness has now for centuries been so puffed up in literature and upon the stages of opera and the theater that an illusion has come to exist that the actual truth concerning them is virtually impossible to discover. But in spite of all the rumors put about by their contemporaries, and the legends which have subsequently sprung up around their names, there still remains as a kernel of fact one particular reason why the Borgias should have become—as they did—the most famous family of their kind: the other papal houses might excel them in violence or in greed, in vengefulness or corruption or immorality, but when these several fields of effort were seen grouped together panoramically, no other family was so nearly excellent in so many of them all at the same time; and it is really upon the broad scope of their evil-doing, more than upon any specific action, that the fame of the Borgias continues to rest.

Before this ambitious house achieved the majesty of the papal throne which was to render its name celebrated and notorious down the reaches of time, it was a line of no special consequence, but (so that its background shall not be underestimated) it was of long-standing respectability, having existed in the town of Jativa in Spain as a family of gentlefolk—provincial governors and soldiers and priests—for more than two centuries before the year 1440, in which one of these priests accompanied his patron to Italy, where, owning a fine legal brain and the ability to rise to certain occasions, he became a cardinal, and then Pope in 1455 under the name Calixtus III. The highest fortunes of the family had, by this lucky stroke, been founded.

Calixtus III was seventy-six years old when he ascended the throne of St. Peter, and in his literal-minded, suspicious old age one of the few persons he felt he could trust was his nephew, Rodrigo Borgia, whom he quickly made a cardinal, and by and by Vice-Chancellor of the Church, a position second only to his own. This Rodrigo was fully equal to the opportunities offered him; and upon his uncle's death he proved to be so deft in fulfilling the duties of his office, so able in conciliating the everlastingly quarrelsome churchmen, and so canny in picking his way among the politics of the Vatican that he contrived to maintain his position as Vice-Chancellor through the pontificates of the four Popes who one by one succeeded his uncle.

And under each of them he gained strength, he corrupted and extended his power, he conducted his fantastic love affairs, he accumulated great hordes of ill-gained wealth, he oversaw the upbringing of his illegitimate children, and he set his cap more and more loosely on his head so that it might at any time be displaced by the triple tiara, the awesome crown of the Popes of Rome.

In the same year as Columbus's discovery of a new continent and a new world, Pope Innocent VIII died. Rodrigo Borgia, now past sixty, had spent thirty-seven years in biding his time against just such a portentous hour, and the hour had now arrived. He had intrigued and plotted and stolen and cheated and murdered; he had forged Church documents, some of them nothing less than papal Bulls, when he saw some profit to be made in this way; he had committed every sin forbidden by the Church; and at last, when he saw the papacy to be almost within his hungry grasp, he was prepared to hesitate at nothing, if need be even to topple the very throne he coveted. If he could bribe every one of the cardinals in order to carry the papal election, it was his intention to do precisely that, and during the days between the late Pope's death and the opening of the conclave mules heavily burdened with gold were to be seen leaving the Borgia palace under guard, destined for the palaces of the other venal cardinals.

As it was seen at the beginning, the contest for the papacy appeared to lie only between the Cardinals Caraffa and Costa, the one affiliated with the Dukes of Milan in the north, and the others with the Kings of Naples in the south. Cardinal Borgia, smoothly and treacherously in the middle, was not thought to be a serious candidate. At the first balloting of the Sacred College he received only seven votes. He was, however, as busy as a mole, burrowing and bribing and cajoling. On the second voting he had risen to eight. At last, when he had drawn into his hands fourteen votes, he was only one short of the majority he needed to win. He knew perfectly who were his friends, who his enemies, and who still swayable. In this last category only one man was left, Cardinal Gherardo, ninety-five years old and senile. His allegiance was finally obtained, and the victory accomplished.

When the remaining members of the conclave saw that the dark horse was winning, they threw in their lots with him—being, to tell the truth, already a little frightened of this human monster—and so he was unanimously elected. The result of the election was announced at the hot, humid dawn of a day in mid-August, 1492. The new Pope, adopting the name Alexander VI, strode out onto the balcony to acknowledge his election, bellowing in uncontrollable joy: "I am Pope and Vicar of Christ on earth!" The Christian world had been purchased by him for cash, like a certain acreage of soil containing so many head of cattle; the issue of religion did not enter upon the scene. The Spannochi Bank, where the Borgia wealth was deposited, nearly crashed as a result of the feverish withdrawals as the cardinals collected their bribes. The eleven terrible years of his reign had begun.

Alexander VI was a man of the flesh, a bull of a man—appropriately enough since his family's heraldic insignia was a bull. He could not get his fill of women, nor apparently could they get their fill of him, for his conquests were legendary, and he is reported by his contemporaries to have been extraordinarily handsome and to have possessed a singular and irresistible charm of manner. He may have had charm—that quality is too elusive to survive the centuries—but his portraits and busts are by no means those of a handsome man: he is shown as having a thick, hooked nose, a pair of small, droopy, bagging, cynical eyes, and a receding chin; but the most prominent features of his face are the lips, heavy and sensual, almost slobbering, as coarse and broad as an ape's.

He was monumental in stature, and under the crusty folds and jeweled embroideries which his office as Pope dictated and his private love of ostentation seconded, he looked a veritable walking mountain. His passions were as gigantic and as grotesque as his façade. All his life he had been subject to spasms of murderous rage; he could never bear to have his will crossed; and once he became Supreme Pontiff these failings swelled to double their earlier proportions.

Erotically he was insatiable, but this seems to have been characteristic of his entire family. He enjoyed all the perversions and eccentricities of the age (it was said that after the taking of Faenza by the papal forces the young lord of the city, Astorre Manfredi, regarded as the handsomest youth in Italy, was lustfully attacked by both the Pope and his son Cesare before having a stone hung round his neck and being drowned in the Tiber); but on the whole he preferred a more conventional satisfaction for his appetites. The number of his mistresses was phenomenal, but in the earlier period of his life, while he was still a cardinal, one of these far outshines the others, a woman of peculiar good sense and lack of affectation named Vannozza. For fifteen years he was as faithful to her as he was capable of being to any woman—which was, in fact, not faithful at all—and by her he had four surviving children: Cesare, Juan, Lucrezia, and Jofre.

These were certainly not all the children he had—and since he was a priest all, of course, illegitimate—but he chose not to acknowledge most of them. The oldest publicly acknowledged was Pedro Luis, for whom his father created the Spanish duchy of Gandia, but he died at an early age. The fact that the future Pope did acknowledge Vannozza's children was not only proof of his fondness for her, and after they ceased to be lovers they remained close friends for the rest of their lives, but also an indication that he saw in them a clearer reflection of himself than he had seen in his other children.

He was a man of stupendous pride and arrogance, and while it has been truly said that he loved these acknowledged children with an unnatural fervor and devotion, he did not love them for themselves, but for what he could find in them of his own self. In his frantic attempts to forge principalities and weld kingdoms for them, to marry or trade them to the greatest advantage, it was his own advantage he saw first, and afterward—leading beyond his vision into the future—he labored for the perpetuation of himself through them. It was neither a normal nor a healthy love.

At the time of Borgia's seizing the papal throne, Pedro Luis was dead, Cesare was eighteen years old, Juan was seventeen, Lucrezia twelve, and Jofre ten. Cesare had already entered the Church, following in his father's footsteps, so the now vacant title of Duke of Gandia was given to Juan, the second surviving son. This was to be the cause of great trouble.

Jofre, being a mere boy, was of slight importance in the family's affairs. He married for political reasons a notably voluptuous princess of the Neapolitan House of Aragon, who was five years older than he. With her loose ways she was perfectly at home among the Borgias; and she became the mistress of both Cesare and the Duke of Gandia.

These two elder sons were made of more rugged stuff than Jofre. They had inherited the sheer animalism of their father—his licentiousness, his mad rages, his toughness and cynicism and arrogance. They were raised and educated as if they were legitimate princes. No restraint was ever placed upon them, and their recklessness was even encouraged. Their father had great plans for them. It was his firm, if insane, determination that Cesare should succeed him on the papal throne, that Cesare should, in turn, be succeeded by his own illegitimate son, and that the papacy should thus become a hereditary possession of the House of Borgia, exactly as kingdoms were the hereditary possessions of their royal families.

The utter foolishness of this project escaped him altogether, while he pondered the almost insuperable difficulties involved in carrying it out (the worst of these was that by Canon Law bastards were strictly prohibited from becoming Pope in the first place). Alexander VI refused to admit that anything he might undertake was beyond his reach, however, so far as the Church was concerned; and this was indicative of a flaw in his character more influential than any of his other faults—it was psychologically impossible for him to comprehend what religion was basically about. To him the Church was merely a state like any other; the College of Cardinals was the equivalent of a house of lords; he, himself, was a king—indeed, the king of kings; and the revenue of the Church had no other use than to be devoted to purely worldly purposes. Because he did not—could not—understand anything beyond his five senses, the niceties of his position were totally lost on him. During a mass he was celebrating in St. Peter's he allowed Lucrezia and her maids-in-waiting to frolic and scamper and giggle in the stalls reserved for the canons. And on another occasion he was so careless in his hurry to finish a mass and be done with it that he actually dropped the Host to the floor and heedlessly trampled on it, having plainly no conception of the enormity of his behavior. The Church of Rome had reached the lowest point in its long and venerable history.

Alexander VI made no effort to hide his contempt for religion; but tiresome and incomprehensible as he might find it, the Catholic millions of Europe who made up his subjects provided him with greater advantages and opportunities than any other ruler could claim. It was his right to impose taxes on men's spiritual lives, as temporal lords imposed them on men's physical lives; and he could always overcome any human obstacle simply by the threat of excommunication, the most fearful weapon in the world at that time. He did not propose that these tremendous sources of power should pass out of his family's hands.

As the first step in his plan for inheritance, Cesare (now a bishop) must be made a cardinal, and the Pope was no sooner established on his throne than he began to work toward this end. The other cardinals were solidly opposed to this invasion of their ranks by a boy who was only now turning nineteen, and they did what they could (which was honestly not very much) to oppose the Pope's wishes; but he soon overbore them. It was not for nothing that he had spent those thirty-seven years battling his way up to this eminence, and he proposed to take full advantage of it once it had been reached. Cesare was duly elevated to the purple.

He was still less suited for a priestly career than his father, for he lacked even his father's sense of using the Church as a tool. Cesare was pleased with the income which his position brought him, but beyond that he found religious matters simply a bore. In his own palace he lived a life of riotous debauchery with his mistresses and hangers-on; he seldom appeared in his cardinal's robes, much preferring the elegant dress of a Roman gentleman; he avidly pursued in public his favorite sports—hunting and bullfighting—and was known to be wildly envious of his brother, the Duke of Gandia, because of the duke's position in the world outside the Church. In his person Cesare was tall, dark-complexioned, and accounted handsome (his surviving portraits bear little resemblance to his buffalo-headed father) except when, being syphilitic as everyone in the family was, his face broke out in horrid pustules. He had inherited all the Pope's savagery of disposition.

The Duke of Gandia was also receiving various boosts from his father. He was sent to Spain—a country which, being the homeland of the Borgias, they always regarded with nostalgia —and there married a Spanish princess. Living in Spain he gave free rein to his fancy, gambled away thousands of ducats, was known to wear what would amount to nearly a million dollars' worth of jewels at one time, and allowed it to be understood that his new wife was so distasteful to him that the marriage had never been consummated. Upon hearing this, the Pope flew into an awful rage; and to placate him the duke by and by did produce a son.

It was Alexander's grandiose idea that while Cesare should inherit the papacy, the Duke of Gandia should conquer numerous of the Italian states which were separately ruled by their princely families, and by riveting them all together should form for himself a unified kingdom of Italy; and with this in mind the duke came home from Spain and began his attempted conquests. Unfortunately for him, however, he had very little military talent, his conquests did not go well—in fact, he became the laughingstock of Europe—and this increased the bad blood between the two brothers, for Cesare was confident that, if only he had the duke's opportunities, he could do the job with infinitely greater competence.

But this was not the only point of dissension between them. They were, as well, rivals for the amorous favors of their youngest brother's seductive wife, the Neapolitan princess, a triangle which, of itself, verged on the incestuous. And to become incestuous in the most blatant way, they were both to some extent in love with their sister Lucrezia, who as time went on was noticeably becoming a woman. She had blonde hair and blue eyes, and was altogether a pretty little thing who, between her two brothers, preferred Cesare but was, at the same time, not averse to Gandia's attention and to the stirring up of a little trouble.

It must have seemed to Cesare at this time that if only his brother were out of the way, every resource would finally be his. He could desert the Church and emerge on the scene of European politics as a great secular prince; Lucrezia's heart would be his alone, as would that of Sancia (his sister-in-law); and he would have the Pope's full support which was now bestowed upon the duke. Matters, then, were reaching a crisis.

On June 7, 1497—almost five full years after Alexander's seizure of the papacy—Gandia was given the lordships of Benevento, Pontecorvo, and Terracina (each one a deeper thorn in Cesare's envious flesh), and Cesare was appointed papal legate to a forthcoming coronation at Naples. And on June 14, the evening before their respective departures, Cesare to Naples and Gandia to his new properties, they were invited by their mother, Vannozza, to an alfresco supper in a beautiful vineyard which she owned just outside the city.

As the summer evening slowly cooled after the heat of the day, the guests sat around the richly laden board, eating and drinking and conversing merrily, Vannozza herself, still handsome in middle age, occupying the head of the table. The Duke of Gandia was noisy and boastful as always, his sycophants and attendants playing up to him. Cesare, in secular dress, was smooth and mannered and watchful. The feast continued until long after dark, and was only broken up at last by a masked figure approaching the duke and whispering in his ear.

No one paid much attention to this mysterious figure—it had been noticed coming and going around the Vatican for the past month—but very shortly the party separated into groups taking their departure by torchlight, Cesare and the duke each surrounded by a small suite of attendants. These last two groups rode together back into the city. It was now two o'clock in the morning.

The city was dark and silent and ominous, but the young Borgias rode noisily through the streets, laughing and talking, until they came to the Ponte district. Cesare was going on across the river to his own palace; but the duke said that he had a tryst, and so they parted company, the duke dismissing all his attendants except the figure in the mask and a single groom, and these three turned down the narrow streets leading into the Jewish quarter. It was the last time the Duke of Gandia was ever seen alive.

As early as the next day there were already rumors of his disappearance, but at first no attention was paid to these in the Vatican. It is true that he was not to be found, but when this was brought to the Pope's attention he turned it easily aside, saying that as his son had specified that he was on his way to a tryst, quite probably dawn had overtaken him still in the lady's house, and he was reluctant to leave in broad daylight for fear of the scandal. But as daylight passed, and twilight, then darkness followed, the Pope became alarmed, and that alarm turned rapidly to fear.

Almost immediately word arrived that the duke's horse had been found wandering loose in the streets, with only one stirrup remaining, the other having been sliced cleanly off. And no sooner was this news absorbed than the next bulletin came in: the groom who, alone of the attendants, had accompanied the duke had been found mortally wounded, beyond the power to speak, and had died while he was being moved into a neighboring house.

This latest word served to mobilize the police, and to set searches and inquiries afoot. All the mercenary soldiers in the employ of the Borgias were put to work patrolling the streets; everywhere there were guards; the city was turned upside down, and in this tumult the great families of Orsini and Colonna saw their opportunity, and swept down in the midst of the confusion to attack one another from their strongholds—this had no connection with the Pope or the Duke of Gandia, but it did seem to be a happy occasion for advancing their famous feud.

Finally, after midnight, as a result of all the inquiries high and low, a Dalmatian boatman was found who had a story to tell. Under the threat of torture he revealed all he knew. His confession was that on the previous night he had slept on his barge in the Tiber because it was loaded with a shipment of lumber; and waking just before dawn he had beheld a curious sight on the bank of the river opposite him. Two men on foot had darted cautiously out of a narrow alley, and scouted the embankment through the darkness. At last, apparently satisfied that the area was empty and unobserved, they disappeared back into the alley. But for a time nothing happened; and then they reappeared and repeated their careful inspection. This time, finding everything exactly as they wished it, they made certain signs of reassurance toward the black mouth of the alley, and out of that darkness came a rider on a white horse accompanied by two more men; and thrown across the back of the horse behind the rider was what appeared to be a dead body, its feet dangling on one side and its head on the other. The servants on either side of the horse were holding the body in position.

This was the very place where the garbage collectors regularly came to dump the contents of their carts into the river, so no likelier spot for the disposal of a body could have been found. The white horse clattered nervously across the stones of the embankment. At the water's edge it turned around, hindquarters toward the river, and the two men who had been walking beside it pulled the body down over its tail, swung it outward between them like a garland, and hurled it into the water with a resounding splash.

The horseman asked whether they had thrown it properly, and the boatman at the far bank heard the men answer: "Yes, my lord." The horseman then, turning, studied the dark water, apparently looking for any trace of his victim, and at length pointed out a dark object floating on the shimmery surface: it was the dead man's cloak, swollen with air like a bubble. The men on foot found rocks and threw them at it until it sank. Then the rider wheeled his horse and, with his attendants hovering close around him, vanished back into the darkness of the alley as mysteriously as he had appeared. The embankment was once more silent and deserted.

The boatman who had observed all this from the other side of the river (for the Tiber is not such a very wide stream) was named Giorgio. He was one of those ordinary—almost anonymous—characters, without substance or personality, who are

fated to stumble upon the scenes of history. There was no reason
why he, rather than another, should have witnessed this particular scene, except that when he was questioned as to why he had
not come forward immediately to report it, he answered with
utter, blank astonishment that in his time he had seen a hundred bodies pitched into the river, and no one had ever troubled
to ask questions before. This left the Pope at something of a loss,
since it was by his command that so many of these murders had
been committed.

It was at once ordered that the Tiber should be dragged with
nets. All the fishermen were impounded for this labor, and on
the afternoon following Giorgio's disclosures, at a point near the
island in the river, the duke's body was dredged up, covered with
filth and weeds and scum. It was significant—if anyone had
thought of robbery as a motive—that the corpse was still fully
dressed, still wore its valuable collar of jewels around its neck,
and that the purse which was attached to its belt was still full of
money. The throat was slit, and the body had been stabbed fourteen times. These horrible remains were carried to the Castel
Sant' Angelo, the papal fortress, where a stripping, washing, and
rerobing procedure took place; and on that same night the funeral procession to the spot of interment was held. The procession, in passing the Vatican, could hear the howls and screams
of the Pope's wild sorrow issuing from a lighted upper room.

This terrible grieving lasted for four days—days, for the Pope,
of no food and no sleep—and at the end of that time he snapped
suddenly back to his normal self. A search for the murderers
was organized; but Cesare had prudently taken himself off to
Naples on his appointed mission, and the murderers were never
officially discovered.

The verdict of history has largely, and logically, been that
Cesare killed the brother who stood in his way in a most expedient fashion; and his future behavior was of a sort to show everyone his powers of dissimulation—such powers, indeed, that he
would have experienced no difficulty in sitting at his mother's
table, laughing and joking with his brother, only hours before he
killed him. For a time following the murder observers could no-

tice a marked coolness between Cesare and his father, but presently the unity of the house was once more established. Cesare gave up his bishoprics, cast off his cardinal's robes, and formally retired from the hierarchy of the Church. He assumed the French title Duke of Valentinois, married a princess of the House of Navarre, and bent his full energies upon the pursuit of a worldly career which had all along been his ambition.

The murder achieved exactly the results he had hoped for. He was appointed Captain-General and standard-bearer of the Church, and set forth on the conquest of the Italian states just as Gandia had tried to do earlier. Events were to show that Cesare's high opinion of himself was justified; he possessed all the military and diplomatic skills, all the instincts for treachery and boldness of action which his brother had lacked. In him Machiavelli, the Florentine envoy, saw the perfect prince.

At the same time as these events were going forward, other matters as well were taking place in the purlieus of the Vatican. Alexander VI accepted it as a matter of course that his daughter Lucrezia was going to be of as much service to him as his sons —indeed, of more service in one way, since it was widely believed that not only her brothers were among her lovers, but that her wild beast of a father was, also.

Lucrezia had, early in life, been twice engaged. The first time was to a Spanish gentleman, and this engagement was broken when a more profitable-seeming offer was made, again by a Spaniard. This one, however, occurred in the last months before Alexander's election to the papacy, and with this glorious prospect facing him he wisely held Lucrezia back in reserve. As the daughter of a Pope she was very much more eligible and would certainly be able to make a better match than as the daughter of a mere cardinal; and as soon as the election had been successfully rigged and the triple tiara borne off in triumph, swarms of matrimonial offers poured in from every part of Europe.

The second Spanish engagement was promptly canceled. The Pope at once had his dishonest finger in the political pie of Italy; and as he had married off his youngest son, Jofre, to the easy-living Neapolitan princess, Sancia, it now seemed expedient to marry Lucrezia into the Milanese family of Sforza, these two factions being among the most dominant in Italy.

As it happened, there was no suitable bridegroom available in the direct Sforza line, but a young cousin, Giovanni Sforza, Lord of Pesaro, was unmarried and upon him the choice unluckily fell. This young man was in no sense a prize, but neither was he a disgrace. He was timid, he lacked all the Borgia qualities of self-assertiveness, and evidently he was bothered by a great sense of his own inferiority—he was, in brief, a frail reed. But even to him it was flattering to receive the hand of the Pope's daughter, as well as the vast dowry which accompanied that hand. And accordingly the wedding took place.

At this time Lucrezia was still growing up, and was housed with her father's currently favorite mistress, the exquisite Giulia Farnese, so a complex situation existed. Lucrezia knew more of the facts of life than many mature women, but bodily she was still a child. So the wedding ceremonies were undergone, but the marriage as such could not be consummated. Giovanni received a part of the dowry, with the understanding that he would receive the rest when he and Lucrezia became husband and wife in fact as well as in name.

Giovanni was forever scampering nervously here and there, back and forth between Rome and Pesaro; and finally, at a moment when Lucrezia was alone in Rome, the Pope announced that the time for the consummation had arrived. Giovanni bolted eagerly back to the papal household, was warmly welcomed, and the remainder of the dowry was paid. Posterity is left to suppose that the consummation did, indeed, take place.

The politics of Italy were always shifting, like so many beds of quicksand, and unavoidably the time arrived, by and by, when an alliance between the Pope's daughter and the house of Sforza no longer served the purpose for which it had originally been designed. On Good Friday of the year 1497—only weeks before the murder of the Duke of Gandia—Giovanni came to his wife's room in the early morning, telling her that he was going to visit the seven major Roman churches; but he was never seen at any

of the churches, and twenty-four hours later he was safely locked
up in his palace at Pesaro, having fled Rome to save his life. It
was rumored abroad that Lucrezia (who had a sort of slatternly
fondness for him) had warned him that he was in the process of
being poisoned by her family, and upon this word he had taken
flight.

In vain the Pope tried to summon him, and then by false
smiles and promises to lure him back to Rome. Giovanni would
not budge. The Pope had, to be perfectly truthful, made up his
mind to do away with Giovanni by poison—to let him, in other
words, succumb to the "Roman fever" which, under the Borgias,
was such a prevalent disease—but the young man was now outside his immediate reach. So in place of poison, a bill of divorce-
ment was taken in hand. Bishops and papal legates were
dispatched to Pesaro to obtain Giovanni's consent; but since this
consent involved his swearing that he was impotent and that
the marriage had never been consummated (then why had the
Pope given him the rest of the dowry?) he naturally withheld
his agreement. As a matter of fact, he was a widower when he
married Lucrezia, by his first wife he had a child, and he was
later to marry for yet a third time, so his virility seems reasonably proven.

All the right was on his side—in addition to which he appears
to have been genuinely in love with Lucrezia—but the power was
all on the side of the Pope. The Sforzas of Milan were more interested in keeping the Pope's good will than in keeping
Giovanni's; and so, betrayed on either hand and lacking the for-
titude of character to support himself, he was forced to sign the
humiliating agreement at last. Lucrezia was officially declared
to be still a virgin.

It was awkward that at the moment when this decree was
made, Lucrezia was visibly six months pregnant—and since
Giovanni had been away from Rome for more than six months
while the wrangles over the divorce took place, there was no possibility that the child was his.

In the course of their separation Giovanni had stated flatly
that the reason why the aging but still intemperate Pope wanted

the divorce was in order that he might have his daughter back in his own bed, and now it was naturally supposed that this child was either the offspring of His Holiness, or that of his son, Cesare. Other rumors were, of course, simultaneously afloat—the most popular being that Lucrezia had had an affair with a Vatican servant, and that Cesare on discovering it had chased the man to the foot of the papal throne with drawn sword, and there had killed him, spattering blood up into the Pope's face. (The body was thrown into the Tiber: no one ever seemed to consider any more novel methods for disposing of a body.) But there were many who continued to believe the story of papal incest, and who supposed that Cesare had slain the servant either to turn the rumors away from himself, or to protect his father's reputation.

Whatever his paternity, the child—a son—was born and promptly spirited off into hiding. Lucrezia with her pretty little doll's face reappeared in the day-to-day life of the papal court; and before long she was ready for a second husband, one who might be of greater political use than her first had been. Again the bidding started—rather like a recurring national lottery—and this time the chosen suitor was an illegitimate son of the House of Naples, a brother of the sensuous Sancia (she was illegitimate, too), the young Alfonso, Duke of Bisceglie.

He came to Rome, and the wedding was quickly celebrated in a somewhat hole-in-corner fashion; but despite this inauspicious beginning, it soon became apparent that this marriage was going to be a good deal more successful than the first one had been. Alfonso, although a year younger than Lucrezia, was said to be exceptionally handsome and amiable, even if he had perhaps less than his share of intelligence; Lucrezia herself was far from intellectual, and it might have been supposed that Alfonso's friendliness and slight stupidity would afford him more protection in this pack of wolves than any amount of brain power could do.

The newlyweds were genuinely in love with each other; and one of the guests at the shoddy wedding feast remarked that quite plainly they could hardly wait to get to bed. The wicked old Pope was pleased to see his daughter so happy and so well satisfied. Everyone was content except Cesare, who was as jealous of Alfonso now as he had been of the Duke of Gandia earlier —and it is not unlikely that at this period Lucrezia's incestuous relationship with Cesare came to an end, since she and Alfonso were so compatible. Cesare was away from Rome much of the time now, conquering more and more of the Italian states to build his kingdom; and it truly appeared that fortune was smiling on the House of Borgia. The Pope was committing more crimes than ever—murder and extortion and the sale of Church property—and Lucrezia and Alfonso passed their drowsy days in love-making and gaiety.

But this state of affairs was so agreeable for everyone concerned that it could only provide a challenge to destiny; and no sooner did it appear that everyone was being given his heart's desire than the state of affairs took a sharp turn for the worse. The ceiling of the papal throne room fell in, and the Pope was nearly buried alive in an avalanche of rubble. Injured as he was, he took to his bed where he was subjected to all the quackeries of Renaissance medicine, and nursed by Lucrezia and Sancia. At the same time, on the political front, the royal House of Naples found itself no longer in such high favor at the Vatican as it had previously been, and as might have been expected, Cesare grabbed at this opportunity to be rid of his second unwanted brother-in-law.

On Wednesday evening, July 15, 1500, Alfonso had taken supper at the Vatican with his wife, his convalescing father-in-law, and Sancia. The meal being finished, he decided to return for the night to his own palace which was only a short distance away, and so he bid good night to the little family circle, and set out attended only by a gentleman-in-waiting named Tomaso Albanese, and a squire. The three of them left the Vatican by an entrance opening onto the square of St. Peter's, and began to walk briskly across that vast, dark, open space.

The Rome of the Renaissance was, at night, a city of utter blackness. The streets and squares were without the slightest illumination except for the occasional shaded lanterns of a

nightwatchman or the flaring torches as the suite surrounding
some great nobleman cantered past. The square of St. Peter's
now seemed almost deserted; and Alfonso paid no attention to
the vague, muffled figures which he could scarcely make out
lounging or lying along the steps leading up to the portico of the
cathedral. The year 1500 was a jubilee year for the Church, and
Rome was packed with beggars and pilgrims, many of whom
could not afford a room in which to sleep. There was no reason
for Alfonso to notice them now; and he was striding on across
the square with his two attendants just behind him when, without warning, the apparently sleeping figures all sprang up soundlessly together, as if at a given signal, and hurled themselves
through the darkness onto him, surrounding him and his companions, and producing swords with which they attacked him.

For a second they had the advantage of surprise; and then he
had drawn his own sword to defend himself. He was greatly outnumbered, and glancing around quickly saw that there was no
chance of making a dash to safety. Albanese and the squire were
not armed, but as the attack pressed in upon him they served at
least to give him a little protection in the rear, and were meantime shouting loudly back toward the closed doors of the Vatican for help. Alfonso was an excellent swordsman, recklessly
courageous, but even so he could not hope to win out against
such numbers as confronted him, however valiant his defense.
The noisy clangor of steel rang in the hot night air; harsh
breaths panted between clenched teeth; the points of the harry-
ing blades began to touch him, to penetrate his guard; an elegant panel of gold embroidery which hung on the front of his
doublet was cut loose and fell to the pavement; the swords
slashed at Albanese's cloak, and he dropped it while he went on
yelling desperately for help. A troop of horsemen, allies of the
attackers, had galloped into the square and were plunging about
loudly on the dark cobblestones at the edge of the skirmish.

One of the swords penetrated Alfonso's shoulder, and then
after a moment another sank into his thigh. Stabbed as he was,
he fought steadily on until at last one darting blade caught him
on the head and, his own sword rolling out of his suddenly limp

fingers, he slumped to the pavement, unable to support himself, his blood pooling around him on the stones. Instantly the assailants swooped down on him, preparing to drag him away with them; but Albanese and the squire were too quick for them. The squire snatched up his master's fallen sword and carried on the defense with remarkable skill, while Albanese began to tug the bleeding body back toward the Vatican. The attackers were still trying to wrestle it away from him when, at long last, the great portals giving onto the square began slowly and ponderously to creak open, throwing a gold panel of light out across the darkness. Immediately the attackers seemed to dissolve, flitting away like ghosts, springing nimbly up onto the hindquarters of the curvetting horses, so that by the time the papal guard marched rattling and clanking out into the square, the only other sound to be heard was the retreating gallop of hoofs through the night.

Although helpless from his wounds, with blood pouring down over him, Alfonso was still half conscious through his pain. The soldiers picked him up carefully in their arms and carried him back into the Vatican, up dim stairways and along flickering corridors, to the room he had left such a short time ago, where the Pope and Lucrezia and Sancia were still sitting just as he had left them. At the sight of the blood-soaked specter dangling in the doorway, clothes sliced to gory ribbons, they flung themselves upon him in horror. Gathering the last remnants of his strength, he lifted his head and mumbled the name of his attacker: Cesare. Then he sagged into unconsciousness, his clotted head falling back, the last of his strength gone, and it was thought that the end was near.

Lucrezia hearing her beloved (and, as she believed, dying) husband announce that her brother was his murderer, had suffered too great a shock; and no sooner had Alfonso lost consciousness, than consciousness deserted her, as well, and she fell back fainting into her father's massive arms. The Pope began angrily to rumble out the necessary orders. Candles and torches were lighted. Footsteps rang through the rooms and halls of the great palace. Ambassadors and priests and doctors rushed in from every quarter. Hasty messages were dispatched to Naples. Lucrezia began slowly to come out of her faint; and the first thing she saw when she opened her eyes was one of the cardinals bending over Alfonso's handsome, death-white face, administering Extreme Unction.

As for the Pope, he was nearly as thunderstruck as his daughter; it was quite plain that he had had no foreknowledge of the attack, no hand in organizing it, and he was tremendously displeased that it should have taken place at all. He had, himself, committed or engineered so many murders that one more or less could not disturb him on the grounds of morality; but this was an affront to his dignity—and before any further steps could be taken to dispose of Alfonso, Cesare was to have to placate his father and talk him round to the point of agreeing.

Meantime, Alfonso was still expected to die at any moment. There could be no question of removing him from the Vatican to his own palace; instead, at Lucrezia's urging, he was carried to a room adjoining the Pope's own private apartments in the Borgia tower where he was put to bed, and by the uncertain light of candles the doctors began tending his wounds. Lucrezia had by now started to recover some of her wits, and was able to give a little thought to her husband's safety, should he survive.

She persuaded her father to station sixteen guards at his door to protect him from any further attack. The doctors, at work under her anxious eye, and that of the Neapolitan ambassador, after what seemed an endless time straightened up from over the bed and announced that Alfonso had a chance of recovery. This was all Lucrezia needed to hear: if a chance existed she would make the most of it.

Naturally the Vatican—and, indeed, all of Rome—was thrown into upheaval when news of the attack broke forth, and no two persons were subjected to more upheaval than Lucrezia and Sancia. The fact that each of these ladies loved Alfonso in her own way was now adequately demonstrated by the devotion with which they attended him. They deserted their personal chambers and spent their days in his company, nursing him, and their nights on improvised pallets under the nightlight beside his bed.

He was never to be left alone and undefended for so much as an instant. They, themselves, cooked all his food there in the room on a camp stove in order to guard him against poison—and poison would logically have been Cesare's next step, had they not removed this opportunity before it came into existence. Lucrezia began laying plans for the future, and even went so far as to make definite arrangements for the hour of Alfonso's full recovery when they would leave Rome for the safety of Naples and his family.

It really began to look as if Cesare were to be thwarted, his blood-lust to remain unsatisfied. Slowly, little by little, Alfonso gained strength and started to recover. As his wounds healed he was able to leave his bed and move about his room. The windows looked out over the Vatican gardens with their walks and flowers and statues; and seated at one of these windows he could soak up the hot, bright sunshine of late July and early August to help the mending of his body and the reviving of his spirits. As his convalescence advanced his thoughts became more cheerful, and when he felt like enjoying company he did not lack for it. His Neapolitan attendants stood always ready to amuse or entertain him; he had a hunchbacked dwarf who sang to him the lilting songs of Naples; and his wife and his sister were always on hand. As the date of the attack in the square dwindled into the past, it must have seemed less and less real, more and more like an unhappy dream.

The Pope, with honeyed words of solicitude dropping from his coarse-lipped mouth, often came to visit; but Cesare was conspicuous by his absence. He came to the room only once, and then he was smoothness and grace personified. He might, had he chosen, have allayed any fears which yet remained, but instead he wished the strength of his purpose to be glimpsed for a moment through the charm of his manner. Looming sleekly over the sickbed, he said in a voice audible only to Alfonso: "What remains unfinished in the morning can be finished at night." His intention could not have been more clearly stated, and terror rushed back in upon them who had nearly ceased to fear. They now knew that he was not to be put off by such trifling defenses as they were able to erect. At any moment he might strike again, and they could only wait, stricken in advance.

They did not wait for long. On the morning of August 18, thirty-four days after the attack in the square, the blow fell. Cesare, with a henchman of his, one Michelotto, came through the guards on duty outside Alfonso's door without meeting the slightest resistance—the guards would not have dared to challenge him or deny him entrance. Lucrezia and Sancia were taken completely by surprise; they threw themselves desperately upon him, imploring and pleading with him, but to no avail. He forced them sternly out of the room, and shut himself and Michelotto in with their victim.

Alfonso must have seen from the men's faces, if he had not already learned it from the frantic behavior of his wife and his sister, that murder was upon him. And this time there was no Albanese to call for help, no squire to pick up his sword and defend him. Brave as he was, with all the courage of youth, he was not brave at this moment; the youthfulness in him could not bear the thought of dying. He was still weak from his earlier wounds; but, as Cesare stood looking on with an air of agreeable, dispassionate interest, and Michelotto advanced across the room, a strangling cord stretched between his hands, toward the bed where Alfonso had been lying at their entrance, he did manage to push himself unsteadily to his feet. His knees almost buckled under him. He raised his hands in a wordless gesture beseeching mercy. The cord went around his neck, and under Cesare's impassive gaze a hideous death entered slowly into him.

In the meanwhile Lucrezia, in a panic of horror, finding the sixteen guards unwilling to interfere, had dashed off frenziedly to search for her father and beg him to protect Alfonso; but the treacherous Pope was nowhere to be found—it was presumed afterward that Cesare had brought him around to his own way of thinking, and that now in order to avoid a nasty scene he was hiding from his daughter. When she saw that her search was hopeless, she rushed back to the room in the tower, only to find that Cesare and Michelotto had already finished their business and gone. The body of her husband, strangled, lay sprawled limply across the bed, the recently handsome face black and contorted.

The fact was that by now even the Pope himself went in mortal fear of his ravening son. In his father's presence Cesare wildly threatened to stab one of the cardinals; and upon the Pope's reproving him, he spun upon the gross old man and screamed that if he didn't hold his peace, he would receive the same. Of course both the Pope and Cesare energetically denied that they were in any way connected with Alfonso's death—giving out that the whole occurrence had been a regrettable accident. But finally, after being badgered into a corner by the Venetian ambassador, the Pope was forced to say pettishly: "If Cesare *did* strike the blow, then Alfonso must have deserved it."

For a time Lucrezia grieved for Alfonso; but while she might deplore his murder, she could not be fundamentally shocked by it. Murder was a part of her life, as it was of her father's and brother's. All the Borgias were accomplished virtuosi in one or more of the three forms of murder—inspiring it, instigating it, and committing it—and it must truly be said that for the most part they restricted themselves to the first two categories. It is not reasonable to suppose that Cesare strangled Alfonso with his own hands, or himself slit the Duke of Gandia's throat; he figures as the instigator rather than the committer. And in the same way, Lucrezia—who may seldom even directly have instigated a crime—certainly inspired many, through lust, natural or incestuous, through ambition, through jealousy, or through frustration. As to the Pope himself, little doubt exists that he committed murders with his own hand, he instigated killings, and he inspired deathly deeds in those who hoped to win his favor—and thus he qualifies in all three categories.

The truth was that the Borgias loved the act of killing in every one of its modes, the most barbaric as well as the most refined. But even in the heat of this general enthusiasm there was one method above all the others which, no matter how intricate or fascinating the rest might be, most particularly appealed to them; and it is upon this as much as upon anything else they did that the reputation of the family is founded, for the Borgias are known to have been among the greatest poisoners of all time.

The dispensing of poison is not a simple matter. Until relatively modern times no serious poisoner would, in any thing less than the direst emergency, have considered so crude an action as feeding his victim a bit of straight aconite or strychnine. Poisoning has often been called an art, and during the centuries of its greatest importance it was exactly that, an art as elaborately organized, as full of rules and canons, and as subject to fashions as any of the other arts. Poisons were distilled and coaxed to perfection and blended as delicately as perfumes or cordials, and with as much care for obtaining a particular desired effect.

Administering poison in the simplest way, that is through the mouth, was by no means the extent of the poisoner's resources —even when the most roundabout methods were employed and, to take an actual instance, the sacred Host was imbued with poison and the victim was thus murdered at the communion rail (which must be considered a devious way of getting at someone), it was still possible to find much subtler approaches. And it must be borne in mind that during the great eras of poisoning, persons who thought they might be poisoned were very cautious about what they ate, and often it was necessary to invent some other method of introducing a toxic substance into their bodies.

For this purpose poisoned gloves and shirts and other garments were devised—and while it was believed for a long time that these romantic objects were merely the products of too-vivid imaginations on the part of the authors who described them, and had never in fact actually existed, it is now thought instead that they may have worked very well. It is almost inevitable that minute lesions exist here and there on the body, particularly on the hands; and if the linings of a pair of gloves were smeared with a tactile poison, such as curare, death would almost certainly ensue. Similarly the thorns of a rose could be coated with poison, or a ring or key could have a jagged poisoned edge which would scratch the skin. Letters were even sent on poisoned paper. In the same way, but using a different combination of poisons, it was possible to prepare lethal bouquets of flowers, or candles which exhaled deadly gases as they burned.

It must not be thought, however, that these murderous marvels were accomplished with simple or unsophisticated poisons. Quite the reverse was true. A singular complexity existed in the business of manufacturing poisons. As long ago as the days of the ancients, Locusta rose to the top of her profession by the masterly skill with which she brewed and mixed and fused her poisons even to the satisfaction of fastidious Nero (concocting a really new poison and observing the effect it had upon its victim must have given its inventor the same thrill as Escoffier felt when he created Peach Melba, or Louis Diat when he created vichyssoise). But even Locusta appeared at an advanced stage in the history of poisoning. She was by no means the first person to engage in this line of work—indeed, she was only a small if spectacular link—for the earliest poisoning dates back to the beginnings of time.

Quite naturally the earlier poisonings were the simpler ones. It is easy enough to feed an enemy the raw root of wolfsbane if he is so simple as to imagine it a horseradish, which it does, in fact, resemble. But like all the rest of the arts, this one rapidly developed from its primitive stages to the first plateau of sophistication, where there is customarily a long halt because of some enormous barrier of ignorance yet to be overcome. In painting the barrier was a lack of understanding of perspective; in medicine the circulation of the blood was a stumbling block; in music it was the equal temperament of the scale; and in poisoning it was the fact that the only poisons known in the world of antiquity were vegetable poisons.

Locusta, for all her blending and the subtleties of her concoctions, was restricted in this way. She had access to, and presumably used, all the corrosive and irritant roots and leaves and berries and seeds and barks and flowers and pods and fruits, but this being the age of purely botanical poisons, she had no further resources than these. She could manufacture belladonna and aconite and many others of that same general family, but the most important poisons were still beyond her reach, and were to remain beyond the reach of even the most ambitious poisoners for a very long time to come. It was not until the thirteenth century that a full understanding of mineral poisoning came about in Europe; and without question this period represented as much of a peak in the mountain range of poisoning as it did in other ranges of human affairs.

(As opposed to mineral and vegetable, there is a third category of poisons: animal. Most prominent among these is cantharides; but in addition there are many further and less-known animal poisons—all the waste products from the human or animal body, and the bacteriological decay which sets into organic matter after death are poisonous—and the ancients were acquainted with all these, and used them to blend with their vegetable poisons. But animal poisons, by their very nature, lack the variety of the other two categories; and so, while they are useful in blending, and are even occasionally used by themselves, they have never reached the same stage of importance as the other kinds.)

In the discovery of mineral poisons a whole new universe had been opened to view. There were suddenly available such reliable, fast-acting, dramatic poisons as sulphuric acid and cyanide and the lead and zinc salts, producing effects which the most ardent poisoners had never before even dreamed of; so it was only natural that there should be a renaissance in poisoning after the slump of the dark ages, as there was in other fields of learning and intellectual endeavor, and there rapidly arose a positive fad for the whole business, as if it were some popular sport. And in order that this sport might be available to all and sundry, an entire class of persons sprang up which lived by the manufacture and sale of poisons.

In every neighborhood, rich or poor, town or village, there was some little shop which sold love philters, or the waters of eternal youth, or elixirs to improve potency or fecundity, or any of a great number of other miracle-working potions; and from these shops there were also to be obtained—if one were prepared to pay for them—the deadly new "essences of widowhood" or "powders of eternity." In major cities such shops congregated into neighborhoods of their own, occupying blocks or even whole streets. In dank cellars and musty back rooms retorts bubbled and cauldrons cooked and alembics distilled. The sale or use of poison, of course, was illegal, and many persons who sold or used it injudiciously were given their proper punishment (as, for example, a young man of San Felice named Gioppu who, making no effort to cover his traces, sent in a dish of poisoned cakes to the wedding feast of a girl whom he had, himself, wanted to marry; several persons were poisoned fatally, and the whole story coming to light, Gioppu was suitably brought to justice, hanged, and quartered for his crime). Nevertheless, the universal taste for poisoning continued unabated.

And among the mineral poisons which made this tremendous vogue was one, the veritable king of poisons, which ever since its discovery has been the most popular single poison over the centuries: arsenic. From the start it had an extraordinary number of points to recommend it, or even to make it the virtually ideal poison. It was white (or when dissolved, colorless) and so in its powdered form it could be mixed with sugar or flour or with many other common recipe ingredients. It was odorless, and this was something of an asset in an age of food-sniffing. And most important of all, it was so nearly tasteless as to make the difference of no great matter. It could be sprinkled on food, especially highly seasoned food, without being detectable (it was the only mineral poison of that period which did not have a distinct and often disagreeable flavor of its own); and it could easily be dissolved in liquids—wine for the banqueter, broth for the invalid, milk for the child. The commonest form of this almost perfect poison is an arsenious oxide known as white arsenic. It is a specific irritant, which is to say that it causes inflammation of the alimentary canal; it is not as quick-acting as, for example, strychnine, or some of the other neurotic or corrosive poisons, and while strychnine usually kills within less than an hour, it requires several hours for arsenic to perform the same function, although this would be no deterrent to those who enjoy the act of poisoning; arsenic's symptoms are violent—nausea, vomiting, intense thirst, diarrhea, extreme tenderness of the abdomen, fever, collapse, and finally death. The Renaissance poisoners found arsenic altogether congenial to their personalities and requirements.

But in this period the great poisoners seldom used simple dosages, and the intricacy involved in their manufacture of poisons did not stem entirely from a desire to produce always better and better merchandise. There was a personal element involved, as well. A certain pride of individualism existed among the large-scale poisoners, who would no more have thought of using an anonymous, commonplace poison than they would have thought of using someone else's coat-of-arms. One's poison was a trademark, something unique and original.

At the present time it would be nearly impossible to reconstruct and unravel the complex formulas for those poisons which, each ingredient contributing some lethal factor of its own, so delighted the great inventive poisoners; and to add still further complexity to the subject, there were two different types of poisoning: direct—which is what passes for poisoning in the ordinary sense—and delayed. Some doubt had been cast upon the real efficiency of this latter method, but persons living in the Renaissance certainly had faith in it. Caterina Sforza, a virago of the age, recorded in a secret manual, in cipher, one of the few surviving prescriptions for a delayed poison, but the gravest doubts exist—in the absence of anyone prepared to test it on himself—as to its producing a delayed murder. (Perhaps it should here be made plain that there are also various substances which, when swallowed, often cause death—ground glass is one of these —but which are not technically poisons, and so do not bear directly upon this subject.)

The basic idea of a personal poison dates from much more ancient days than the Renaissance. In the family of the Caesars there was a famous poison chest (something like a spice cabinet, one supposes) which contained all the fundamental poisons from which the recipes were made up. (This was before the time of Locusta, and the emperors and empresses still concocted their own poisons.) This bizarre piece of furniture with its horrid contents first came to light in the possession of Caligula, but it was guessed to be a hereditary belonging of the family, possibly originating with Livia, the most important poisoner of them all. When Caligula was assassinated, the great cabinet passed into Claudius's hands; and being one of the less murderous members of his family, he resolved upon its destruction. Taking it with him to the seacoast, he had himself rowed out into deep water and pitched the monstrous object overboard, thus effectively disposing of it. The only unhappy result of this disposal was that when the tide came in it brought with it thousands upon thousands of dead fish whose bodies littered the neighboring shores and teemed in the waves, belly up, for days afterward to the serious inconvenience of the local fisherfolk.

From the viewpoint of historical research it seems a pity that this remarkable chest was not preserved for posterity; it could have thrown a brilliant light on the somewhat murky subject of the poisons of the Caesars, and would surely have given an indication, at least, as to which poisons were Livia's personal favorites, which Tiberius's, or which Caligula's. But poisoning has always, by its very nature, been an obscure and secretive business; and even in the field of more recent trademark poisons, only a slightly ampler body of knowledge exists.

In seventeenth-century France, the Marquise de Brinvilliers and her lover, Sainte-Croix, decided to do away with the marquise's family. Sainte-Croix, finding himself in prison earlier, had taken the occasion to study the art of poisoning under one of his fellow inmates, the celebrated Italian poisoner, Exili; and upon his release he set up a laboratory and proceeded to doctor and improve on Exili's prize formula. Then, at the completion of each of his experiments, the marquise tested the workability of the poison on a number of innocent persons—mostly invalids in hospitals which she charitably visited with pots of poisoned soup or toxic stews—until, satisfied at last, she went ahead to murder her father and brothers. Eventually she was caught and beheaded. Sainte-Croix met with a more poetic end: while working in his laboratory he was overcome by the fumes of his own poison, and so asphyxiated.

Samples of his distillation were, of course, found when Sainte-

Croix's laboratory was entered (his body was lying sprawled there among broken phials and overturned chemical equipment), and were sent off to be analyzed. But although the physicians to whom this task had been entrusted were both willing and capable, finally after a great deal of work they were forced to make the humiliating admission that the job was too much for them: the poison was of such a complicated nature that all their efforts to break it down were unavailing, and its components remain obscure to this day.

Unfortunately this is true of the majority of the most famous or most interesting poisons in history. Calculated guesses are often made later, and probably with excellent results—the Sainte-Croix poison is thought to have contained nitrate of silver, vitriol, opium, and antimony, as well as other undecipherable ingredients (the problems involved in making such a poison are readily seen to be legion)—but no one can now ever be sure that the formula reconstructed from the symptoms of the victims is the true one, nor even actually know what form the poison took —liquid or solid, harsh or bland.

This utter degree of uncertainty is not, however, quite so extreme where the private family poison of the Borgias is concerned. It was, to begin with, seen and described for coming generations by the Bishop of Nocera, who says that it was "a sort of whitish powder, like sugar, with a faint and not unpleasant savor." A tremendous amount of speculative discussion has been devoted to the composition of this celebrated powder. The faintness of the savor, as well as the color and texture, strongly suggest that arsenic was a principal ingredient, and the action of the powder also bears this out. Death came with a certain deliberation which, along with various clinical symptoms, inescapably suggests arsenic. There were all the agonies of the digestive system; there was the characteristic feeling of heat inside the victims; and there was an erupting and peeling of the skin.

But it is not to be imagined that, living in the age of labyrinthine poisons, the Borgias would be content with arsenic pure and simple. There were, for one thing, symptoms which were not compatible with arsenic alone. Occasionally, although not regularly, the poison also attacked the nerve centers of the spine and the brain, so it is evident that a complex substance had to be involved. In some cases there was even the suggestion of some strange "delaying" agent reminiscent of Caterina Sforza's delayed poison; but it may reasonably be presumed that no such agent actually did exist.

Among all the guesses concerning the composition of the Borgia powder, however, one stands out above all the others as the most popular choice. Its recipe is said to have been as follows: pure arsenic, employed as the basic ingredient, was lavishly spread in the open abdominal cavity of a freshly slaughtered animal, preferably a pig, pork being more given to immediate spoilage than other meats. The presence of the arsenic on the rotting flesh considerably delayed the rate of decay, but did not by any means halt it altogether; and the resulting putrefaction was of the utmost deadliness. At last, when this revolting mess was thoroughly decomposed, the liquorous fluids were strained off and reduced once more to a powder, while the rotted intestines were also dried and powdered and the two substances combined to form the final poison which now contained not only arsenic, but the deadly animal alkaloids as well. With the substance in hand, then, and given the character of the Borgias, it only remained for the poisonings themselves to be committed.

First, there were all the slaves and prisoners, persons of such menial degree that their deaths would pass almost unnoticed, upon whom the poison was continually being tested. Lacking the precise chemical methods of later times, each new production of poison had to be tried for efficiency, and so, as the Bishop of Nocera goes on to say, it was fed to a great number of innocent persons. This, in itself, was no very novel proceeding. Locusta, in addition to trying out her poisons on different animals, had also used humans—had, in fact, very much preferred humans for this purpose, as being a surer gauge of her art—and the practice was to continue long after Madame de Brinvilliers and her hospital patients.

The poison being, then, demonstrably workable, the more important murders could be committed, and toward the end of

Alexander VI's life his reputation was so fearful that any Roman possessing a fortune of the slightest consequence took it for granted that sooner or later he would be dispatched and his goods seized. It made no difference if he had not left his goods to the Church; the Pope seized them anyway. Even in the cases of natural death, there was a great scramble to lay hands on the estate of the deceased. This happened at the demise of Bishop Duerkop—and again with Cardinal Sclafenato—and again with the Bishop of Cortona—and again with Cardinal Fregoso—and yet again with Cardinal Zeno (except that in this case there was a tug-of-war between the Pope and Venice, with Venice managing to secure the bulk of the fortune)—until finally, in order that there might be no further confusion on this subject, the Pope ruled firmly that the cardinals did not have the right to appoint their own heirs or dispose of their own fortunes, a ruling which was necessarily the final word on the matter.

But even while all this pirating took place, there were now and again persons who did not die naturally when the Pope wished them to, and so they were sped on their last journey by means of the poisoned cup. The Bishop of Calahorra was arrested on the obviously trumped-up charge of maintaining the Jewish faith; he was imprisoned in the Castel Sant' Angelo, his immense fortune was immediately confiscated, and he was given the poison.

Cardinal Giovanni Battista Orsini (the whole family of Orsini had a run of bad luck under the Borgias) rode into the Vatican unsuspectingly one day with his retinue, and was set upon by a body of armed men and taken to the Castel Sant' Angelo after watching all his horses and mules being calmly led off to the papal stables. All his goods were at once requisitioned, "even to the straw from his stables." His mother begged frantically for his release, offering a huge sum of money to ransom him; and his beautiful mistress, disguising herself as a boy, succeeded in reaching the Pope's presence and offered him a magnificent and very famous pearl which belonged to her, and which she knew the Borgias coveted. The Pope agreed to accept the money (which the cardinal's mother had great difficulty in raising among her friends and relatives) and the pearl; and in return he poisoned the cardinal and handed over his corpse to those who had loved him.

Cardinal Ferrari was poisoned with the Borgia powder by a certain young favorite of his named Sebastiano Pinzon, a tool of the Borgias. This cardinal had rendered the Church great service in the post of treasurer, displaying an avarice nearly equal to the Pope's own; but the size of his personal fortune was too tempting to be offset by mere gratitude. Pinzon was publicly rewarded for the poisoning by the Pope, but subsequently, under Pope Leo X, he was tried for the crime and beheaded.

A similar poisoning was that of the wealthy Venetian Cardinal Michiel. The poison this time was administered by his secretary, Asquinio Collorado, who was paid a thousand ducats for carrying off the job. (Like Pinzon, he was later to be brought to trial and executed.) The Borgian greed was such that, upon Cardinal Michiel's murder, the body was not cold before the Pope had sent the Governor of Rome to the cardinal's palace for the specific purpose of plundering it; and by the following morning the building had been picked as clean as a bone. But the cardinal had possessed also considerable property of value in his see of Porto (this bishopric had been the bribe he received for his vote at Alexander's papal election), so the Pope in person hurried straightway off to Porto to see what the gleanings there might amount to and, as the Venetian ambassador remarked gloomily, returned to Rome some days later looking very cheerful.

Where there was a gain to be made, or a person to be murdered, not even the closest degree of family relationship was honored among the Borgias. The Pope may not have considered killing any of his children; but no such scruple occupied Cesare when he brought about his brother's death and publicly threatened his father with stabbing; and certainly more distant relatives were not entitled to expect protective courtesy merely on account of a blood relationship. The Cardinal of Capua was a Borgia—the grandson of the Pope's sister—but his birth failed to keep him safe from harm. While away on his travels he was suddenly and inexplicably struck with a bout of fever so virulent that it killed him within only a few hours. Of course, everyone presumed the worst, particularly as he was buried with the most indecent haste (the Borgias often did this to their victims) and was not even accorded the honor of a tombstone.

Another relative was the Cardinal of Monreale, the Pope's nephew, who was unexpectedly taken off only sixteen days before the death of the Pope himself. At this time there was conveniently a small epidemic of malaria abroad in Rome, and so the cardinal's death was blamed on this. (The Pope's death was presently—and unconvincingly—to be blamed on the same cause.) But the Pope, far from showing any grief, even a pretended one, for his favorite nephew, was reported the next day to be joyously closeted with his new wealth, counting the money and fingering the jewels; the Cardinal of Monreale had been the miser of the family, and this latest windfall was a particularly sumptuous one.

And so it went.

The poisonings, while decidedly the form of murder dearest to the Borgias' hearts, were far from being the limit of their crimes. Cesare, for instance, was extremely addicted to strangulation. He had finally resorted to it for the removal of Alfonso of Bisceglie when less obvious methods failed; and in other cases he was forever falling back on it. And for all his generalship, Cesare was not finding life so easy. He was always short of money with which to pay his armies; and he was not surrounded by much affection there, for his followers were attracted to him by thoughts of self-interest such as did not breed loyalty in their hearts; they were faithful to him only so long as it was to their profit to be faithful, and were prepared for treachery should a worthwhile opportunity present itself. Thus, from time to time, Cesare's captains banded together among themselves to enforce their wishes upon their master, and finally this course brought them to open rebellion. It must be said, however, that they mistrusted one another as much as they feared and hated Cesare, so no real concord existed in their ranks. It was not, then, difficult for him to lure them back into his service with blandishments and promises. And so, one by one, betraying each other as they had betrayed him, they arranged to meet with him once more. He had them all tied up and strangled when they came to the meeting place at Sinigaglia (a curious case of historical onomatopoeia: the name Sinigaglia sounds, itself, like the rasping choke of strangulation), and with the rebellion quenched, he held the entire center of Italy firmly in his palm. Two members of the Orsini clan—Paolo Orsini, and the Duke of Gravina—were among his victims. Affairs for that family were progressing from bad to worse. (The Pope, as an act of sheer mental cruelty, imprisoned Giulio Orsini, Lord of Monterotondo, in the Castel Sant' Angelo so as to frighten the family, and then by and by turned him loose again. At the sight of him alive and unharmed, his mother dropped dead from joy.)

Meantime, while all these matters were taking place, the private lives of the Borgias were continuing on their customary course. A new husband had been selected for Lucrezia—Alfonso d'Este, heir to the duchy of Ferrara. There is no question but that this was the choicest of her three marriages. The duchy of Bisceglie and the lordship of Pesaro were as nothing to Ferrara, and the Este house was one of the oldest, the proudest, the haughtiest, and the most exclusive in Italy—so much so, indeed, that the Estes regarded the Borgias quite correctly as being crude, lacking in taste or refinement, and insufferably bumptious. All the same, the Borgias had the weight of power on their side; and since the marriage seemed desirable to them (not alone because of the Estes' social status, but principally because of Ferrara's strategic location between Cesare's half-soldered kingdom and the mighty Republic of Venice), the arrangements were duly made.

Some eighteen months elapsed between the murder of Alfonso of Bisceglie and the marriage to Alfonso d'Este; and if any misgivings remained in Lucrezia's mind where the first Alfonso was concerned, she seemed to have no difficulty in hiding them, for she was never gayer, never more laughing, nor was her behavior ever more scandalous than during this recess between marriages. For her, life in the Vatican was now one prolonged festivity, and the banquets of the Caesars were never more arresting in their details. As if realizing that life in Ferrara would be far different from that in Rome, she was crowding every possible pleasure into her last days of freedom—with the willing help of her father and brother, who were enchanted to arrange such spectacles as would give her delight.

One day in November of 1501, not long before her departure for Ferrara (she had to go to the Estes; they would not come to her as Giovanni and Alfonso had done), a certain peasant had walked into Rome from the country leading two mares laden with bundles of wood. It was his misfortune that his course took him across the square of St. Peter's; and he was just below the Vatican when a group of papal servants and men-at-arms swarmed out upon him, took the two mares from him, threw his precious bundles of wood onto the pavement, uncoupled the harnesses, tossed them aside, and retreated back through the gate into the Vatican courtyard, taking the mares with them. There was, of course, nothing he could do about it.

Once the mares were safely in the courtyard, four stallions were fetched from the papal stables, and at the sight of the mares they began to battle among themselves furiously for possession of them, biting and striking out with their hoofs, rearing and whinneying loudly. Finally the two victorious stallions took charge of the mares, all of them in a state of such frenzy by now that the mares were severely hacked and wounded. Presumably the Pope arranged this little divertissement for his daughter, because the two of them watched it throughout from His Holiness's window over the gate, laughing and evidently enjoying themselves. It must have made a pretty picture of domestic felicity, with Lucrezia jumping up and down and clapping her little hands for glee, while beside her the Pope's mountainous bulk quivered with excitement and gratification.

But this business was a mere trifle as compared with another which had taken place two weeks earlier, the high point of recorded debauchery in the lives of the Borgias, and perhaps one of the great orgies of all time. It is known in history as the ballet of the chestnuts, although it was a ballet only in the loosest sense of the word. It was arranged by Cesare for the amusement of his father and sister, and took place in his apartments at the Vatican.

The Pope and Lucrezia, along with various members of the papal court, were invited by Cesare to attend a sumptuous banquet; and to lend a certain spice to the occasion he also invited fifty of Rome's most famous courtesans (a distinction being made here between the relative status of a courtesan and that of a common prostitute). The beginning of the evening was sedate enough. Waiters passed in and out, and servants slipped deftly through the crowd. Everyone was very festive. There was music, and under the flickering light from the great candlesticks the courtesans began to dance for the guests; then presently they began to dance *with* the guests, and with the servants, too. It appears that the guests were really more interested in watching than in participating, so by and by the servants virtually stopped waiting on the table and gave themselves up altogether to treading through the pavanes and romanescas.

At first the whole scene appeared respectable; everyone was clothed, at least; but then the courtesans began to disrobe. The Borgias did not find this action unsympathetic, and watched with increasing interest as more and more nudity was exposed. The guests had all, by now, reached the point in the feast where they were lolling back, full of food and wine, toying with a bowl of chestnuts; and it was at this point that one of them had a singular and original notion. The lighted candles were removed from the table and set about on the polished floor to form a sort of gymkhana course; the courtesans, stripped quite naked, got down on their hands and knees; and a wild race ensued as they scrambled slipperily about, trying to grab the chestnuts which were tossed clattering down from the table, without overturning those candlesticks or letting hot wax drip on their bare skins.

Cesare's hospitality was, however, by no means exhausted by this game. When the chestnuts had been disposed of, and the girls were back on their feet, a very considerable air of lustfulness had been generated; and sensing that the time was now ripe for the climax of the occasion, he brought out and displayed an impressive collection of clothes and jewels—silk capes, brooches, hose, and other luxurious objects—and these were promised to those among the waiters and manservants who proved able to enjoy the greatest number of courtesans. These menials there-upon also stripped and, selecting partners without further ado, proceeded to their business quite publicly there on the floor, showing no signs of embarrassment.

The spectators, among them the Pope and Lucrezia, watching with zest, were to act as a board of judges in this contest. For a while the entire floor was a writhing mass; but then, inevitably, as time went on the initial impetus began to slacken a little, and the servants exhausted themselves one by one and had to fall out. In this way the ranks were slowly thinned until, some hours later, only a handful of men possessing extraordinary prowess remained in action. These were acclaimed as the victors, and the rewards were divided among them. On this jaded note, with these acro-bats sluggishly pulling their clothes on again, the orgy dissolved and everyone retired to bed since the whole night had passed and it was now dawn. The Pope was so wearied that he slept straight through his mass the next morning.

From this peak there were really few greater debaucheries to-ward which Lucrezia might strive, and after her marriage to Alfonso d'Este and her removal to Ferrara her life became con-siderably calmer—in fact, even a little dull. Her court paid a good deal of attention to her; and of course she was not the least bit faithful to Alfonso; but somehow her later amours lack the brio of her earlier ones. Toward the end of her life she be-came inexplicably religious, and is supposed to have worn a hair shirt next to her skin. She died in childbirth in 1519, still a rea-sonably young woman.

At the time of Lucrezia's last marriage, the end of the terrible eleven years was approaching, and when the collapse came she was fortunate to have the sanctuary of her position in Ferrara. When the House of Borgia fell it was with a mighty clamor, a sudden fearful crashing down of everything which the eleven years had been spent in gaining.

There was no warning that the end had arrived. The Pope, in his early seventies, was the embodiment of good health; he had always been a powerful, robust man, and he had lost none of his vigor, either physical or mental, with the onset of age. He was as lusty and strong and worldly as he had ever been. As for Cesare, he was not only in the prime of life and in perfect health (aside from his syphilis), but also at the crown of his political career. His kingdom was taking firmer and firmer shape in the middle of Italy; he was one of the most powerful men in Europe. Only a single dull note, a foresound of doom, was heard in this halcyon air. The Venetian envoy, Capello, was approached by Cesare, who was attempting to get into the good graces of the Republic of Venice. Capello answered him sagely: "You are very wise, my lord duke, for should the Pope die, you would be reduced to nothing within four days." It was an eerily accurate prediction.

The Pope did die with startling suddenness, and that is the only indisputable fact. All else is obscurity and conjecture, a series of skirmishes between rival theories. The most interesting, and perhaps the most plausible of these centers around Cardinal Adriano di Corneto; and this story, whether or not it is the true one, rounds out the history of the Borgias with incomparable neatness and polish.

Cardinal Adriano was the Pope's former secretary, and he had amassed a very large fortune which, needless to say, the Borgias coveted; so they resolved that he should be given a dose of the white powder and sent to join all the other cardinals who had fallen by the way. Everything the Borgias did seems to have taken place in the most intense heat, and now in the year 1503 it was once again the month of August. Every possible measure which might combat the tropical temperatures was put into operation; and it happened that Cardinal Adriano possessed a beautiful vineyard just outside the city (it appears that everyone who had the slightest claim to distinction owned a beautiful vineyard just outside the city in those days) where the heights of Monte Mario were raised above the perpetual humidity of the Tiber Valley, cool evening breezes blew away the daytime heat, and luxuriant grapevines perfumed the air of a villa's handsome banqueting hall. Here the cardinal decided to hold a feast. Both the Pope and Cesare were invited and, perhaps seeing their opportunity presented to them, they accepted.

This much is known to be true, but what occurred at the banquet itself is not so clear.

The cardinal made all his careful arrangements, and so did the Borgias, in a different way, make theirs. The most popular of many stories is the one in which Cesare, impatient to hasten the cardinal's death, bribed with money and promises and probably also with threats, one of the servants who would wait on the banquet so that he should poison a quantity of the cardinal's wine and serve it to him—this being the old standard theme of the Borgias. For their parts, they were cautious about having the poisonings take place at banquets which they gave in their own names, although it seems naïve for them to have imagined that by this childish gambit they could divert suspicion from themselves. In any case, the transfer of poison was arranged, and it reached the servant's hands; he found occasion at some point before the banquet to put it into a sizable amount of wine where it would instantly have dissolved and become tasteless, then to pour the wine into a very large and special carafe, and finally to set this carafe on one of the serving tables which lined the room, there to be ready at hand for the moment when it should be poured into the cardinal's goblet. Unpolluted wine was, presumably, to be served to everyone else.

At this point, however, if the story is to be believed, fate entered the picture in a stagey manner. The poisoned wine was prepared. The cardinal was fussing over last-minute details with his steward. The sun was setting and the air was growing cooler. The guests were starting to arrive, and among the earliest comers were the Pope and Cesare. At this date there were no cocktails, no pre-prandial drinks; guests were received and taken directly to the table, as the Borgias on this occasion were led to the seats of honor.

But now, for one reason or another, the venal servant had to leave the banqueting room. In his absence the Pope grew thirsty and called for wine; and that wine was poured for him from the poisoned pitcher by another servant who was not in on the plot. The Pope accepted it without the slightest suspicion. It was a very good Trebbia, and even though the Pope was not a heavy drinker, he tossed it off neat. Cesare was also thirsty, and also called for wine, but then he diluted his with water as was the common custom of the age. Other guests were coming in, too, all this while, and were being seated and given refreshments. One may suppose that at some point in the proceedings the original servant returned to the room and discovered that matters were now out of hand entirely, but nothing more is heard of him.

The logical alternative to this whole story is that Cardinal Adriano somehow got wind of the plot and rebribed his servant to switch victims and poison the Borgias instead of himself; and this would be quite credible except for one significant fact: while the poisoned carafe was being passed, the cardinal also drank of its contents and was poisoned, as were many of the other guests. The cardinal was, in fact, poisoned so severely that for a time his life was despaired of. It may be presumed that this was not some intricate countermaneuver on his part; so only an accident such as this one could account for all the poisonings which took place. There must have been a great quantity of the evil wine mixed, too, for not only were the host and his guests poisoned, but also some of the servants who must have drunk the leftovers; a cook and a carver who had drunk the most heavily died of it. But in the meantime the banquet went on its way with the vine leaves whispering and the candles burning down in their sockets under the breeze, and the guests drinking and drinking without having any suspicion of what would follow. The Borgia powder was always slow to act.

But none of this is known to be absolutely true. Historians cannot even agree as to the date of the famous banquet. All that is certainly known is that on August 9 both the Pope and Cesare had fallen unexpectedly ill, and it must be said that no sooner did they take to their beds than rumors of poison began to circulate, especially when it was understood that Cardinal Adriano and others who had attended the banquet were also sickening simultaneously. Of course, all the enemies of the House of Borgia were at once on the alert for every bulletin. The Vatican, in turn, became tight-lipped and secretive.

The Pope had himself bled by his physicians—some persons said that as much as fifteen ounces were let out of his veins at one time—and while his friends and allies thought this injudicious in the face of his age and the hot weather, his enemies prayed that it would weaken his system. It was given out that he was suffering from tertian fever or malaria (in fact, people were asked to believe that all the cardinal's guests had contracted malaria at the same time), and it became known that he was vomiting intermittently.

A certain amount of time had now passed since the banquet, and the poison was nicely impregnating his system.

As a little more time passed, two or three days, the vomiting became more persistent, and it was understood that it was accompanied by violent intestinal spasms—more and more symptoms of the poison were steadily showing themselves. By August 12 the Pope's state of health had grown much worse; his fever was rising—in spite of the bloodlettings which his doctors, in desperation, continued, and which were altogether useless—and it was now widely known that he was suffering from great agony of the stomach, and was vomiting a yellowish humor (*citrina* was the word used in describing it).

His condition was obviously so serious that he sent for the Bishop of Venosa (who was also sick in bed) as well as another doctor, both of whom he wanted in attendance; and when they were seen entering the Vatican but not leaving it again after a few hours, the rumors increased apace. The Pope's enemies were, by this time, almost jubilant, but the end was not to be yet. In fact it almost appeared for a day or two that a plateau in his malady had been reached. Perhaps that elusive delaying agent was taking effect. He did not improve, but neither did he worsen. Blood was let on the thirteenth, and again on the fifteenth—each of these involving the loss of something like a pint—but even through the fog of these extraordinary medical practices it can be seen that the symptoms of malaria or tertian fever do not accord very well with the symptoms of the Pope's ailment. Cesare, it may be noted, was following substantially the same course as his father; and in both cases there were none of the ups and downs characteristic of malaria, nor is it associated with the awful pain and terrible stomach cramps which Cardinal Adriano and his guests were experiencing, and which are so frequently an associate of arsenic poisoning. And, as if the field had not been sufficiently plowed, there was one of the doctors (naturally none of them even breathed the word "poison") who, because he was unable to reconcile all the symptoms, optimistically suggested such a remote disorder as apoplexy, thereby intimating that some reaction existed, also, to the animal alkaloids of the Borgia powder.

Cardinal Adriano himself was undergoing a dreadful time. He had all the Pope's symptoms as well as a burning sensation throughout his innards (which the Pope probably had as well), and his skin erupted to the point where at last it peeled off all over his body. No one knew who might survive the poison—it would not have been survivable in earlier days, when the poisoner would have been on hand to administer further doses as needed —but there was a grim anticipation all through the Vatican that the Pope was to die several days before the actual event took place; and while it is typical that his passing should be in the center of this holocaust, it is satisfying to think that he perished by his own murderous vehicle.

After the relative leveling off of the thirteenth, fourteenth, and fifteenth of August, on the sixteenth there was a decided change for the worse. The ambassadors were severed from any contact with the papal court, and the Vatican was sealed up tightly. The few persons able to get in were all prevented from leaving again. Those who had valuables on the premises began to smuggle them out by night; coffers filled with precious objects and gold and silver were carted away to various safer destinations through the darkness. And Rome was hastily and uncertainly filling with large bodies of troops against the hour of emergency.

On the seventeenth the Pope took a little food, and the outsiders who received this word were led to understand that it was with good result. But before long the truth became known, that his vomiting and paroxysms continued. An atmosphere of hushed tension smothered the entire palace with its waiting army of servants and priests and courtiers. It is possible that during much of this time the Pope was unconscious (although on the fifteenth he had rallied sufficiently to play a game of cards with members of his household; but this does not mean that his strength lasted for more than an hour or two, for his will was as imperious as ever); the idea of partial unconsciousness was given birth by the fact that he never once spoke the name either of Cesare or of Lucrezia, nor did Cesare—who was now, himself, beginning to recover, and who was frantically but vainly trying to read the future—make the slightest effort to see his father.

On the morning of the eighteenth the Pope was visibly sinking, but he was able to hear mass and receive communion. His intestinal spasms had continued all through the previous night, and he mumbled to those around him that he felt deathly sick. As the day passed he sank deeper and deeper until, with the shades of late afternoon drawing inward, he was given the last sacrament. After that he lay in a frightening silence, like an animal in a torpor, his huge bulk and twisted brain stripped of everything but their essential elements, until at last, almost without any change, the mountainous bundle of flesh and bones was dead.

The hour of vespers had come and gone, and no sounds of prayer drifted up from St. Peter's to the darkening windows of the Pope's bedroom. The red sun had set over the Tiber's luminous haze, and night was beginning to fall. As if the Pope had been kept alive—and then briefly dispatched—to observe a special, honorary function, this day stood marked as the third anniversary of the murder of Alfonso of Bisceglie. So passed the Vicar of Christ.

But even though his spirt had departed, this was not yet an end to the adventures of Alexander VI in the form of his mortal remains. His body was bathed, dressed in white robes with a gold chasuble and velvet slippers, and laid out on a catafalque draped with crimson satin between two candles. But there were few persons who even came to stare at this sight inquisitively, and the prayers for the dead were completely forgotten. The whole of the Vatican was suddenly in a fine uproar upon receiving news of the death; and the servants, discovering themselves without a master, rushed hungrily about pillaging and sacking the great palace, stealing everything of the slightest value, and even carrying off the papal throne.

But if the inhabitants of the Vatican were indifferent to the dead Pope, everyone on the outside was agape with curiosity. And following the customary usage of centuries, the body was removed from the Vatican's despoiled chambers the next morning and taken to St. Peter's for the formal lying-in-state to which the public was admitted. During the transferring of the body, however, it occurred to some of the cardinals in attendance that there would almost certainly be persons among the crowd who might wish from motives of vengeance to harm or mutilate the corpse; so they had it placed in one of the side chapels, protected from the file of visitors behind a stout if ornate iron grille. And at last the public was allowed in for the viewing.

But by now a very dreadful thing had started to happen. The body had not, of course, been embalmed; and it was slowly, of its own inhuman volition, beginning to puff up into a hideous monstrosity. And while it puffed, it turned black and revolting to the eye. And to complete this horrible scene it emanated the foulest stench imaginable through the iron bars. These sights and this smell made, quite naturally, a profound impression on the viewers; those who maintained that the Pope had died of his own poison took this as further proof of the poison's effect, while the partisans of a natural fever blamed everything on the August heat. There were even those who, being impressed by the devilish look of the corpse, went still farther and swore that they saw remarkable visions round the catafalque—fiends and evil spirits and demons of every type. A pact with the unholy one was said to be known as an accomplished fact.

After a few hours of this, the churchmen in authority saw that the situation was rapidly becoming impossible. The corpse was by this time so blackened and bloated and misshapen that it no longer bore any resemblance to the human form, but seemed merely to be an offensive mound of rotten meat. So it was decided that it might be less distasteful for everyone if it were displayed to view at night only, by candlelight, and were covered

over in the meantime; and accordingly this was done. But with
the arrival of night a shock lay in wait. The chapel was entered.
The candles were held aloft. The sheet was pulled back; and what
had been merely disgusting by daylight was positively ghastly in
the wavering glow of the candle flames under the high, shadowy,
beamed ceiling of the ancient cathedral. Putrefaction did not
wait on time, and the thing upon the catafalque was disfigured
past belief. The Venetian ambassador describes the body as "the
most hideous, monstrous, and horrible corpse that was ever seen."
And the Ferrarese ambassador says, "never in Christian times
was there a more monstrous or terrible object."

It could very plainly no longer be shown either by day or by
night, nor could the awful thing even be allowed to linger in the
open precincts of St. Peter's. Very little ceremony, beyond the
baldest of attentions, had been tendered upon the Pope's death
or in the time which had since passed; and in view of this careless
and hasty attitude it was now thought only sensible that a tremendous papal funeral might very practically be foregone. The
body of Alexander VI needed burial, and buried it should be
without any further ritualistic delay.

In accordance with this matter-of-fact decision gravediggers,
carpenters, and porters were summoned to do their jobs. The
heap of flesh was carried out of St. Peter's into the nearby church
of Santa Maria della Febri, where a hurriedly built coffin awaited
it. By now it was late at night. The bloated carcass was trans-
ferred to the coffin, but then it seemed to hang there upon those
wooden rims like a rising bubble: it was so swollen that it would
no longer fit into the area designated for it. The terrible thing
had outgrown its own resting place.

At this point in the affair every scruple had long since departed;
and so, while several of the late Pope's prelates stood watching, a
nightmarish scene took place in the flickering light from the
torches. Rather than knocking together a new coffin to contain
the carcass, it was decided that the carcass must be forced into
this coffin. Two of the most powerfully built servants were given
this task, and with much swearing and panting and perspiring (it
was very hot and intolerably smelly) they managed somehow by

pushing and thumping and shoving and pounding and tugging to squeeze the huge, flabby, bulbous object into the long wooden box. Once it had been crammed in, with no regard for the science of anatomy, the lid was quickly put down on it, and it was buried without ado. This was the final end of Alexander VI, the terror of Italy, France, and Spain, the horror of Catholic Europe, the most detested man of his time. The little company which had seen to his interment was happy to be done with him, and hurried away out of the dark church leaving him under his stone without pity or sorrow.

This was the real end of the House of Borgia. As to Cesare, he had been nearly as sick as his father, but he had undergone a treatment which the doctors feared to try on a man of the Pope's age—the belly of a mule was slit open, and he was doubled up inside it; then he was plunged into ice water. Whether it was because of this odd treatment or some other, both his health and his looks were ruined, but his life was saved. The Venetian ambassador, in conversation with one of the papal physicians before the Pope's death, was told of Cesare that "he is in no danger whatever, is without fever, and can rise from his bed whenever it pleases him." But it did not please him to do so at once, even though his father lay dying in the rooms directly below his own. He was waiting to see what direction affairs would now take.

The Pope had not been dead for more than a few minutes when the tramp of feet was heard outside his door and a group of Cesare's men under the trusty Michelotto burst in and demanded the Pope's chests of treasure—or, if these were not at once given them, they proposed to throw the papal treasurer out the window. Without much argument they bore away the coffers of gold and silver, although in their haste they neglected to take along the most valuable coffer of all, that containing the Pope's superb collection of jewels.

In spite of the doctor's report, Cesare was still pretending to be at the threshold of death; but now (without altering his story one tittle) he left the Vatican and moved to the more defensible Castel Sant' Angelo, where he barricaded himself in, and once more sat down to await further developments. But he could not stay there in isolation forever, so two weeks after his father's death he decamped for the castle of Nepi. Then he came back to Rome again. All his comings and goings, his intrigues and plots and counterplots, appear both futile and pathetic without his father's support. A new Pope, Pius III, was elected, and died three weeks later. Another Pope was elected, Julius II, a long-time enemy of the Borgias, who spent some little while in playing a delicious cat-and-mouse game with the powerless Cesare, imprisoning him, turning him loose, making promises and then deliberately breaking them. Finally Cesare was maliciously allowed to go to Naples (a foolish and shortsighted move on his part, since the Neapolitan king was the uncle of Alfonso of Bisceglie), and there he was quickly arrested and sent as a prisoner to Spain.

After being locked up in one castle after another for two years, he contrived to escape from his jailers and made his way to the court of his brother-in-law, the King of Navarre, where he was unenthusiastically provided with a refuge. It must have been a dismal period for him, stagnating in this provincial capital after the vivid and commanding life he had led. It lasted only for a few months, though; and on March 12, 1507, while involved in a war-like sortie against the neighboring Count of Lerins, he was assaulted in an ambush, wounded, killed, stripped of his clothing, and left lying naked on the ground. He was thirty-three years old. He was given Christian burial, but a few years later his body was disinterred as being a thing unclean and sacrilegious. Where it may have been taken is not known, nor is there any trace of his grave.

The other members of the family had not climbed as high as Cesare, nor did they fall as low. Lucrezia reigned until her death as Duchess of Ferrara, and her children carried on that dynasty and, by their marriages and offsprings, spread the blood of the Borgias through the royal houses of Europe. Jofre still held the principality of Squillace. And the long-dead Juan, having given his Spanish wife a son and a daughter, had laid the foundation stones of the ducal house of Gandia. But for all these titles and trophies of power, it was unmistakable that the Borgias had passed altogether out of the mainstream of history, and were never again to achieve their former eminence.

Yet there was still one final circle to be closed, one last significant act to involve a member of this family. And it was brought to pass when, in 1572, Francesco Borgia, grandson of the Duke of Gandia, great-grandson of Pope Alexander VI, was canonized a saint. It was the ultimate Christian irony that the Church should at last be able to salvage some good from the family which had done it such irreparable and grievous harm.